PLAYBACK

PLAYBACK

A NEWSMAN/RECORD PRODUCER'S
HITS AND MISSES FROM THE THIRTIES
TO THE SEVENTIES

BY DAVE DEXTER, JR.

BILLBOARD PUBLICATIONS, INC., NEW YORK

Library of Congress Cataloging in Publication Data
Dexter, Dave.
　Playback: a newsman-record producer's hits and misses
from the 30s into the 70s.
　　1. Dexter, Dave.　2. Music, Popular (Songs, etc.—
United States—History and criticism.　3. Music trade—
United States.　I. Title.
ML429.D5A3　　338.4'7'789912　　76-000777
ISBN 0-8230-7589-3

First Printing, 1976

TO MICKIE
and "our" Anja, Kamala, and Davey Django

INTRO

People often complain that music is too ambiguous; that what they should think when they hear it is unclear, whereas everyone understands words. With me it is exactly the opposite, and not only with regard to an entire speech but also with individual words. These, too, seem to me so ambiguous, so vague, so easily misunderstood in comparison to genuine music which fills the soul with a thousand better things than words.

—FELIX MENDELSSOHN

PERHAPS YOU RECENTLY read a report in *Publishers Weekly*, as did I, disclosing that 40,846 new and reissued books were published in the United States last year. It's plain that still another is just what everyone craves.

I have an excuse. There has never been a book devoted to my business by a man who has survived some 40 years either writing about phonograph records or producing them, and even that sounds lame.

I drive home every evening feeling somewhat like the aged chimpanzee observed in the 1960s in the eastern Congo by the eminent Dutch scientist Adriaan Kortlandt. The elderly chimp paused at the same grassy site every night at dusk, sat down, and then stared wonderingly at the vivid, changing colors of the African sunset.

"When it became dark," Dr. Kortlandt reported, "my simian friend turned slowly and retired to the forest without halting to pick a pawpaw for his evening meal."

All of us, at times, should retire to the forest to sort out our thoughts. That's the logic behind these pages. But I missed no evening meals writing them.

A clever man, an accountant with whom I have worked for several years, drew a pocket calculator from his jacket at lunch recently. He poked a few buttons and cheerily announced that a man 65 years old will have enjoyed a single childhood, 3,380 weekends, and 23,741 nights away from his job. He appeared pleased with his calculations.

Yet to a record man his workdays, evenings, and weekends all blend into one extended, blurry, exciting workshift. He either is out pursuing new talent and tunes or he is recording and editing tape while the sane world sleeps. His bosses demand that he conform to the strict nine-to-five office routine accepted by his fellow employees. No one understands a record man—not even another record man.

The versatile and knowledgeable Orson Welles composed a flattering foreword to the first book I attempted, at the close of World War II.

"Dexter cheerfully avoids the chi-chi of the specialist," Welles opined. "You'll find nothing in it of that sentimentality and spurious mysticism which muddy many earlier treatments of the jazz subject. I find myself in some disagreement with a few of Dexter's evaluations but I salute him for his wholesome approach and for his painstaking documentation. I like his writing because a square can understand it."

Thirty years later I hope the squares will understand this rambling, name-dropping, memory-provoking tome, and I wish even more fervently that the hip and the erudite bestow their approbation as well. Books are like records. You can't please everyone. Sometimes you can't please anyone.

I watch young producers strut about Hollywood boasting of their million-selling albums and singles and I wonder how long—how many years or decades will pass—before they realize that some 212 million Americans did not buy their chart-topping disc, and that an overwhelming majority of those millions was never aware it existed?

Still, people like them are but a portion of a vast tribe of contrasting personalities comprising the world of records. Ours is a sort of overcrowded palette jammed with uncountable variations of male and female humanity; one watches them all with a kind of mesmerized fascination, much as amused children observe monkeys at a zoo.

There is, for the record, one species of monkey that ranks its male members by the color of their scrotums, which vary from a deep indigo to a pastel turquoise blue. Curious scientists a few years back painted a less-endowed male with vivid dye, then watched him win instant deference—his choice of food and females—with his falsely acquired status symbol. I have known several bigwigs at Capitol Records and elsewhere who may well have won their lofty vice-presidential positions similarly.

What happens when the dye wears off?

I know. They write books.

In the chapters that follow I have attempted to credit the many persons who extended a hand to me along the way. I am most grateful to my family, including my niece Marjorie Jean Dexter at a Texas college, and Mrs. Janie Croswhite, who insisted I continue when I was about to chuck numerous early pages of my manuscript into a Yucca Street sewer. I am indebted as well to the many present and past employees of Capitol Records who have shared with me the wins and losses, the several agonizing management upheavals, and the debilitating grind of seeking the big smash hit in the dank atmosphere of profits come first, or else. All corporations are, of course, like that, and in the recording industry they are all getting worse.

Mrs. Charles (Anne) Davis and Miss Natha Witt made personal sacrifices to type this manuscript into legibility. Marvin Schwartz will be remembered for his generosity and assistance. Lee Zhito and Hal Cook had faith when others did not.

The author also expresses appreciation to New York editor Margit Malmstrom for her efforts in preparing *Playback* for publication.

Working with records the better part of one's lifetime is as punishing, at times, as pro football. But for this portly veteran of the wars it's always been the only game in town.

DAVE DEXTER, JR.
Hollywood, California

1

In the beginning
God created the heaven
and the earth.
The record business
with its phonies
and no-talents
came along
a little later.

—GLENN EVERETT WALLICHS

SHE WAS BLONDE with a Joey Heatherton body. Short hair, immaculately coiffured. A silky, buttoned blouse topped a modish miniskirt and ultrasheer charcoal nylons. Her gleaming patent pumps complemented an attractive near-thirtyish face as she quickly strode into my office and took a chair.

She kicked out her foot and pushed the door shut.

"You're a busy man," she said. "I won't waste time. I'm here because I want to make records. I'm a hell of a singer. I look good. I hope you'll work with me."

She began unbuttoning her blouse. Now she stood up. Her blue-green eyes looked directly at mine across the desk. "This is yours whenever you want it," she said, lifting her left breast from a lacy, well-filled bra. "And so is this." She pushed the other breast up and cupped it as if she intended to weigh an oversized grapefruit.

"This goes along with the boobs, of course," she smiled, using both hands to raise her bright blue skirt to her navel and reveal bright, transparent apple red panties under a slender white garterbelt. She stared at me intently.

"Just tell me where and when, Mr. Dexter."

By now I was shocked. Why, for God's sake, did a pretty, impeccably-dressed young woman spoil such an intimate moment by choosing to wear *red* panties with her tasteful sky blue blouse, bra, skirt, and shoes? I resented her slatternly taste, her impertinence. The apple red panties *clashed*.

A great many things clash within the record business.

°   °   °

There are no rules, no boundaries. What clicked today may flop tomorrow. A Frank Sinatra will reign as top cat one year and lie moribund and ignored another, then crawl off the floor and become The King again. Or you may watch a

Nat King Cole whose records have all been failures instantly become a consistent top seller on a different label. And why does a great act like Les Paul and Mary Ford, with a dozen million-selling discs to its credit, abruptly turn cold overnight and never sell again?

How is it that delectable, gorgeous Lena Horne is acclaimed throughout the world as a superb showman, a gifted singer, and a surefire attraction who commands as much money at the Waldorf-Astoria as any act in show business, and yet is rebuffed, year after year, by the unpredictable, vacillating masses who unfailingly refuse to purchase her discs no matter which songs she sings so expertly?

Liza Minnelli. She's won more awards in two years than her mother did in a lifetime. Judy Garland sold millions of records. Liza lacks disc appeal. In three years she's drifted from Capitol to A&M to Columbia, a failure on all three labels. Why?

You don't analyze the paradoxes and peculiarities of my business. You accept them.

Producing records is a vocation only for the courageous and the stupid. It is Russian roulette on a roll of tape. Stomach ulcers are as much a mark of the career man as are a coal miner's black lungs or a catcher's crooked, fractured fingers. Fewer than 20 percent of today's creative men in the producer's booth will be in the business five years from now.

One lives and dies every week by the charts—those lengthy lists of the best-selling record singles and albums so carefully compiled and published every Monday by the major music periodicals—the trade sheets, they're called—*Billboard*, *Cash Box*, and *Record World*. The masters you bleed to create while normal folk are asleep must make those charts at least occasionally or you are jobless. Some 500 aggressive rivals are trying just as determinedly as you to dominate the listings. Yet no matter how large the plate, one can pile only so much caviar—or even oatmeal—on before it slops over and lies wasted.

With records, the spoilage runs into millions of dollars in losses, money that remains unrecoverable. No one will buy a flop, even for a dime. You cannot give away a failure, a stiff. I know. I've tried. But thousands will pay $10 and even $20 or more for a yet-unreleased LP by Elton John just to possess it a few days before it goes into the stores, or on the racks, at $6.98.

That's the record business today.

Those in our industry—and it is an industry rather than the profession it once was—are violently opinionated. A grocer finds little difference in Armour, Roth, Swift, or Farmer John hams; Detroit motor car makers couldn't care less if their new models are tired by Goodrich, Goodyear, Michelin, or Firestone so long as the supplier's prices conform to their specifications.

Pop music is different. Like the unseeing quarterback being rushed by an enraged linebacker, we who create music are afflicted with irremedial blindspots that emphatically affect our judgment, our success or failure as producers, and our jobs.

No matter what the financial rewards might be, not in a thousand years would I record performers like Johnny Mathis, Yoko Ono, Frank Zappa, Sonny and/or Cher Bono, or those of the stripe of David Bowie or Alice Cooper. Either their performing styles are repugnant to me or their personalities are offensive and intolerable. They are, of course, privileged to say the same of me.

One can only ruminate as to why one act makes it big and another flops, everything apparently being equal. Dave Garroway, to cite an exemplary instance, featured a brunette singer named Connie Russell for several seasons on his memorable Chicago NBC television series in the 1950s. Connie had it all—intelligence, dramatic ability, poise, graciousness, performing skill, a beauteous face and, most important, a voice and the inherent musicianship that typifies artistic excellence.

Garroway's not only was the best of the variety shows in those early days when we on the Pacific Coast awaited it every Sunday via snowy kinescope, but it also was one of the two or three most-watched programs by the nation's viewers. Miss Russell, moreover, was plainly its main attraction. After her first solo records on a rival label failed to sell, I confidently moved in with an offer to produce her future discs in California for Capitol. I promised her better songs, stronger arrangements, better accompanying orchestras, more promotion, and, obviously, hit singles and albums which would sell into the millions throughout the world.

Connie accepted my offer. Never was there a more cooperative artist. No act ever worked more diligently, or followed more suggestions, yet her records bombed dismally despite widespread airplay on more than 2,000 radio stations in every state of the Union. Why?

Was it the songs we selected? The arrangements? Or was it the wrong time, or the wrong place, or the wrong singer? The Good Lord only knows why people will ignore a Connie Russell and buy a Johnny Mathis.

I seek consolation in recalling that Mildred Bailey and Billie Holiday sold only to a few appreciative musicians. And they were the most talented female pop singers this nation has yet produced.

Connie Russell wasn't alone in failing to grab the brass ring. There have been many. June Hutton is one of a legion who deserved better. The personable, petite sister of sexy Ina Ray Hutton (the bandleader), June was merely marvelous as a singer with the old Charlie Spivak orchestra and as the girl who succeeded Jo Stafford with the popular Pied Pipers vocal group. On her own, no singer except Ella Fitzgerald was blessed with more perfect intonation, easy phrasing, and voice quality, but, like the ravishing Miss Russell, June failed to move up among the elite on records.

She and her husband, Axel Stordahl, one of the most versatile of all arrangers and conductors, are remembered by few for the role they played in dragging a moody, bitter Frank Sinatra from the depths in 1952–53 and helping him establish a vastly more successful career than he had enjoyed a decade earlier as the bow-tied idol of immature, bobbysoxed little girls shortly after he had left his singer's spot with Tommy Dorsey's band.

All the time that I was striving to bust out with a smash disc with June, she and Axel persistently nagged me to listen to their old friend Sinatra. He had been fired from his network radio series and his early films at RKO and MGM were long forgotten. Frank's eight years on the Columbia label had ended in rancor and no other company had accepted his agency's pitches to sign him.

Sam Weisbord of William Morris doggedly tried to arouse interest in Frank, but every producer knew of his long string of stiffs, a chain that remained unbroken when his unsympathetic producer, Mitch Miller, finally insisted that Sinatra team up on discs with a singularly unmusical television personality named Dagmar whose awesome, oversized bosom had given her a fleeting place in the sun. On their duet, Frank gamely tried to sing a sickly novelty, *Mama Will Bark*, but it came off as a hopeless and cruel burlesque of his immense talent and he ended up yelping like an Airedale in what stands as one of the most frustrating and humiliating incidents of his career. He and Columbia then parted.

Agent Weisbord contacted all the waxworks: the majors, the minors, the high and the low of the industry, but he got no bites. Several record execs bluntly told Sam that his client was through as a performer. All of them agreed Sinatra had lost his appeal. Some confidentially declared he had "lost" his voice. Yet through those many despairing months and despite the negatives that had infiltrated all of show business, June Hutton and Axel Stordahl constantly implored me to take on their frigid friend from the old Dorsey days. "He's singing better than ever," June insisted. "We hear him at parties around town and in our own Encino home and he's great again."

I knew Sinatra well, if not intimately. I had met him when he was with Harry James' dance band in 1939 and I watched him work in his first job outside his native New Jersey at Chicago's Hotel Sherman. I listened to his nightly broadcasts, and his first records with James, 10 in all, were good things like *All or Nothing at All, Melancholy Mood, From the Bottom of My Heart,* and *On a Little Street in Singapore.* Later, with the Dorsey band, he had been assigned even more songs, some of them ill-chosen. Frank sang some of them unemotionally and unimpressively. As a *Down Beat* editor and reviewer I judged them that way. Far more frequently, I praised his work and generously devoted space to his activities and first fan clubs.

And so I made a decision. Without hearing him, I accepted the judgment of the Stordahls. I went to my boss, Capitol's artists and repertoire chief Alan W. Livingston, and urged him to call Sam Weisbord and draw up a Sinatra contract.

"I don't know if he can come back on records," I told Livingston, "but I promise his output will be musically good—you won't hear any barking dogs. And I'll use full orchestras with him, not just a piano, drums, and a Schick electric razor."

Livingston contracted for Sinatra through Weisbord and a few days later telephoned Frank to find him not only jubilant over a fresh, new chance on records, but optimistic that the role of Maggio in the Columbia motion picture version of James Jones' *From Here to Eternity* might also be awarded him by producer Buddy Adler. Things suddenly were looking up for the discouraged, abandoned bobbysoxer idol whose marriage to a childhood sweetheart, Nancy Barbato of Jersey City, had recently collapsed.

Livingston advised Sinatra that Capitol would like to huddle with him in the office and go over songs, discuss his choice of arrangers and agree on the type of orchestra that should accompany him.

"Your producer," my boss enthused, "will be Dave Dexter. He's raring to help you kick off a whole new career."

Livingston heard only silence from Sinatra's end. And then, explosively:

"That bastard? I won't work with him. He's the jerk who rapped my records in *Down Beat*. Screw 'im, who needs 'im?"

Livingston, shaken and embarrassed, then walked into my office and told me exactly what Sinatra had said. I flared up like a Saturn 5 rocket, grabbed the four songs I had carefully selected for Frank's first session (*Lean Baby* and *I'm Walking Behind You* were among them) and stuffed them into Livingston's hands. Then I realized how funny—how incredibly ironic—the situation was.

I turned to my boss, and we both started grinning.

"Here's a guy who is dead on his ass," I said. "He's been deserted by all but a few of his friends, he's without a job, and he's brushed off every day by the record companies, the picture studios, and the radio and television networks.

"But I believe in his basic talent just as the Stordahls do, and I'm the only guy in the world who's willing to risk my job in spending $100,000 or more of my company's money trying to bring the son-of-a-bitch back—and he fluffs me.

"Next time you talk to him, Alan, tell him to shove it. The feeling is mutual."

Livingston assigned Sinatra to a more placid producer named Voyle Gilmore, who took *Lean Baby* and *I'm Walking Behind You* and enjoyed an immediate hit single with Frank. He was, indeed, singing well again. Better than before his long hiatus. *From Here to Eternity*, of course, helped bring Sinatra additional kudos, an Academy Award, and a wondrous, rejuvenated, new life at the top. Within months, Capitol had dropped the Hutton-Stordahl team as if they'd been smallpox carriers. Sinatra employed Stordahl as arranger and conductor on a session or two and then, at producer Gilmore's suggestion, canned him in favor of Nelson Riddle.

That's the record business.

There's a minor postscript. Livingston generously tried to assuage my ire with Sinatra by finding another baritone of Italian heritage. He asked me to be his producer. "I think he can become.even bigger than Sinatra," my boss confided, "and just think how Frank's going to feel when your boy tops him on the charts."

The baritone's name was Bobby Milano, a pleasant, ambitious young man. I gave up on his chances in the producer's booth before he finished his first song.

Ingrate or no, there's only one Francis Albert Sinatra and in 987 years there will never be another quite like him. Perhaps I might blame our conflict on our birthdates. Our impenitent, dogmatic, and often-pugnacious traits as fellow Sagittarians may be the basis for the friction. Under other signs of the zodiac we might well have become another Frick and Frack.

o   o   o

The record business is much the same throughout the world.

For almost eleven years, my job was to audition samples of every type of pop music sent to the Capitol Tower in Hollywood from affiliated companies in many lands, issuing those which had—based on a strictly subjective opinion—hit potential. Every couple of years I flew out to visit as many of those sister companies as was feasible. There I listened to 45 and 33 rpm samples and sat in the producer's booth watching records being made. Only the musicians were different from the sessions we have in Hollywood and New York.

In Hong Kong, Buenos Aires, Rio de Janeiro, Milan, Helsinki, Cologne, London, and Paris, wherever I visited, my colleagues said the same thing: "Competition is the toughest in the world right here. Even if you make a hit you've got to come up with two more a month later just to stay in business."

Most producers—they are also known as a&r men because of their involvement with artists and repertoire—are not active long. Scoring that first smash is, oddly, easier than popping through with a second and third chart-topper.

But as they've said for more years than I can remember, there's no law that says a man can't try.

2

If we could devise an arrangement
for providing everybody with music in their homes,
perfect in quality, unlimited in quantity,
suited to every mood, and beginning and ceasing
at will, we would have the limit of human
felicity already attained.

—EDWARD BELLAMY (1876)

It all began with Thomas Alva Edison of Ohio and Emile Berliner of Germany. Edison's choice for reproducing sound was the cylinder, which he developed using tinfoil in 1877. Berliner, who had invented the telephone transmitter after he moved to America, favored the flat disc and demonstrated its superiority to the cylinder in 1882.

Americans were buying 100,000,000 records annually by the middle 1920s and arguing the respective merits of wood, steel, and cactus-thorn needles on their fashionable, hand-wound Victrola, Graphophone, Panatrope, and Gramophone playing machines. Engineers at Bell Laboratories introduced electrical recording, a revolutionary new sound-capturing process which spectacularly increased the frequency range up to 5,000 and down into the bassy 100 cycles. For the first time in 40 years, music and speech as recorded through microphones, electrically, could be heard with a reasonable degree of fidelity.

Is there anyone around today who remembers the Little Wonder series of discs?

They gave me my first exposure to the world of music back about 1923, in Kansas City. The label featured a line drawing of a magician. It was a five-inch platter selling for a dime in the Kresge and Woolworth five-and-ten chain stores. Little wonder that Little Wonder singers and orchestras were anonymous. They deserved to be. But the repertoire offered all the popular hits of the Coolidge era and children's songs and stories as well. I played my collection until the grooves disappeared.

Kansas City's preferences in music were mightily influenced in those distant days by stations WDAF, owned and operated by the powerful Kansas City *Star & Times*, and WHB, an affiliate of the Sweeney Automotive School. Most of us who resided in Jackson, Clay, Johnson, Wyandotte, and Saline counties first heard radio broadcasts while wearing earphones on crude, cat-whiskered crystal sets.

It was the time of Paul Whiteman's twin million-sellers, *Whispering* and *Three O'Clock in the Morning*, and Enrico Caruso's gut-busting arias from Verdi and Leoncavallo operas. Millions danced the Charleston. Girls marcelled their hair and were called flappers. *Time* magazine was born. Red Grange, Babe Ruth, Bobby Jones, and Bill Tilden were the sports heroes.

I played records.

And because I had acquired a scalp ailment known as barber's itch, my mother boycotted our neighborhood shop and sent me all the way downtown by trolley to enjoy the tonsorial services of my dad's barber, Louie Stone. Occasionally, as I underwent his snipping scissors, Frank Spina in the adjacent chair would attend to the requirements of an agile, bespectacled little man he called—with due deference—"Captain." The talkative customer told funny stories and rated far more respect from the barbering corps than any of the other patrons. "Captain" was friendly enough with me, patting my head from time to time as he fished around in his pants for a quarter tip for barber Spina.

Later, as I got older, the same little man was known as "Judge." He still told hilarious jokes and he tipped Spina without fail. I had never seen a gratuity given by anyone but "Judge" for services rendered, and along about the fifth or sixth grade it occurred to me that Louie Stone deserved a little extra for his efforts, too. A dime was the best I could do.

"Judge" became "Senator" when I was in high school and he commanded even more respect inside the Tenth Street shop. The glib, gregarious little man from Independence whose last name I had never known was to have yet another title years later, in 1945, when he became the thirty-third president of the United States upon Franklin D. Roosevelt's death. Harry S Truman continued to patronize Frank Spina whenever he was in Kansas City. To this day, whenever I leave a tip for anyone, I think of the feisty little guy who advanced from haberdasher to Jackson County judge to U.S. senator to the White House.

President Truman and Spina, who had served under Truman in France in World War I, died within months of each other.

I never suffered barber's itch again.

o   o   o

Whiteman's success with his dance band kicked off a revolution in popular music. Paul was a good-natured, obese, impeccably dressed Coloradoan whose father, Prof. Wilberforce Whiteman of Denver, had taught his son well. With his hit records, a tour of Europe, and a tidal wave of international publicity following his debut performance of George Gershwin's *Rhapsody in Blue* in 1924, the shrewd and showmanly Whiteman was established as the biggest attraction in show business. Many called him the King of Jazz.

Whiteman's unprecedented triumphs quickly attracted competition. From Canada, Guy Lombardo and his brothers began their climb to prominence in Cleveland and Chicago. Fred and Tom Waring, Vincent Lopez, Isham Jones, Don Bestor, George Olsen, Duke Ellington, Fletcher Henderson, Ted Weems,

Ted Lewis—suddenly there were scores of new dance bands making records and performing in hotels, ballrooms and speakeasy nightclubs where spiked beer, wine, and rotgut booze were illegally served in violation of the Volstead Act.

Radio equipment improved; clumsy crystal sets disappeared, and now it was bulky superhetrodynes with a bewildering variety of dials that were in fashion. In 1928 record sales slumped. They dropped even lower in 1929. By 1930, with the great American economic depression evident, sales were plummeting to new lows, an alarming trend which, Whiteman told me a decade later, was "tragically understandable."

"Why," he said, "should a family buy records when a radio was in every home with the most popular entertainers performing for free? Some of us forget that the market crash in 1929 brought about the most devastating economic situation in America's history."

Crash or not, and with the Dexters struggling like millions of others to remain solvent, I bought and borrowed records regularly. Didn't one of the finest dance bands ever assembled play nightly—and at lunchtime matinees—downtown at Kansas City's Hotel Muehlebach? It was the Carleton Coon–Joe Sanders Nighthawks, and I treasured many of their black and gold label Victors. One, *Slewfoot*, I still have. Another local maestro, the black Bennie Moten, likewise recorded for Victor. I didn't comprehend the titles of Moten's swinging instrumentals like *Rit Tit Day*, *Rite Tite*, and *Boot It*, but they were all brisk sellers with black buyers, and I liked them, too.

Somewhere along the way, as a third grader at Thacher School, I had started lessons on a silver-plated Conn alto saxophone which my dad lugged home after his day's work in an advertising agency. Forming an embouchure wasn't difficult, nor was the fingering. But sight-reading stopped me. It required a mathematical mind. Soon I knew that I would never become a Rudy Wiedoeft.

Record sales had peaked at 106,000,000 in 1927 and dived to a minimal 6,000,000 in 1932. The major stars of the twenties—Whiteman, Gene Austin, Al Jolson, Rudy Vallee, Ruth Etting, the Two Black Crows, and the unknown cretin who bastardized the trombone in fashioning a belly-splitting smash out of the Okeh *Laughing Record*—no longer were valuable attractions. Nor was anyone else. Bing Crosby got off to a strong start as solo act after he departed the Whiteman and Gus Arnheim orchestras, but his Brunswick biggies rarely attained the 25,000 sales level.

Victor engineers in 1932 were attempting to develop a long-playing, microgroove disc. Their experimental platters failed to impress buyers and the idea was abandoned. Two British orchestras (Ray Noble and Jack Hylton) sold as many records as their American rivals; the novelty of the Boswell Sisters, Cab Calloway, Kate Smith, and the four Mills Brothers aroused new enthusiasm in the industry. I had them all and more in my growing collection—even things by Boyd Senter's Senterpedes and a *Peanut Vendor* recorded in Havana. I collected the warped, 15-cent Hit-of-the-Week discs made of laminated paper which were sold only in drugstores.

You listened to a Hit of the Week with a certain anxiety. After a half-dozen plays, the music faded away into insufferable surface clatter. I still have several of those dreadful, misshapen rarities. I don't want to hear them.

Students at Northeast High School were just like a jillion other teenagers in those wretched, Depression-tainted days of the early 1930s. We cut classes occasionally. Sometimes we took the trolley downtown to attend the infamous "businessmen's luncheon" at the Chesterfield Club, where for a dollar you were entitled to tip the pretty waitresses, after hamburger and French fries, with any combination of coins you had handy. Some of us stacked up pennies, others left a thin dime, but it didn't matter to those obliging, skillful girls. They worked nude (except for their shoes) and collected their gratuities by daintily squatting momentarily over the coins, their legs wide apart, then strutting around to display their grabbing, grapling techniques at other tables.

Few of us had money in those days.

We tried to fatten our meager allowances from parents with a dance band led by Wilber (Bonyo) Cromwell, who bought the stock arrangements and fronted our group at the few gigs we secured. I played bad alto sax and doubled on a borrowed baritone. Irving Berlin's *How Deep is the Ocean* was—and still is—a lovely melody, well endowed with big, long, lovely whole notes. That's the only tune in the Cromwell book where I dared to use the big sax.

Eddy Morgan's, on Fifteenth Street, was the class of the Kansas City speakeasies in 1933, thanks to its strategic location near the teenager's hangout, Dixon's Chili Parlor. Youth then was much like youth today; we talked of the movies (*Flying Down to Rio, King Kong, Forty-Second Street, Tugboat Annie, A Farewell to Arms*) and of President Franklin D. Roosevelt and his New Deal. We argued baseball and pondered our chances of entering college. We discussed the Richard Byrd Antarctica expedition, the numerous lynchings of "colored people," and coming—on December 5—ratification of the Twenty-first Amendment that would legalize all alcoholic beverages.

Kansas City was a world unto itself in that era, a little universe of 400,000 persons bossed by moon-faced, rotund Thomas J. Pendergast. As czar of all Missouri Democrats, his political influence extended east to St. Louis, south to the Arkansas line, and north to Iowa. Gambling was wide open around the clock. Nightclubs flourished, attracting some of the nation's best acts and musicians, who sought to escape the soup lines of Eastern cities.

John Lazia controlled the city's underworld; John Dillinger excepted, America's most daring criminals visited Kansas City frequently or made it their home with impunity. Clyde Barrow, Bonnie Parker, Charles (Pretty Boy) Floyd, Harvey Bailey, Fred (Killer) Burke, Wilbur Underhill, Adam Richetti, Verne C. Miller, Frank Nash, and Ma Barker all frequented the cow town so proudly hailed by Conrad Mann's Chamber of Commerce promotional literature as the "Heart of America City."

Kansas City's teenagers took it all in stride, and so did their elders. There was one year when the *Journal-Post* angrily publicized the city's murder rate as 16 for each 100,000 population; Chicago in the worst days of the Capones, O'Banions, Gennas, and Aiellos reached a peak of "only" 13.3 homicides.

We found ways to break the monotony of gangland killings and widespread poverty. Harold Kratky, Frank McCrae, and I bummed our way to Los Angeles on freight trains, ostensibly to see the Olympics, but for all our adroitness in avoiding the vicious billyclubs of belligerent railroad brakemen, we stood around the colorfully decorated Memorial Coliseum unable to raise the price of tickets. Mildred (Babe) Didrickson won all three of her gold medals that summer without three 16-year-old Kansas Citians in the stands.

In 1933 I hitchhiked to Chicago, alone, with enough cash to see the Cubs edge the Giants (Lon Warneke vs. Carl Hubbell) at Wrigley Field, my first major league ball game. I saw Ben Bernie's band and Sally Rand's provoking fan and bubble dance at the World's Fair. I even got into the Aragon Ballroom to hear Wayne King and his waltzes. Not until later did I learn that Chicago's *good* music emanated from the crowded South Side.

Two years at a friendly little Presbyterian college, Missouri Valley at Marshall, followed high school. I took my saxophone along. Few asked me to play. But football, basketball, and track kept me active during the day; and at night, while others studied, I twirled the radio dial, seeking dance-band broadcasts. It was while I was still a freshman that I began writing record reviews for the Missouri Valley weekly *Delta* newspaper. The Kansas City *Star* sent me checks varying from $6 to $10 a month for my services as sports correspondent covering competition in the Missouri College Athletic Union.

By now it had become the spring of 1935 and I knew what I wanted.

My father had been a newspaperman—one of the best—and it appeared to me that writing might offer a vocation which, at its worst, would never be dull. In September I matriculated at the University of Missouri's School of Journalism.

I left the saxophone at home in Kansas City.

Sergei Rachmaninoff playing the piano on a basketball court in Columbia, Missouri, now appears as incongruous as Scoop Jackson making a friendly appearance in Moscow. But it happened that the dour, unsmiling Russian appeared there during the winter of 1935–36, at a time when he had not yet finished his *Third Symphony in A Minor*. I attempted to contact him, hoping to elicit something in the way of quotes that might make a feature for the Kansas City *Star* or at least a stick of type for the *Missourian*, on whose staff every journalism student at the University was automatically enrolled.

The maestro was not to be found at any of the hotels in town, so I had to elbow my way down front at his concert at the Brewer Field House if I was to have any chance at an interview. Rachmaninoff performed brilliantly, mixing Chopin with his own preludes, and he ended his recital with his own *Prelude in C Sharp Minor*, a work he had grown to detest. By the time he walked off the portable stage I had maneuvered to the foot of the stairs, but it was the green rookie against the aging but still-smart vet who knew all the tricks, and all I got of him was a glimpse of his back moving away from me into the limousine that was to carry him straight to St. Louis.

The evening was not a loss. I had never heard a pianist—or a musician—with talents like Rachmaninoff's. Nor have I since. One can play his records today and still hear his peculiar, near-incredible genius.

So it was back to jazz and pop for Dexter, reviewing records and radio remotes for *Showme*, the University humor magazine, and zealously promoting the then-new music of Benny Goodman, Jimmie Lunceford, and, among others whose orchestras brought about the Swing Era, Jimmy and Tommy Dorsey and Glen Gray and the Casa Loma band.

The year I spent in Columbia attending the first, the oldest, and the finest journalism school in the world was memorable for the education I obtained outside the Neff Hall classrooms, listening to bands long after midnight, night after night, and recognizing their differences, appreciating their singers and solo instrumentalists, and with it all, learning the songs of that period.

Came May, the end of my junior year, and a summer job with the Kansas City *Journal-Post* opened up.

It was a smaller daily newspaper than the rival evening *Star* with its morning *Times*. And it was understaffed; a *J-P* reporter and his photographer would arrive at a major fire and watch three reporters and two photogs arrive for the *Star*'s coverage. The *Journal-Post*'s daily circulation of about 150,000 was one-third of the *Star*'s readership. But I like to think that the old *Journal-Post*, where my dad had worked before me, had character and guts and a spirit among its staff that few other metropolitan dailies had.

I checked off campus on a Friday and the following Monday morning I walked into the *J-P* city room and meekly introduced myself to the boss—my first boss—the city editor. He was tough-looking guy, and built solid, like a fullback. I looked him over for a moment and felt like sprinting around end in the direction of home. But it was too late to retreat.

3

Music is now so foolish
that I am amazed. Everything
that is wrong is permitted,
and no attention is paid
to what the old generation
wrote as composition.

—SAMUEL SCHEIDT (1651)

UNLESS A ROOKIE reporter—they are called cubs their first year on a newspaper—shows extraordinary literary ability in his first few weeks in the city room, he is destined for several months of dreary, unbylined toil writing obituaries and peewee items of little news import. I fell into this class, of course. Missouri's School of Journalism was the first in the world and has remained the best for more than 60 years, but there are still things aspiring newsmen must learn outside the classroom, on the job.

The city editor of the Kansas City *Journal-Post* was Eddie Meisburger, an old friend of my father. His face was that of a punchy, battle-weary light-heavyweight with his ever-present cigar. Meisburger's background included a distinguished World War I combat record in France serving under Harry Truman.

Meisburger listened patiently while I explained, my first day on the job, that I was a nut on anything pertaining to show business, music in particular. The incomparable Goodman Ace had made his reputation on the *Journal-Post* and left for New York acclaim only weeks before I signed on with the paper. Meisburger, chewing his stogy, softly advised me that Lowell Lawrence was the *J-P*'s new show-biz editor.

"But," he said tactfully, "we'll see what comes up in the music field." He handed me a half-dozen death notices from the morning *Times*, our competitor, for rewrite.

I soon got to know, and became a friend of, every mortician in Jackson and Wyandotte counties. But I was hardly ready to settle for that distinction as my life's achievement. Two weeks after I came on I went to Mina Wilcox at Jenkins Music and borrowed nine new pop records, took them into a booth, played each side twice and took notes. At home that night I churned out my first *J-P* record review column. Meisburger accepted it and ran it in all three Sunday editions. The column was in no way memorable but no one objected to my copy and we got a few letters from readers asking for more.

Meisburger, in my third week, asked me to go to the Hotel Muehlebach and interview a man who had just checked in. "Who is he?" I asked.

"Rudy Vallee."

Vallee was as big as they came, then or now. His Thursday night *Fleishmann Hour* was one of the three most popular programs on network radio, and he had been featured in numerous motion pictures. Rudy's records for seven years had been best sellers, his *Maine Stein Song* ranking as one of the all-time top hits.

I called his room at the Muehlebach and got no answer. Rushing into the hotel's ground floor coffee shop, I saw Vallee at the counter drinking coffee. He was wearing dark glasses, movie star style. He refused to acknowledge my self-introduction, and a greasy little man with a strong New York accent seated next to the Great One spun around and informed me that Rudy wasn't meeting the press that day.

I humbly asked the obnoxious Vallee aide a number of routine questions, trying to figure a local angle, and got curt, stock replies. After about five minutes I returned to the city room.

Never having met a performer of Vallee's exalted rank previously, I wrote six favorable paragraphs about his being in Kansas City and included an undisguised plug for his in-person performance that night. In my innocence I assumed that *all* big names were difficult and rude. Vallee didn't deserve six words.

Just days later, I was assigned to interview the prominent opera star Lawrence Tibbett. I knew nothing of opera and I knocked on his door at the Muehlebach fearful that I'd lay an egg. A staff photographer was with me.

Tibbett welcomed us as if he had known us for years.

"What can I do for you, gentlemen? I'll stand on my head if you think it will make a picture."

He was what we, at that time, called a "longhair," but his warmth was overwhelming. He spoke of the roles he had played, the arias he had sung, the libretti he had memorized, the cities throughout the world in which he had appeared, and he said it all with becoming modesty and high good humor.

Tibbett has been dead many years now. May he rest in peace. He taught me that the world of entertainment is not all Rudy Vallees. And the feature—with pictures—I wrote about him brought me a number of compliments from Meisburger and others in the city room, the first praise I had merited.

From Hollywood came Tom Mix and his Tony, perhaps the most successful western duo in cinema history. I accompanied the dour-faced, tight-lipped cowboy actor out to the Northeast section of the city for an appearance before hundreds of ailing and crippled children at Mercy Hospital. He was, of course, a sensation as he put his educated horse through a series of tricks which I found, as did the youngsters, highly amusing. But Mix obviously was an insecure, unhappy man. He was later killed in an Arizona motor accident.

Col. Clarence D. Chamberlin flew into town in a specially made experimental Lockheed Sirius low-wing monoplane, the fastest craft in the skies. He had flown the Atlantic, with his backer Charles Levine as a passenger, immediately after Charles A. Lindbergh's New York–to–Paris nonstop hop had won the $25,000 Raymond Orteig prize. I don't recall all the things Chamberlin said in an interview and in a second session following a thrilling flight—at speeds up to 400 mph in long, graceful power dives—but one prediction he made sticks in my memory: "We will be flying passengers and freight across the Atlantic to London and Paris within two years. Boeing and Sikorsky already have the planes on the drawing board."

He was right. I got not one but three readable features out of Chamberlin, and I've often wondered why his sleek, powerful Sirius never was produced on a Lockheed assembly line.

Fred Waring and Cab Calloway were delightful to a cub at the Mainstreet Theater between shows. Waring's humor has always been enviable, and he's a longtime expert in public relations. His Pennsylvanians were all superb showmen and musicians. The flashy Waring finale took place on a dark stage with everyone playing instruments outlined in luminescent paint.

Because of the songs he sang, things like *Minnie the Moocher, Cokey Joe*, and explicit lyrical references to narcotics in other repertoire, Cab Calloway was rumored to be an addict—they were called dope fiends in the 1930s. I sat in his dressing room at the Mainstreet, astonished by his handsome, clean-cut physique and his verbal eloquence; a quick-witted, well-read, highly aware man who appeared, close up, about a foot shorter than he did prancing about the stage in his long white tails. He had studied in college to be a lawyer, he told me, but music became his passion.

Cab was anything but an addict. He bagged more space in the *Journal-Post* than Waring. Most of the Calloway musicians were Kansas Citians, and thus the local news interest was stronger.

If Mary Pickford at one time had been America's Sweetheart, Sonja Henie was no less than the World's Sweetheart when she visited Kansas City with her spectacular ice show. She was fresh from her dazzling figure skating triumphs at the 1936 Olympics, with a series of profitable motion pictures at Twentieth Century-Fox yet to come. The rival *Star* had one of its best young reporters, Berton Roueche, at the Muehlebach the same time I arrived at Miss Henie's door. She was sitting on a sofa, attired in mink, a tiny, extremely beautiful young blonde who patiently and honestly answered dozens of questions directed to her by Roueche and me. I obtained so much material on her background—in Norway and Hollywood—and her future plans that I spent a weekend at home writing an article for *Photoplay* magazine. I sent the editor in New York a half-dozen excellent photos of the skater which George Cauthen of the *J-P* staff had made during the interview, but within a week my manuscript and the pictures were back with a cold form-letter rejection. However, my feature on Miss Henie did run in the Sunday *Journal-Post* under a three-column head, which was more space than Roueche was given in the *Star*.

Sonja Henie, Norwegian ice skater, Olympics champion, and Number One motion picture box-office star being interviewed by Dexter in 1937 for the Kansas City Journal-Post *at Kansas City's Hotel Muehlebach. (Hubert McClain)*

Bert didn't slash his wrists. Today he is a nationally popular author of books and one of the most capable and literate contributors to the *New Yorker* magazine.

I continued to handle more than my share of obits, and from day to day I was sent out to cover accidents, fires (the most difficult of all news to report) and civic events in that lusty Pendergast-controlled county. Memory is tricky. You forget the week-by-week drudgery, the rushed 30-minute lunch periods, overtime in the city room on Saturday nights, and the monotonous, never-ending rewriting of news items culled from the morning *Times*. But I haven't forgotten a sunny afternoon riding a city ambulance to the far South side of the city to help pull the body of a handsome, freckle-faced boy of nine from a pond. He had drowned only moments before we arrived with a pulmotor. I picked up his little blue pants, seeking identification, and found two pennies and a scared baby frog in one pocket.

Nor can I erase from memory the plight of a woman—she was black—whose legs were not only fractured, but crushed, as we lifted her to a stretcher from a demolished sedan. She survived a double amputation at General Hospital. Where is she today? And what might the nine-year-old lad be doing now had he not elected to swim that warm, lovely spring afternoon in Johnson county?

There is pathos in show business as well. The alcoholic Helen Morgan came to Kansas City in a revival of Flo Ziegfeld's *Follies*. I took a stock 8 by 10 glossy publicity photo of her to the interview. She looked at it, handed it back and suggested she autograph a "better" likeness. From her trunk she withdrew a more recent pose, addressing it to me personally. "I'm not young anymore," she said. "Why try to kid anyone with a picture made 15 years ago?"

Soft and feminine, sweet and helpful to a young reporter, the attractive Miss Morgan of *My Bill* and *Can't Help Lovin' That Man* fame poured a drink. "You're welcome to one if you like," she said, a bit pensively. "But after what it's done to me I don't push booze on anybody."

She was 36 years old. She died, five years later, in 1941. Most of the autographed photos I collected as a cub reporter have been lost, lent and not returned, and some I threw out long ago. I still have the Helen Morgan print. And I feel almost tearful when I hear one of her ancient records.

Fish gotta swim, birds gotta fly. Life goes on, for some of us.

Ben Bernie: The ole maestro, yowzah. An amiable, cigar-puffing businessman who was extremely publicity-conscious and an ideal interviewee. "Write about my feud with Walter Winchell," he asked me. "That story's kept me and all my musicians in the big money for years. You needn't mention that Walter and I have been close friends through most of our lifetimes."

Bob Burns: Dumb like a fox, as they say. A rube from Arkansas whose rustic humor and primitive bazooka music brightened dozens of Paramount movies and Bing Crosby *Kraft Music Hall* broadcasts. Wonderfully friendly, providing good copy on interviews.

Dave Rubinoff: Does anyone remember this forerunner of Liberace, a violinist with an uncontrollable temper, and a mean, unbearable bastard with news-papermen? He was one of the nation's biggest names in the early thirties, earning millions and then sliding off into oblivion.

Harry Richman: He stopped off in Kansas City with his pilot Dick Merrill, to refuel their big Bellanca monoplane stuffed with ping pong balls, en route to New York and an attempt to break the transatlantic speed record. Another acutely publicity-conscious showman, Richman said crazy things and made insane predictions to be sure he made the papers. He was a prime favorite of America in theaters, cabarets, and on records and network radio as a singer but, like Rubinoff, he too faded fast. When he died in 1972 in California, broke and helpless, hardly anyone remembered him. I suspect a motion picture based on his career will eventually be produced.

Hal Kemp: Never a jazzman, he moved out of North Carolina with one of the most musical dance orchestras in history. I first talked with him at the Tower Theater while he tried to listen to Ravel, Stravinsky, Debussy, and Schoenberg records on a small portable phonograph he carried with him on the road. He provided little that was newsy. Hal was too retiring, too introverted, to make headlines until he was killed in a California highway smashup in 1940. He was 36, and some of the unusual voicing of woodwinds he featured for the first time outside the classical sphere are still in use today.

Amelia Earhart: Long before I graduated from high school I enjoyed a period of four years in which I hung around Kansas City's Municipal Airport washing planes, selling sightseeing rides over the city, and monkeying around with student pilots as they learned to fly. Miss Earhart glided down in her famed Wasp-powered Lockheed *Friendship* one afternoon enroute to Los Angeles, not long after she had become the first woman to fly the Atlantic in 1928. No one expected the world's most popular aviatrix in Kansas City; she climbed down from the cockpit and asked for a weather report. I ran over to the National Air Transport hangar, grabbed a bulletin and rushed it back to her. She stood around for a half-hour while her *Friendship* was fueled and its cockpit glass washed and she treated the three or four of us as cordially as if we were a civic welcoming committee. A charming, completely feminine woman despite her long, drab coveralls and goggles, her disappearance on a mystery flight in the South Pacific in 1937 hit me hard.

No one could get near Charles Lindbergh on his occasional Kansas City visits following the epochal Paris flight. I saw him three times, but he said nothing to anyone and always managed to hide somewhere in one of the airport hangars, Howard Hughes style. Little Wylie Post appeared friendlier, like Miss Earhart, when he and his purple-striped *Winnie Mae* set down in Kansas City just before he set a solo 'round-the-world record of seven days, 18 hours and 49 minutes in 1933. I remember his black eyepatch and the way he squatted on the cowling of his Lockheed as he carefully directed refueling. Also what he yelled, peering down from his high perch:

"Hey kid, why the hell ain't you in school?"

He and Will Rogers died in an Alaska crash in 1935. I haven't hung around airplanes since.

o   o   o

Memories, memories. Maybe they add up to something.

I huddled with George Cauthen and Homer Hale in their photo darkroom and we listened to a British King abdicate the crown to spend the next 35 years with "the woman I love" and to drop from a full-blown king to a mere Duke of Windsor. "Some company ought to be recording this speech," I told Hale in the dark. "It would sell a million." American Brunswick did. It didn't.

My Sunday review column had attracted enough readership to motivate Columbia, Decca, and Victor distributors to send me review copies of popular and classical discs. And in October of my first year on the *J-P*, I wondered what my assignment would be when Franklin D. Roosevelt arrived in the city on his campaign to win reelection over Alf Landon, a local favorite. I learned soon enough. Meisburger sent me out on the streets as a roving sidewalk reporter, jotting down quotes from adult and juvenile spectators, but I at least got to see the big black open car carrying the President from Union Station to the Muehlebach. Landon took a dreadful beating a month later. Roosevelt, it seemed, was an even more beloved local favorite.

I spent as many nights as I could mingling with musicians. They intrigued me. Julia Lee was an overweight black pianist and singer whose unfailing humor, combined with her top-drawer musicianship, made her a favorite with middleclass whites all over the city. She worked every night at Milton Morris's homey, unpretentious tap room in midtown. I got to know Julia well, and wrote a few letters to New York record executives urging them to consider her discs, but no replies ever came.

I did better with Jay McShann, though. He had just arrived from Muskogee and was working as a non-union single, at the piano, at the Monroe Inn out in the northeast section of the city where I lived with my parents. He had style, particularly with the blues, and was so likeable I began a minor crusade to establish his name nationally. *Down Beat* in Chicago published my McShann rave (along with a photo) and soon Jay was working better jobs—union jobs— with a bassist and drummer. I wrote Decca Records in New York urging that they consider him for recording, received a cordial letter of thanks from Decca boss Jack Kapp, and four or five years later his brother Dave Kapp *did* come out to the Middle West to record McShann. One disc, *Confessin' the Blues,* was an instant smash.

I remember another youngster, Charles Parker, who played alto sax ineptly and hung around all the bands and combos bugging the musicians to allow him to sit in and blow. He called me "Dexterious" and bummed cigarettes and dollar bills. Even then he was on narcotics, but eventually he was hired by McShann and mastered his instrument brilliantly. I never liked him as a person. Nor did many of the black Kansas City musicians.

Andy Kirk was still in Kansas City seeking bookings even after his *Until the Real Thing Comes Along* broke as a hit on Decca. I had followed him for several years, at Fairyland Park, Winnwood Beach, and the Pla-Mor Ballroom in Kansas City. He dropped by the *Journal-Post* city room one afternoon at my request, bringing glossy publicity pictures and a fat scrapbook, and I spent more than two hours recording the evolution of his Clouds of Joy.

Between Kirk, McShann, Miss Lee, and the late Bennie Moten's cousin, Bus Moten, I began to compile a notebook filled with material on Kansas City jazz. It seemed unbelievable that so many nationally noted musicians were veteran members of Local 627 of the American Federation of Musicians on Highland Avenue in the black section of the city. Count Basie was one. He was a New Jersey native, but had formed a small band for an engagement at Kansas City's Reno Club at Twelfth Street and Cherry in the black ghetto. There he had been discovered by the ever-alert John Hammond who heard a late W9XBY broadcast of Basie's nine-piece group while sitting in his car in Chicago.

"I remember Basie when he was with Bennie Moten," Hammond told me later, "but this little outfit at the Reno was better than Moten. The saxes were Lester Young, Buster Smith, and Jack Washington. Brass comprised trumpeters Oran (Lips) Page and Joe Keyes—a drunk—and Dan Minor on trombone. The rhythm was Walter Page on bass, Jo Jones on drums, and Basie was of course at the keys. It was the most exciting band sound I had ever heard."

Hammond pulled the band out of the Reno, installed Willard Alexander as Basie's agent, and the Count was off and running. He still outswings everyone in the 1970s.

Everyone I've met in the record business swears he used to sit in the Reno enjoying Basie's rock-solid combo. They lie. Hardly anyone knew of the Reno Club, unless they were black adults and as enamored of jazz as I was. I confess I entered the place only once. It was small, crowded, dirty, and rough. The thick mixture of tobacco and marijuana smoke was stifling. It just wasn't for me. But I helped publicize the place, and Basie too, before he moved on to the Grand Terrace in Chicago and national recognition.

I also wrote copy for *Billboard,* the theatrical weekly edited in New York, published in Cincinnati, and read everywhere. Its music editor was a modest, hard-working man named M. H. Orodenker. He guided me, suggested stories, and wrote me long letters that were helpful in my acquiring space in the sheet. They paid correspondents 25 cents a column inch. Some months I earned checks running as much as $12. That was a full week's cub reporter's salary on the *Journal-Post* in 1936.

With Orodenker's helpful hand, I did a long feature about Basie, Kirk, McShann, Harlan Leonard, Ben Webster, Pete Johnson, Joe Turner, Mary Lou Williams—she was Kirk's pianist and arranger—and many others who called Kansas City home. Orodenker ran it in a *Billboard* special issue, playing it over a full page with a continuation jump. Oro even ran a box, with picture, describing the author's background—God knows it wasn't imposing at the time—and interests.

The *Billboard* blast did a lot for me, but not inside the *Journal-Post* city room. Meisburger read it, puffing his cigar nervously, then set it aside without comment and handed me a stack of obituaries.

"Here, Deems Taylor, get these ready for the noon edition."

No one got a big head at the *Journal-Post*.

I decided not to go back to the university for my senior year and a B.J. degree. Newspaper jobs were too hard to find. Unemployment was still high as the Great Depression continued. Radio's big names were Boake Carter, Kate Smith, Edgar Bergen, Major Bowes, Rudy Vallee, and Goodman Ace with his *Easy Aces* series out of New York.

A "candid camera" craze swept the land. And as the New Year of 1937 began most of us were whistling *Pennies From Heaven*, *It's D'lovely*, *There's a Small Hotel*, and *When My Dream Boat Comes Home*. The mighty German dirigible *Hindenburg* exploded in New Jersey in May, killing 36 of its 97 passengers; San Francisco's Golden Gate bridge was completed; Arturo Toscanini was named conductor of the reorganized NBC Symphony Orchestra; and swing music had caught on with everyone under 30—Benny Goodman's band suddenly was the nation's most popular; Joe Louis won the heavyweight title by flattening Jim Braddock in the eighth in Chicago; Joe DiMaggio left the San Francisco Seals to join the New York Yankees; in Europe, Gen. Francisco Franco's legions besieged Madrid in a move that led to the end of the Spanish civil war; Adolf Hitler repudiated the Versailles Treaty of World War I and declared the German Reichsbank would not pay other nations reparations dating back to the 1914–18 conflict; and we were all dancing the Big Apple.

I was kept busy telephoning funeral parlors. When they picked up the phone I asked a single question: "Who's new over there today?"

All music is nothing more
than a succession of impulses
that converge towards
a definite point
of repose.

—IGOR STRAVINSKY

CITY EDITOR MEISBURGER pointed his cigar at me one morning and looked at his watch. "Take a run over to the Muehlebach and see if there's a story in Benny Goodman."

I beamed. For months I had awaited the Goodman orchestra's booking at the Municipal Auditorium. His Victors were the most exciting records being released in 1937, and although I had seen him work once before, at the Congress in Chicago, I now gloried in the opportunity to meet him personally.

Leonard Vannerson, Benny's dapper manager, met me at the hotel and took me up to Goodman's room. He was showering, but from a steamy, overheated bathroom Benny yelled a "hello" and emerged in a towel.

He was 28 and looked younger, without his eyeglasses. He extended his hand. "Basie came out of Kansas City," said Goodman. "Who else good is around here?"

He spoke with a rounded Alabama accent. He still does today. Yet he was born and reared in Chicago and has resided below the Mason-Dixon line only on one-nighters. No one, not even Benny, can explain his odd speech pattern.

I told him of Jay McShann, Julia Lee, Joe Turner, Pete Johnson, Herman and Woodie Walder, Bus Moten, Tommy Douglas, Jesse Price, Buster Smith, Countess Johnson, and the excellent Harlan Leonard orchestra. "There's lots more," I said with home town pride, "where Basie came from."

He said he would like to hear them, and invited me to go backstage at the Municipal Auditorium that night and meet the men in his band.

I returned to the office, rapped out a lengthy feature on Goodman, and at shift's end rushed back to the Auditorium. Soon I was standing by Lionel Hampton's set of vibes, gabbing with Lionel as he practiced. He was always first on the job. I was introduced to Teddy Wilson, an extremely shy man, who was my favorite pianist in 1937 and remains my favorite pianist today. I met Ziggy Elman, Jess Stacy, Art Rollini, and Benny's brother, bass-fiddler Harry Goodman. And then the most famous drummer in the world, Gene Krupa, a handsome, black-haired, gum-chewing showman who could set audiences into a frenzy with his cymbals and tom-toms. "I didn't get your name," he said, friendly enough as he tightened a snare. He said the same thing a dozen times in the years to come. Great hands, bad memory.

Harry James didn't show. He was ill, and a local trumpeter sat in his chair while Elman played Harry's solos. But it was a memorable evening. When the Goodmans slowly swung into view on the city's first-ever revolving stage, blowing their *Let's Dance* theme, the crowd cut loose with the most massive roar, the likes of which I didn't hear again until a Beatles concert in Nevada.

It was all a part of the city's Jubilesta celebration, a sort of indoor festival which City Manager Henry F. McElroy and Mayor Bryce Smith wanted to be a nationally known annual civic entertainment spectacular. Spectacular it was. The hottest act on radio, Edgar Bergen with his Charlie McCarthy; popular singer Frances Langford; the orchestras of Isham Jones and Ted Weems; the Ben Yost vocal troupe; Gertrude Niesen; and other brilliant attractions of 1937 all appeared in person, in addition to the Goodman band.

After it was over, someone discovered that the city would have lost $100,000 on the project even if the Municipal Auditorium had been twice as large and sold out every performance. That ended the Jubilesta.

I wrote stories on all the acts. Awaiting Weems' arrival one evening, I sat down in a box with one of his singers, a Valentino-type with heavily oiled, wavy hair. His name was Perry Como. I remember the incident only because of his despondency. "It's just too hard to take, month after month on the road," he said, looking forlorn and forgotten. "I was happier cutting hair. There's no future singing with a dance band."

I kept looking for Boss Weems to arrive so I could interview a big name. But I sympathized with the homesick baritone. I had his Decca record of *That Old Gang of Mine* at home. Like Bob Eberly and a host of other band baritones, Como brazenly imitated Bing Crosby.

"I'll give it another month, until we get back to Cleveland or Pittsburgh," Como mumbled. "This is no life for me."

I left him sitting in the box, lonely, blue, and unbuoyed by my compliments and well-intended encouragement. Weems turned out to be a nice guy, but he didn't say anything newsworthy. Miss Langford was gracious, warm, and lovely to look at. Bergen was equally hospitable; it turned out that he and I were Delta Upsilon fraternity brothers. I got autographed photographs from Bergen, Miss Langford, Weems, and Goodman. Como had no pictures to autograph and I could find none of him in the *Journal-Post* files kept so efficiently by Margaret Moorhead. It didn't matter. He wasn't much of a name. And after all he would soon quit singing.

I met Goodman again in Kansas City when he returned to play a theater, but again I missed Harry James. He was in one of the numerous Baltimore Avenue bookie joints playing the horses with Benny's brother Harry. Between shows, before shows, and after the final show every night, hot hornman James bet the bangtails.

Benny asked me to show him around one night—he actually *was* interested in Kansas City jazz. Out on Troost Avenue he nursed a single drink carefully and enjoyed Julia Lee's heavy-handed piano and big blues pipes. He savored the juicy shortribs at the Kentucky Barbecue. Along about 3:30 a.m. I left him, and manager Vannerson, so I could change clothes and report for work at 7:30 at the *Journal-Post*. I suspect Benny heard several other local musicians, particularly Pete Johnson and Joe Turner, after I checked out.

In Chicago a couple of years later, Goodman asked me to take a walk with him between shows at the Chicago Theater. We ambled by Marshall, Field & Co., one of the world's nicest department stores. "Gee, I keep forgetting," Benny exclaimed. "I need a new hat." With his accent, he sounded like a julep-sipping plantation owner. We went inside, Benny found what he wanted and tried it on in front of a mirror.

"You're Benny Goodman, aren't you?" the alert clerk asked. "This is quite a coincidence. Years ago, when Kay Kyser first came up here from North Carolina, he walked in here just as you did and bought a hat from me." "Yeah," Benny mumbled, "he's still wearin' it."

Kyser, Rudy Vallee, Horace Heidt, and Lawrence Welk are renowned among musicians for being low-pay maestri. But Goodman, eccentric in several ways, never was cheap around me. He grew up in poverty. His father, an unemployed tailor, was killed by a car while operating a newsstand at Chicago's California and Madison streets. "I can remember," Benny recalled once, while indulging one of his rare, talkative moods, "we lived in a basement, all ten of us, and there was no heat during the whole winter. A couple of times there wasn't anything to eat. I don't mean *much* to eat; I mean *anything*. I haven't ever forgotten it."

Through the years I became one of Goodman's most vocal champions. Not only for his musicianship (even his detractors acclaimed him as the best), but as a human being. He still is absent-minded: he once got in a cab, shut the rear door, leaned back, looked around, opened the door, left the cab and inquired of the waiting driver, "how much do I owe you?"

He has an Achilles heel—drummers. There's a certain sound, a specific beat, that Benny insists on, and when it's missing he slowly turns to the guilty one and stares him into humiliation. It's called the "death ray," and drummers dread it.

Benny drove me all over Bucks County, Pennsylvania, one rainy Saturday in May, 1938, the day Lawrin won the Kentucky Derby. Now affluent and famous for his music throughout the world, he wanted to purchase an estate in the country. We stopped at several places. We walked through them slowly, seeing old but classic mansions with five to eight bedrooms, spacious grounds, and stables. Benny soon realized he knew nothing about houses. He had spent most of his lifetime in hotel rooms in hundreds of cities. "Maybe," he said finally, "Moss can help me."

"Who's Moss?" I asked. "Oh, my friend Moss Hart. He writes. He lives around here close."

Benny found the Hart country house—it looked like Buckingham Palace to me—and drove up the curling driveway in the rain, and honked. Whoever it was that opened the door said Mr. Hart wasn't at home.

We drove on to Pottstown or some such place for a one-nighter, talking music, arguing about musicians and trying to stay on the road in the driving rain. Only then did I learn that Gene Krupa had left Goodman's band and that little Davey Tough was his replacement; Bud Freeman had also joined on tenor. In those days that was stop press, page one news. It was like David Cassidy joining the Osmond Brothers with Sly Stone coming in on guitar. Big.

Benny ended up waiting a while before he bought a house. First, he got married, to Alice Hammond Duckworth, sister of the jazz writer-producer John Hammond. They finally settled in Connecticut and are still devoted to each other. But Moss Hart lost a hell of a potential neighbor out in that lovely pastoral Pennsylvania country when he was someplace else one rainy May afternoon long, long ago.

❖   ❖   ❖

Louis Armstrong was known for his screeching, above-staff notes when he brought his trumpet and orchestra to Kansas City in 1937, and the audience stood around the stand shouting "higher, Louis, higher" every time he soloed.

Backstage, he delicately applied salve to his lips while we talked. He affected a dark brown beret-type lounging "hat" made from a silk stocking. I inquired as to his favorite musicians of the moment. He quickly named several jazzmen. "But the orchestra I've enjoyed for so many years is Lombardo's," he exclaimed with surprising exuberence. "He lays down that good danceable music; his saxophones are the mellowest."

Guy Lombardo? The Royal Canadians? To every musician I'd ever met the Lombardo sound was a joke. Most of the cruel barbs and gags within the profession centered around saxophonist Carmen Lombardo's nannygoat vocals. Louis thought otherwise.

Armstrong was then 37, in his prime as a trumpeter but dangerously overweight. He shuffled on and off the stage. Yet his showmanship and formidable horn gave him an undeniable rapport with his audiences. He was not the articulate, sophisticated man I had found Calloway to be. Louis grew up on the streets and in the whorehouses of New Orleans. Calloway had studied law. Disparate as their backgrounds were, each had much to contribute to the world of popular music.

I was to encounter Armstrong many times in the future. Occasionally he would personally type a short note and mail it off to me. All were signed in green ink, "Red Beans and Ricely Yours, Louis." Louie found no red beans and rice, his favorite dish, in Kansas City. Instead, he cheerfully settled for barbecued shortribs and boiled Missouri River crawdads.

Eddy Duchin played the new Municipal Auditorium at a time when his cross-handed piano style was selling innumerable records for Brunswick. He

Louis Armstrong through the years wrote Dexter letters in green ink, and he invariably signed them "Red Beans and Ricely Yours, Louis." He and Duke Ellington, the author believes, have had the strongest influence on American jazz in the twentieth century. (Charlie Mihn)

was billed "New York Society's Favorite Maestro" and his satin tuxedo lapels reflected his image of the suave New Yorker slumming in the boondocks of western Missouri. He was curt, almost rude, to me, evasively mumbling one-syllable answers to friendly interrogation. I left him with an empty sheet of notepaper. Nor did I try to write anything, as I had naively attempted with the pompous, unbearable Vallee two years earlier.

Duchin won several of *Down Beat*'s polls of musicians as "corn pianist of the year," a dubious distinction, but compared with his son, Peter, the old man was a Horowitz. At least he had style and a knack for choosing classic, long-lived songs.

An occasional encounter with a grump like Duchin would send me to the city's black musicians for the music and people I enjoyed. Jay McShann was getting better jobs month by month. He featured a good bass player, Gene Ramey, and a shy alto saxophonist, John Jackson, who worked compatibly with McShann's piano. Gus Johnson played superb drums.

One night I noticed a number of empty nutmeg packages strewn on the floor behind the bandstand. Nutmeg in a nitery? Why?

It soon became apparent as I watched the musicians on their rest breaks between sets. They stood around drinking milk or cola beverages, as innocent-appearing as a Brownie meeting. Then they pried open the top of a nutmeg package and poured the powder into their half-filled glasses. Nutmeg with a Pepsi?

They explained later, ribbing me for being a naive ofay—a white—that the combination produced a mild, sudden high much like one gets after downing a six-pack of Schlitz. It's cheaper than beer or booze and neither their bosses nor the paying customers suspected the mixture's potency.

It didn't appeal to me enough to try it, but I considered it hilarious. And I've seen hundreds of nutmeg empties around musicians since McShann's men gave me an explanation—and demonstration.

McShann always led a small combo in Kansas City. He didn't organize his full-sized orchestra until John Tumino took over his management and booked him into New York in 1941. Harlan Leonard piloted the most exciting big band in Kansas City after Bennie Moten died and Basie and Kirk trekked east to more lucrative pastures. A saxophonist of serious mien, Leonard's group probably was more precise and showmanly than Basie's Reno Clubbers, but it didn't swing like Basie's. No band did.

I wrote about them all in *Billboard* and *Down Beat*.

And I continued to cover fires, hospitals, and everything down to cat and flower shows for the *J-P* as I started my third year under Meisburger's tutelage. One day I took a phone call from a young guy whom I had encountered around town on news assignments; he was employed as a one-man news staff by KCMO and he sounded almost secretive as we talked:

"Are you happy there on the paper?" he asked me.

"Well, sure . . . I guess I am," I responded. "I learn a few things every shift."

"I'd like for you to come over to KCMO and work with me on the news," he confided. "Are you interested?"

"What's the salary?"

"You will start at $12 a week and you'll have every opportunity to advance. We enjoy fully paid vacations, too."

I paused for a moment. I had worked up from $10 to $12 weekly pay under Meisburger in two years and I had everything I wanted except a car, good clothes, and money in the bank. But was I qualified for radio? My vocal equipment wasn't enviable and the only experience I'd had at a mike was substituting for John Cameron Swayze on his noon WHB news segment two or three times.

"I'm probably an idiot to decline your offer," I told my friend, "but I'll stick to the city room. Thanks, Walt, and I'll see you at the next big fire." I hung up on Walter Cronkite and pondered my decision. But only briefly. Even in 1938 I wasn't anywhere near his class.

o   o   o

Morton Downey, the tenor; Elsie Janis, the singer who entertained American troops in France so gallantly; the Broadway comedians Willie and Eugene Howard; Clyde Beatty, the intrepid animal trainer and circus star; Charles (Buddy) Rogers, the handsome movie actor from nearby Olathe on the Kansas side of the state line—Meisburger sent me out to interview them all.

But it was the touring bandleaders and their sidemen who got the full treatment from my big Underwood upright in the city room. Glen Gray and the Casa Loma orchestra performed in formal tails in 100-degree temperature at Fairyland Park. It was the classiest band I ever saw. Even in the dreadful humidity of Kansas City on a sweltering July night they looked as if they were playing a New Year's eve soiree up in the Rainbow Room of the RCA building in Radio City.

Manager Eddie MacHarg set up a lunch date with Glen and his star sidemen, Kenny Sargent and Pee-Wee Hunt. They made me feel like I was important. That's an art hardly anyone in the music business knows today. Making friends, everywhere a singer or a band travels, no longer is popular.

Bob Crosby's band appeared at the Pla-Mor, a midtown ballroom heavily patronized by college and high school kids in the cold months. Bing's younger brother possessed little of Bing's vocal talent but he looked good fronting the band; like Glen Gray, Bob worked hard to be sure his outfit was liked. My excitement that night, though, came from meeting and talking music with the group's manager, Gil Rodin, whom I had been reading about in trade journals for years.

It was Rodin who had discovered Jack Teagarden and set his glorious trombone in the Ben Pollack orchestra, in which Rodin played saxophone. The same Rodin had done much for Benny Goodman and Glenn Miller back in the twenties when they were not much more than amateur Midwestern musicians dreaming of a place in the sun. Unaffected, soft-spoken, and sincere, Gil gave me valuable insight into the music business: how a band is formed, how financial backing is secured, how bookings and recording deals are made, all fascinating inside information one doesn't find in trade papers.

Rodin remained active 35 years later as a valued executive of MCA Records in Los Angeles. No one in the profession had more friends. He died in 1974.

There were other attractions who regularly made Kansas City a stopover on tours. Noble Sissle had the poorest black orchestra I ever heard—they couldn't even play stock arrangements competently—but his soprano saxist and clarinet soloist, Sidney Bechet, impressed as an outstanding jazzman. He later moved to France, became a national hero there, and when he died in Paris in 1959, was ranked alongside Maurice Chevalier and Edith Piaf in public popularity.

Red Nichols was edgy and uncommunicative the first time I met him, at the Muehlebach. For a few moments I thought he had been taking charm lessons from Rudy Vallee.

"I'm a little hungover," he admitted, sipping hot coffee and blinking frequently. "These road trips are too much. I wake up some days not knowing what town I'm in."

Red had played Kansas City hundreds of times, invariably with a "Pennies" orchestra comprised of raw, untried kids who were eager to work for flat union scale wages. The band never had the fine, clean sound of his records, made by New York's best pros. I suspected it was the music he was purveying, not the booze, that made Red feel poorly that day I met him for the first time. We later became dear friends in California, where he was careful to employ only the best sidemen.

◦   ◦   ◦

The *Journal-Post* was in serious financial trouble by mid-1938. Month by month the powerful *Star* & *Times* grabbed a larger share of advertising lineage. Dan Kelliher and some of my colleagues on the *J-P* succeeded in founding a Kansas City chapter of the Newspaper Guild headed in New York by Heywood Broun. I was quick to join.

Carrying a CIO labor card in my thin billfold got me no salary increase, and at summer's end the paper's management was forced to terminate a number of employees. The future of the *Journal-Post* was plainly precarious.

I was typing up a stack of obits one afternoon when the aged postal telegraph operator in the city room laid a message from Chicago across my Underwood:

CAN OFFER YOU TWENTY-SEVEN DOLLARS FIFTY WEEKLY TO WORK HERE AS ASSOCIATE EDITOR WITH EVERY OPPORTUNITY TO ADVANCE STOP WIRE ANSWER SOONEST.

CARL CONS
DOWN BEAT

I walked over to my old Postal friend and asked him to put a message on the wire:

WILL BE REPORTING FOR WORK TWO WEEKS FROM MONDAY STOP THANKS STOP REGARDS.

DAVE DEXTER
JOURNAL-POST

I had few clothes to pack and no furniture to ship. I had no car. But I owned thousands of shellac records and some of them I dared not trust to a shipping van. Going through them one by one, I chose my most precious 50 discs and divided them into two large cartons. The artists included Bessie Smith, Count Basie, Benny Goodman, Sergei Rachmaninoff, Mildred Bailey with Red Norvo, Andy Kirk, Louis Armstrong, Teddy Wilson with and without Billie Holiday, Duke Ellington, Jimmie Lunceford, the Philadelphia Orchestra conducted by Leopold Stokowski, Jack Teagarden, Walter Gieseking, Artur Schnabel, Bing Crosby, Chick Webb with Ella Fitzgerald, Artie Shaw, and perhaps several others I've since forgotten.

Off to Chicago I went with a college suitcase and two heavy cartons, in a drafty Santa Fe chaircar.

I'll admit it now. I was 22 and scared.

5

Music is more than
a combination of sounds.
It is colors, too. I see
the different keys like a rainbow.
The key of D is daffodil yellow,
B Major is maroon, and
B Flat is blue.

—MARIAN McPARTLAND

CHICAGO IS ANYTHING but the "toddlin' town" it sometimes is called. The Windy City, yes. My memories of the Illinois metropolis begin and end with the frigid, unending gales blowing off Lake Michigan from October through April, but intertwined with that unpleasantry are other recollections, the good things that occurred when I worked on South Dearborn Street as associate editor of the musicians' monthly newspaper, *Down Beat*.

I was forced to adjust to a strange situation. Carl Cons was the publication's editor but he never edited anything. His partner, Glen Burrs, was co-owner and publisher and his efforts centered around selling advertising.

I moved into the small *Down Beat* editing-writing room as innocent as a newborn squirrel. Within a few days I was writing, or rewriting from a dozen unpaid volunteer correspondents in the major cities, at least 80 percent of the news and features in each issue. I selected the photos and composed their captions. I pasted up the dummy of each page, corrected typographical errors, and arranged the physical layout of each story, writing every headline myself.

Cons was a former pianist, a Kansas Citian like myself, who had bummed his way to Chicago on a freight train, met Burrs, and magically transformed Burrs' cheap little four-page gossip sheet into the readable national monthly *Down Beat* had become. I had known Cons in Kansas City. He was a fair, honest, straight-shooting young man who aspired to write great plays and novels of international social significance. Burrs was taller, slimmer, and balder, an ex-saxophonist who conceived the original *Down Beat* as an insurance-selling aid to his many musician friends. I liked him. I liked Cons. But they were unlike in so many ways, as incompatible as any two men could be. To me they were the original Odd Couple.

I had much to learn. The big bands ruled show business. In Chicago, there were 10 bands to every one in Kansas City. The Blackhawk, the Aragon and

Trianon, the Sherman, the Edgewater Beach, the Palmer House, the Black-stone, the Drake, the Grand Terrace, the Congress, the Bismarck, and various smaller niteries along Rush Street—all presented nationally popular orchestras and acts.

By walking around the Loop and riding the dirty elevated trains, I made the rounds in wintry blizzards as best I could. There were many sites of news, and I already knew, from my days in Kansas City, that working musicians were the most fertile sources.

The hell of it was, Cons and Burrs expected me to cover all those news sites *and* build up sources without an expense account, but never having enjoyed one anyway, I made the rounds sipping a single Budweiser or lingering over a dish of ice cream. Headwaiters hated me.

After a month or so, Cons made a wise move. He brought in a former drum-mer, Ted Toll, to work with me in handling news and feature material. Toll was tall, a pipe-smoking picture of serenity. His easy-does-it approach con-trasted with my eager, aggressive manner, but he got the job done. We made a good team.

Cons poked his head into our cubicle one morning and saw that I was busy laying out page one. Swiftly, he strode to my desk.

"Here's what I want to see in this spot," he said

He took a pencil from his pocket, outlined a large two-column area and wrote a head to go above one-column photos of Benny Goodman and Artie Shaw. The head:

SHAW STABS GOODMAN WITH PARING KNIFE

"Or it can be vice versa," he told me as he stepped back to admire his art-work. "We must have something absolutely sensational in every issue, Dex. If it doesn't happen you must make it happen. Call up bandleaders and the top sing-ers. Get them to make wild statements. Feuds are what we want, anything to make bold headlines. We're not the Chicago *Tribune*. We reflect the mores and behavior of the professional musician."

He spun around and walked out. I suspect he was an admirer of the William Randolph Hearst school of newspapering. I was not. But I got his message.

Toll and I worked together harmoniously and sometimes made the rounds together at night. One evening we went to the Sherman Hotel's colorful Panther Room with *Down Beat's* piano columnist, Sharon A. Pease. Harry James' new band was the attraction. Pease got Jumbo Jack Gardner, James' pianist, in a corner and took notes for a column. Toll and I spent our time be-tween dance sets jawing with Harry and, at a table far to the side, Harry's new singer Frank Sinatra.

Nancy Sinatra sat there that night, pregnant with their first child, Nancy, Jr. She and Frank were visibly exhilarated, not only because of her pregnancy but also because of a letter she held in her hand.

"It's from a girl in Aurora, Illinois," she explained. "She says Frank is the best singer she's ever heard broadcasting from the Sherman Hotel. What a nice thing to tell us."

"We'll go out and thank her personally on my day off," Frank humbly chimed in. He was almost euphoric in describing his pleasure in working with the James band and appearing for the first time in Chicago. He also was flattered that someone from *Down Beat* would seek him out.

"The only other writer I've ever talked with was a guy named Simon with *Metronome*. He said he would give me a break in the next issue."

George T. Simon did. His complimentary notice of Sinatra's high baritone contributions to the James band beat mine out by a month. They were the first notices Sinatra ever got in national publications.

Frank in 1939 sang with less assurance than later. His voice was pitched two tones higher, at least. Yet he displayed an inborn, natural way of phrasing which was distinctive and extremely musical. He looked as if he weighed around 115 pounds. The jacket he wore was too large. A scar on his face was noticeable to dancers. Yet it was obvious that he was not just another band singer.

"I'm pleased that you like the Sinatra boy," James told me that same night. "He once sang in a Major Bowes amateur group but this is the first job with a band. I think he'll get better.

"One thing," James added as he turned to the bandstand to kick off a new set. "Don't write anything about him in *Down Beat* right now. He's been with us a couple of weeks, he's just a raw rookie, and he doesn't know how to dress, but already he's badgering me for a salary raise. He's got a lot of moxie. I've never seen a beginner with more."

James pegged him accurately. In a few months Sinatra left him and joined Tommy Dorsey's orchestra, a vastly more popular unit than Harry's. To Harry's credit he found a more than adequate replacement in Dick Haymes, who had a ballsy, deep-throated baritone voice that has become a legend. Haymes couldn't phrase a line like Sinatra, though. He couldn't squeeze maximum meaning from a lyric, or even a single word from a song as Sinatra has for nearly 35 years now. And I think it's a little ironic that James made his killing with a supersmash record (*You Made Me Love You*) a couple of years later without the help of any vocalist. Harry's horn did it alone.

º   º   º

An alto saxophonist playing the Liberty Inn on the city's North Side never became a big star, but three full decades later I rank him as one of the two or three most unforgettable men I ever knew.

Boyce Brown was his name. His eyesight was failing. He managed to read constantly despite the handicap and he knew more about the world's philosophers than anyone outside a university campus. He believed in all sorts of strange things, including metaphysics. He relaxed by writing sonnets.

42

He named his saxophone Agnes when he acquired the instrument in 1928. He believed that it was an extension of his own physical being, not an inanimate object. I sat with Brown one night at the Liberty Inn for several hours, taking notes as he gently discussed his life and the world about him. He proved to be the most delicate, sensitive musician I ever met, and I said so in a *Down Beat* feature.

Brown's elderly father came to my office later and presented me with a glossy 8 by 10 photograph of his son's alto sax, lying in its case without a mouthpiece and flanked at both ends by lighted candles. Boyce had typed on the attractive folder in which the macabre photo was mounted this eerie testimony:

Her voice now is mute. While life was breathed into Her, She revealed to me in audible measures many of Her faults, and delicately intimate moods found expression through Her being; though She was wholly mine, I never was Her master—quite. Having fully enjoyed the completeness of Her unquestioning service, it is with no great sense of sorrow that I lay Her away. As into the beautiful silence that precedes the touch of the Great Master.

For 12 years Brown went to work every night at the Liberty Inn. Then one day he joined the Servite Order and entered their monastery, where he was known only as Brother Matthew. In 1956 he briefly reappeared in public with an Eddie Condon jazz band for an ABC-Paramount album; he took part in a New York television show and merited a full-page feature in *Time* magazine. Then, just as strangely, he returned to the monastery and died of a heart attack in early 1959.

Whenever I think of Chicago I think of cold winds and Boyce Brown. He helped me to appreciate many facets of the maturing process I hadn't learned in Missouri. Today, I believe that all of us are perhaps the strange ones, not him.

◦   ◦   ◦

Hitler's mechanized Nazis were overrunning Western Europe and his dive-bombing Stukas were destroying entire cities by late 1939. Most of us in Chicago were more concerned with the Cubs and the National League pennant race as baseball observed its 100th birthday.

It was the era of *Deep Purple, Oh, Johnny,* and *I Get Along Without You Very Well.* We sometimes tuned in CBS Radio to hear Ed Murrow's evening war report from London. In San Francisco they were boasting that the Golden Gate International Exposition was by far the most spectacular event of its kind ever to be held west of St. Louis. Franklin D. Roosevelt played host to England's King George VI and Queen Elizabeth, feeding them hot dogs at his Hyde Park residence.

People were reading *Kitty Foyle, The Web and the Rock,* and *Collier's, Liberty,* and *The Saturday Evening Post* every week. *Life with Father* was the smash on Broadway; Hollywood's most successful films included *Dark Victory, Mr. Smith Goes to Washington, The Wizard of Oz,* and *Wuthering Heights.*

Benny Goodman no longer ruled the world of pop music. Artie Shaw had risen to at least equal popularity and a newcomer who had failed previously, Glenn Miller, was threatening to exceed them both in national favor. His group won our 1939 *Down Beat* "best band" poll.

I had never met Glenn Miller, his orchestra having played neither Chicago nor Kansas City. But at Christmas I took the drafty all-night New York Central chaircar to New York to set up a minor promotion for *Down Beat* at the Pennsylvania Hotel, which required Miller's cooperation.

Inside the lobby was a beautiful black Buick sedan, wrapped in a big red ribbon. It was a gift to Miller and his wife Helen from the members of his band. I had never seen such a gorgeous vehicle, nor such a lavish present.

Miller wasn't like all the other big-name leaders. He studied me carefully. He was cautious, weighing every word carefully and probing me like a lawyer. All I asked was that he allow me to appear on his high-rated CBS Chesterfield radio show to present him with a trophy commemorating his victory in *Down Beat's* annual poll.

"If the ad agency okays it, it's okay with me," he finally agreed. He expended words like Lawerence Welk gives away hundred-dollar bills.

The agency proved cooperative. I went to the studio in my Richman Bros. suit (two pairs of pants, a jacket, and vest for $22.50 in Chicago) and checked in with a tuxedo-clad producer.

"You will, of course, wear formal attire tonight for the broadcast," he advised me sternly, after going over the portion of the script in which I spoke to Miller for about 30 seconds.

"Shucks," I told him. "I've got no tux. I don't even have money to rent one."

"Let the kid wear what he's wearing." It was a loud, commanding voice and it carried authority. I looked around to see who had entered so providentially into our conversation. The voice was that of a big, beautiful man who obviously bossed the program—Paul Douglas.

"Who the hell is gonna see him?" Douglas shouted at the producer. "He looks all right!"

Then he walked closer and introduced himself. "Just be here on time," Douglas said. "But don't fluff a lot of words, as I do every night."

Bless Paul Douglas. He had been a superb sports announcer before he signed an exclusive contract reserving his announcing skills for Chesterfield programs. Paul was a man's man, gruff and masculine, and a sex symbol to every woman who met him. His later triumphs in Hollywood as an actor were among the most deserved in Movietown's history. He is still missed.

The broadcast went well. The Andrews Sisters had a jumping two-minute spot, shouting *The Yodeling Jive* just as they did on their hit Decca record, to wild audience response. Miller's band had an even creamier reed sound than on discs. Glenn took me over to the Pennsylvania Hotel later, and when the job ended around one in the morning, he and Helen Miller treated me to jelly pancakes at Lindy's on Times Square.

The Millers became my dear friends on that freezing December night. So did the Andrews girls. But my luck wasn't all good. I never encountered Paul Douglas again.

o   o   o

Carl Cons and Glen Burrs were ideal bosses. They left me alone. Toll and I got the *Beat* to press on time every month, something the owners had never come close to achieving. Our circulation climbed. Advertising increased despite a higher rate card. With Toll's support, I urged Cons and Burrs to publish the sheet twice monthly.

"But won't that double your workload?" Cons asked, sympathetically.

"About 60 percent," I answered. "But we'll have a better, newsier, and more influential newspaper. And after the first year your annual profits should be doubled."

My logic scored. Soon we were issuing twice as frequently, and we began to use color on certain pages. Each issue got fatter. Cliff Bowman, Tom Herrick, and Harold Jovien boosted our advertising lineage while Toll and I worked an average of 16 hours a day writing, editing, and making the rounds. We persuaded well-known musicians to write columns: George Wettling on drums, Dick Jacobs on arranging, and others. I was so markedly impressed with the record collection of George Hoefer that I urged him to do a regular column on collecting. He wasn't a writer, nor was he in the music business, but from his notes I ghosted a column under his name for several months until he got the hang of putting sentences together; his *Hot Box* became not only the most popular column in *Down Beat* but the longest lived, running until Hoefer's death in the late 1960s.

My salary was boosted by Cons and Burrs to $35 a week. The Depression was ending. But I still didn't merit an expense account.

o   o   o

Most jazz buffs move through a youthful period in which they renounce all the big name "commercial" performers in pursuit of long ignored discs by obscure performers of merit. I did, in Chicago.

The lure of the oldtime blues singers was enough to set me off on tours of Salvation Army depots, private houses, apartments, and sidestreet shops in search of rare shellacs by Leadbelly, Bea Booze, Fannie Mae Goosby, Ardella Bragg, Scrapper Blackwell, Barefoot Bill, and Ishman Bracey. They all shouted the blues in the 1930s but only blacks purchased their records. Columbia, Decca and Victor featured them in their "race" series.

I remember more: The Honey Dripper, Roosevelt Sykes; Aunt Jemima, Tess Gardelle; Bumble Bee Slim, Amos Easton; Black Boy Shine, Harold Holiday; and my favorite name of all, the Devil's Son-In-Law. That was the name adopted by a man baptized Peetie Wheatstraw.

The sexiest, most insinuating voice of all belonged to a woman, Georgia

45

White, but her records were never found in the jukeboxes of your favorite malt shop. Georgia's all-time hit was *Don't You Feel My Leg,* on Decca. I paid a nickel for it and a battered copy of Bessie Smith's *Put a Little Sugar in My Bowl* while going house to house on Chicago's South Side seeking rarities. Compared to Georgia or Bessie, Marlene Dietrich sounds as sexy as Bert Parks.

I recall the Henrys, too. There were four of them. Sloppy Henry sang with Eddie Heywood's band for Okeh. Shifty Henry worked solo. Columbia recorded a man named Too Tight Henry whom I rated a peg above Shifty but hardly the equal of Sloppy.

Hound Head Henry waxed for Vocalion, sometimes with Chicago pianist Cripple Clarence Lofton, a popular cabaret entertainer on the city's South Side. Hound Head discs were the most prized of all Henrys; in a swap with a fellow collector you might get three shellacs by Fess Williams and his Royal Flushers for a single chipped Hound Head.

Does anyone remember Ham Gravy? He once recorded with the nationally known Big Bill Broonzy for Vocalion. Gravy chose to feature one of his own works, an opus he titled *Who Pumped the Wind in My Doughnut?*

I never have acquired a disc I coveted for years. It's a blues, *Levee Camp Holler,* made in 1933 in Parchman, Mississippi, for the U.S. Library of Congress. The singer? It was, so help me, a man named Crap Eye.

.   o   o   o

I was living in the Windy City at the right time. Most of the gangsters were gone. Al Capone, Dion O'Banion, John Dillinger, and Arthur (Bugs) Moran and their associates were all dead, in prison, or semi-retired. The only mayhem I witnessed in my nearly three years there was perpetrated by the invincible monsters of the midway, George Halas' Chicago Bears.

Many of America's most listened-to network radio shows emanated from the Merchandise Mart just outside the Loop. It was the largest building in the world until the federal government completed the Pentagon outside Washington, Red Skelton, Vic and Sade, and even Orson Welles and his Mercury Players aired from the Mart.

I walked across the Chicago River Bridge and into NBC's swank studios there one afternoon to watch Mildred Bailey rehearse the *Camel Caravan* program with Bob Crosby's Dixieland band. She was my favorite white singer; we had met in Kansas City. She was noted for her juicy, generous use of expletives. No word, no phrase, was an obscenity to her. She gave me a long report on the antics of her two dachshunds. No news worth printing, though.

I then headed for the band and Gil Rodin, Crosby's manager and saxophonist. He was always a delight and on this day he seemed excited. "Dave," he said, "sitting down there below the stage is a nice young lady I want you to meet. She has just joined our band as vocalist."

"Who is she?" I inquired, taking a pencil out of my pocket.

"She's from Cincy. Worked with Barney Rapp's band and we heard good reports. Her name is Kappelhoff."

I left Rodin and went down into the seats. "Kappelhoff" was all alone, a delicious-looking peaches-and-cream blonde. I introduced myself.

"You don't really use that name professionally, do you?" I asked her.

She sized me up, then:

"What name?" she asked, her big eyes staring me down.

"Kappelhoff," I responded. "It sounds like a German pretzel maker."

She laughed.

"That's my family name, Kappelhoff. I sing under the name of Doris Day."

She was something special; feminine, neatly dressed, and modest. Moving up to the Crosby band and broadcasting twice nightly from the Blackhawk Restaurant on a national network was the biggest thing ever to happen to her. She was jittery. Once she had studied dancing, she confided, and just about the time she was to get a job and work regularly, she broke a leg. End of D. D. terping career.

"Miss Day, I don't know how you sing," I told her as the rehearsal broke up, "but you needn't ever worry about your future. Just stand up there in front of the band. They'll love you."

Doris Day, it turned out, was a hell of a singer. And unlike so many other writers who use the device over and over again, I'm not going to end this incident by asking whatever happened to her. How can a Kappelhoff disappear?

6

To the music of Rimsky-Korsakoff
I could never take my corset off
And where are the sailors who would pay
To see me strip to Massenet?

—GYPSY ROSE LEE

SHE WAS THE SECOND most profane woman I ever met, and one of the most beautiful. She was hooked on narcotics in her teens and before she died in the prison ward of a New York hospital at 44 she admittedly had balled "hundreds of guys" whose names she could no longer recall.

Billie Holiday, someone has written, "died of everything."

Singers like her come along rarely. I sat with her from 2 until 6 o'clock in the morning at the Offbeat Club listening to her talk in the first in-depth interview she had ever undertaken.

Among musicians she was revered and renowned. To the public she was an unknown. The illegitimate daughter of Sadie Fagan of Baltimore and Clarence Holiday,[1] the constantly traveling guitarist of Fletcher Henderson's swinging dance band, Billie as a small child had survived the terror of a frightened grandmother clutching her so tightly in a death lock she entered a hospital for a month to overcome her fright. She was 10 when she suffered the horror of an attempted rape—and spent two days in jail being questioned about it. At a Roman Catholic home for needy children, nuns locked Billie in a room overnight with a dead girl in an inconceivably cruel punishment for a minor offense.

Her mother was 13 years old when Billie was born. When Billie was 13, she quit school after finishing the fifth grade and never returned to a classroom.

Billie's fortunes improved but little when she and her mother left Baltimore for New York. Papa Clarence had long ago abandoned them. Billie went out on the street and worked as a two-dollar whore on Harlem's 141st Street while she was 15 years old. She thought of suicide but feared it would be painful.

"This is the truth," she told me. "Mother and I were starving. It was cold. Father had left us and remarried when I was 10. Mother was a housemaid and couldn't find work. I tried scrubbing floors, too, but I just couldn't do it.

"One day we were so hungry we could hardly breathe. I started out the door. It was cold as all hell and I walked from 145th to 133rd down Seventh Avenue going in every joint and trying to find work. Finally, I got so desperate I stopped in the Log Cabin Club run by a Jerry Preston. I told him I wanted a drink. I didn't have a dime. But I ordered gin—it was my first drink; I didn't know gin from wine—and gulped it down. I asked Preston for a job. Told him I was a dancer. He said to dance. I tried it. He said I stunk. I told him I could sing. He said sing. Over in the corner was an old guy playing piano. He struck *Travelin'* and I sang. The customers stopped drinking. They turned around and watched. The pianist, Dick Wilson, swung into *Body and Soul*. Jesus Christ, you should have seen those people, all of 'em started crying. Preston came over, shook his head and said, 'Kid, you win.' That's how I got my start.

"First thing I did was get a sandwich. I gulped it down. Believe me, the crowd gave me $18 in tips. I ran out the door. Bought a whole chicken. Ran up Seventh Avenue to my home. Mother and I ate that night and we've been eating pretty well since."

We sat at a table at the Offbeat Club staring at each other. The musicians packed up and left. Now we were alone except for a porter placing chairs on vacated tables.

Billie lighted one cigarette (tobacco, not marijuana, that distant morning) after another and toyed with a dying white gardenia she was wearing.

Journalistic conventions in those days precluded the publishing of the raw obscenities she used in her conversation, but for all her course, gutter level talk, she was marvelously frank, lucid, unevasive, and helpful in baring her scarred young soul to a writer-editor exactly the same age as she.

It was in Harlem, at Monette Moore's speakeasy on 133rd street, that Columbia Records' John Hammond saw Billie. It was he who took her to Benny Goodman and then produced her first records—*Your Mother's Son-in-Law* and *Riffin' the Scotch*. That was in 1933.

"I have that coupling," I told Billie. "You were pretty lousy." She grinned.

"But I was only 17 then. I was scared as hell."

"Why do you sing as you do?"

"Look, Dex," she answered. "I don't think I'm singing. I feel like I'm playing a horn. I try to improvise like Lester Young, like Louis Armstrong, or someone else I admire. What comes out is what I feel. I hate straight singing. I have to change a tune to my own way of doing it—that's all I know. You can't copy someone else. Without your own style whatever you do amounts to a big nothing."

Billie had worked, briefly, with the Artie Shaw and Count Basie bands. "I'll *never* sing with a dance band again," she said. "Too many managers, too many jerks telling me what to do, when to do it, how to do it—screw 'em all. I'll make it solo or not at all."

Billie had never been married. I asked her why. She was blunt: "Hell, I've known so many guys I don't even remember them. I loved three of them. One was Marion Scott, when I was a kid. He works at the post office now. Another was Freddy Green, the guitarist with Basie. But his wife is dead and he has two kids and somehow it didn't work out for us. The third was Sonny White, the pianist, but like me he lives with his mother and our plans for marriage didn't jell.

"I ain't sure getting married is the answer, anyway."

But ten months later she took her first husband, Jimmy Monroe. The marriage lasted only briefly.

I look back at that long-ago rap session with Lady Day, as saxophonist Lester Young named her, and note my concluding paragraph from the *Down Beat* feature I wrote:

"Billie says she isn't satisfied now. She wants to get somewhere. Maybe on the stage, acting. She wants to make money, lots of it. She wants to buy a big home for her mother. She doesn't expect any happiness. She is used to hard knocks, tough breaks. She admits she is envious of Maxine Sullivan and other colored singers who have gotten so much farther ahead than she. Someday, she thinks, she'll get a real break. But she's not very optimistic about it. Billie Holiday is convinced her future will be as unglamorous and unprofitable as her past."

Her life story recently was filmed with skinny Diana Ross playing buxom Lady Day. Hollywood as always distorted the truth grotesquely. I walked from the theater admiring Miss Ross's spectacular histrionics but I was irate and disappointed with the hokey screenplay by Terence McCloy, Chris Clark, and Suzanne de Passe, whoever they are.

I think I know the Holiday story reasonably well. From that first meeting in 1939 when we both were 24, our paths crossed many times in New York, in Chicago again, and in Los Angeles. We reviewed new records together with Al Jarvis over KFWB; she posed for a photo session with Charlie Mihn at my request; and we renewed a fond, warm acquaintanceship—if not on an intimate friendship basis—from time to time when she came to Southern California to work the small time, low-pay niteries to which she seemed sentenced. When Billie spent time at the federal hospital in Kentucky, vainly trying to overcome the heroin habit, we exchanged letters and my urging readers of *Metronome* and *Capitol News* to write her just might have given her a lift, some surcease from the misery she endured throughout most of her doomed life. We even talked of making records, and how we would come up with "something different," but it never happened.

She died in New York's Metropolitan Hospital in uptown Harlem on a hot, noisy July day in 1959. She was under police guard, as a narcotics addict. Strapped to one of her emaciated legs were fifteen $50 bills. Her bank passbook showed a balance of 70 cents. Alcohol had rotted her liver. Heroin had destroyed what was left. And when I heard the news, I thought of what she had predicted 20 years before, and how different it might have—should have—been:

Someday, she thinks, she'll get a real break. But she's not very optimistic about it. Billie Holiday is convinced her future will be as unglamorous and unprofitable as her past.

*   *   *

Mildred Bailey was the most profane woman I ever met. She was short and

(Above) Billie Holiday, the ill-fated Lady Day of American Jazz, rehearses with Duke Ellington and Dexter for a radio broadcast in Hollywood. Billie was a teenaged prostitute before her records made her a favorite with musicians; she died of narcotics and a combination of ailments. (Charlie Mihn)

(Left) At the Hollywood Palladium in the golden era of the big bands of the 1940s. From left, Mildred Bailey, considered by many musicians to be the most gifted of all white jazz singers; Mannie Klein, trumpeter; Milton K. Ebbins, talent manager; Dexter; and the founder and long-time president of Capitol Records, Glenn E. Wallichs.

fat and quick to lose her temper. She was hooked on food as a child and she died in poverty, at 43, alone and—unlike Billie Holiday—virtually forgotten by the musicians and few fans who adored her remarkable, childlike but ever-swinging voice.

I regarded Mildred with the same veneration I had for Lady Day. She was the only female singer as talented as Holiday, yet I loved her for vastly different reasons.

She was part Indian, as proud of her racial heritage as she was of her tiny, doll-like ankles and feet. Mildred left her home state of Washington in 1925 for Los Angeles, worked the usual speakeasies for low pay, and was hired by Paul Whiteman for his orchestra. While with him, she was instrumental in persuading Whiteman to sign as an extra added attraction two young men who sang as a team. One of them was her brother, Alton (Al) Rinker. The other was a heavy drinking, hell-raising girl-chaser named Bing Crosby. Mildred told me how it happened. She repeated the story many times during her career.

"Al and Bing had a little six-piece outfit in Spokane while they were attending Gonzaga University," she reminisced. "I tried to help them by giving them records, good jazz things by the Wolverines, the Memphis Five, Miff Mole, and Red Nichols. The two kids would copy those records note for note and they got to be pretty damned good.

"They did as much for Whiteman as he did for them. He paid them $150 a week each and they broke in in Chicago at the Tivoli Theater and later took on a helluva fine young songwriter, Harry Barris, to form the Rhythm Boys. *Mississippi Mud* became one of Whiteman's biggest hits, and several others sold big, too."

Mildred married Whiteman's shy xylophonist, Kenneth (Red) Norvo, and struck out on her own. And, as with Billie Holiday, musicians quickly made her a favorite, but she failed to attain the heights of other femme vocalists of the thirties—Ruth Etting, Frances Langford, Jane Froman, Ethel Merman, Ethel Shutta, Kate Smith and others—singers with clearly lesser talents. Musicians blamed her appearance, her obesity. But Kate Smith in those days outweighed Mildred by plenty.

I first met Mr. and Mrs. Norvo in Kansas City during their first Tower Theater engagement. That was 1937. Norvo's band was marvelous, and the jazz-oriented Bailey's swinging vocals were easily the best—artistically if not commercially—of any band singer's. They took me to Kaycee's black section one midnight after their last show.

"I'll have your largest plate of shortribs loaded with sauce," Mildred told a Kentucky Barbecue waiter. "And when I'm about to finish that plate, bring me a second order just like the first. For starters I'll have a platter full of French fries—be damned sure it's a king-sized platter."

Red and I finished our meal and waited for Mrs. Norvo to consume her second serving. "Shit," she said, turning to me with a gorgeous smile. "I'd order a third round but you might think I'm a God-damned glutton."

I wrote features and ran pictures plugging the Norvo-Bailey orchestra in the *Journal-Post*, sent in a rave review which *Billboard* promptly published, and pestered radio stations WHB, KMBC, KCMO, and WDAF to play their exciting Brunswick and Vocalion records. I planted a feature story in *Down Beat*. I implored at least three operators to push Norvo-Bailey discs in their jukeboxes around town.

But for all my enthusiasm and efforts, and even with nationally known music scriveners like George T. Simon, John Hammond, M. H. Orodenker, and George Frazier writing similarly enthusiastic features and reviews, the orchestra and Bailey never approached the popularity of Benny Goodman, Artie Shaw, the Dorseys, Charlie Barnet, Hal Kemp, Freddy Martin, Wayne King, and the perennial box-office king from Canada, Guy Lombardo.

In later years I was to accompany Mildred on shopping tours in Chicago, helping her restrain her inquisitive dachshunds, Hans and Fritz, as they strained at their leashes in some of the hinctiest shops on Michigan Boulevard. I was to sit with her in the Sherman Hotel's Panther Room appreciating the talents of Fats Waller, Bunny Berigan, Muggsy Spanier, and other jazz titans of the era. She was to come out to my ratty little Drexel Boulevard apartment and listen to records until dawn. She once denied ever recording two of the 78s I spun on my battered turntable one night. "Well, hell," she admitted after hearing them two or three times, "it just shows what kind of shit is being written these days. Bad lyrics, bad melodies—you sing'em once on a record date and they're not worth remembering."

More Than You Know was her favorite song. She always sang the verse as well as the chorus. *Old Rockin' Chair* was her radio theme. "I hate it," she told me. "It's a hopeless piece of shit."

Mildred made hundreds of records with Benny Goodman, Teddy Wilson, Mary Lou Williams, Bunny Berigan, the Dorseys and other top-rank musicians, but none was a hit. In 1941, just ten years before she died, I met her late one night in New York. We went to Kelly's Stable, where Billie Holiday was appearing.

"Do you like that black slut's singing?" she asked me as Lady Day, white gardenia in her hair, walked to the microphone.

"Of course," I answered. "She's the only person in the world as great as you."

"I despise her rotten black ass," Bailey replied, looking for a waiter so she could order a thick steak.

Billie went through a couple of songs with the tasteful piano of Bobby Tucker behind her, in the dark. And then she softly swung into *Solitude*, creating a mood so intensely personal, so deeply moving, that even the bartenders stopped their work and stared.

Mildred tugged on my arm somewhere in the last sixteen bars of the classic Ellington song and I turned to her in the dim light. Immense tears were rolling down her fat, flabby cheeks.

"Jesus Christ," she whispered in her tiny little-girl voice. "That bitch is the greatest who ever lived, the fuckin' best. Let's get the hell out of here before I collapse."

Out we went, as *Solitude* ended. Mildred got into a cab and I walked to the subway. I never saw her again.

But I still spin her records. And I think of her dying, overweight and alone, long divorced from Norvo, unappreciated and incapable of singing again—the greatest non-black jazz vocalist of all time. I still read and re-read the beautifully written tribute by Bing Crosby contained in Columbia's priceless gift-box set of three long-playing Bailey discs: "In her goodness of heart, Mildred took in those two strolling players," Crosby writes, referring to the time in 1926 when he and Al Rinker accepted her bed, board, and entree into some of the Hollywood booking offices on their first trip away from Washington in search of careers as singers. "There it was that she introduced us to Marco of Fanchon and Marco, at that time a very big theatrical producer, and we were on our way—with a lot of her material, I might add.

"Ah. She was *mucha mujer*. A genuine artist with a heart as big as Yankee Stadium, and a gal who really loved to laugh it up. She had a beautiful sense of humor, and a way of talking that was unique. Even then I can recall her describing a town that was nowhere as 'Tiredsville'. . . .

"And Mildred's singing," Bing's homage concludes, "how timeless it is. Just as appealing now as it was then. Certainly seems to me that Columbia has put between the covers of this album things of Mildred's that prove this over and over again. Things that prove there's just nothing like style—and this lady had it in great abundance. All of it good. I surely hope this album meets with the great success it deserves."

Crosby's words are from the heart. They speak for those of us who loved the squatty little fat gal with the foul mouth and one-in-a-billion vocal chords. But I think of the thousands of Kraft Music Hall radio programs Crosby aired over three decades, and the dozens of motion pictures in which he was featured and, perhaps cynically, I inquire of him why he failed to lend a hand to the proud and uncomplaining Mildred. She deserved better.

Like Holiday, but in a different way, Bailey was one of a kind. I don't anticipate hearing anyone as gifted as they for the rest of my life. And I'll always feel embarrassed that I didn't work harder to record them.

In this business, heartaches come easy.

7

There's something of the opium eater
in your jazz cultist. His enthusiasm affects
him like a drug habit, removing him, it seems,
from the uninitiated and less paranoid world
about him and encouraging many of the
attitudes of full-blown megalomania.
—ORSON WELLES (1946)

I SUPPOSE MILLIONS of Americans would find nothing fascinating in attending a recording session.

When John Hammond arrived in Chicago from New York in 1939 to produce four tracks by Count Basie's orchestra for the old Vocalion label and urged me to be his guest in the booth, I showed up an hour early. It was my first session. I've never forgotten it. The combination of Hammond, Basie, the musicians, and the engineer was to change my life.

They recorded on wax in those days, utilizing ugly, fat master discs spinning at 78 rpm—chunky platters which could be shaved and used again. Hammond preferred one overhanging mike, with a second mike centered between Basie's piano and the greatest rhythm section ever assembled—Walter Page's string bass, Freddie Green's unamplified guitar and Jo Jones' drums. A third mike was used for vocals.

There was no tape machine. There were no stereo or quad effects. I watched Hammond "mark" each master by reading aloud a series of numbers over his intercom system. With each selection permanently identified, he would then signal the waiting Basie to start the music.

Basie's band was clean, precise, and eager. Singer Helen Humes knew her lyrics. They had rehearsed four tunes on the road and minimal preliminary takes were required. Hammond suggested minor emendations to the ever-amenable, happy-to-oblige Count. Within the three-hour limit, avoiding overtime payment, Hammond had the masters he wanted and courteously excused the engineer and the musicians. The titles included three vocals by Miss Humes: *You Can Count On Me*, *You and Your Love*, and *Sub-Deb Blues*. Rotund Jimmy Rushing howled the blues with *How Long* as his vehicle.

"Nice session," said Hammond to Basie as the musicians drifted out.

"Enjoyed it. My pleasure," Basie answered.

"See you in New York next month," Hammond said.

That was it. Cool. I returned to my office on Dearborn. but the emotional impact of seeing one of the two or three best bands in the world producing music which I might enjoy 30 years later was so overwhelming I had difficulty tapping my typewriter. I was entranced with the miracle of recording and the beauty of the music I heard from the Hammond-Basie collaboration.

Nor could I erase one thought that kept recurring as I took the el home that evening:

Hammond gets paid doing the thing he enjoys most.

o   o   o

Many recording dates followed Basie's in Chicago. I sat in with the rotund sepia bullfrog Thomas (Fats) Waller at RCA Victor. No one in show business had a better sense of humor than Fats and he was all alone as a successful pianist and jive singer.

His little combo put each tune together in 8- and 16-bar segments, ad-libbing every note. Gene Sedric blew beautiful tenor and clarinet. Waller took longer than Basie, and the engineer repeatedly lifted off the big, heavy wax cake from its turntable and inserted another when musical errors spoiled a take. There were no tape splices in 1939.

Gene Krupa recorded for Brunswick. His band was little more than one year old. He didn't recall meeting me in Kansas City when he was with Benny Goodman at the Jubilesta but he was friendly nonetheless, and even asked my opinion of *Drummin' Man*, his new specialty which sported an Irene Daye vocal. It was one of his big sellers a few months later.

Some say that Krupa sounded old-fashioned in the 1970s, but for at least 15 years in and after the Big Band era he undoubtedly was one of the most accomplished and envied percussionists in the world. I still enjoy his records, and mourn his 1974 passing.

Duke Ellington recorded classics like *Little Posey, I Never Felt This Way Before, Grievin'*, and *Tootin' Through the Roof.* Anything Ellington recorded was good. The sessions I witnessed in Chicago were memorable mainly because they were the first Duke attempted after hiring the best bassist in jazz, Jimmy Blanton.

For two years Jimmy astonished musicians with his technical prowess and fat sound. He then became ill with tuberculosis and was forced to leave Ellington to enter a hospital. He died less than three years later. Musicians still talk about him, for Jimmy Blanton was three decades ahead of his contemporaries.

I remember Ellington's Chicago records for another reason. His sidemen lacked the spirit and discipline of Basie's—every session went into overtime. Duke would be sketching charts between numbers. Nothing seemed rehearsed. But once the date ended Ellington's complex music stood supreme.

o   o   o

Toll and I pushed *Down Beat* out to the newsstands every two weeks, on

56

time. It was a wild-looking sheet with screaming headlines ("I Saw Pinetop Spit Blood") and provocative photographs, most of them leggy girl singers who were acutely aware that a daring cheesecake pose would insure national publicity. Boss Cons checked into the office occasionally and there were times when he might even compose a stirring editorial, but Toll and I were told that he devoted most of his efforts to writing unpublished plays. Burrs dropped in every day urging Ted and me to devote space or a picture to some of his old friends like Joe Sanders, Orrin Tucker, or Wayne King, musicians we deliberately ignored because "their bands don't swing."

Editing the copy mailed to Chicago by the profession's best-known writers became one of my more delightful daily chores. The subject always revolved around jazz, and the musicians who played jazz best. John Hammond worked for a record company as a producer, but his copy was never prejudiced. He was a Yale dropout, scion of a wealthy New York family, and a pro-Roosevelt liberal whose music business experience had included recording the Empress of the Blues, Bessie Smith; Fletcher Henderson's excellent orchestra; a young and unknown Billie Holiday; Count Basie's band; Benny Goodman, and others at a time when good jazz was strictly an underground cultural phenomenon ignored by other record companies. Hammond contributed to *Down Beat* only sporadically, yet his opinions were highly regarded by readers. A rave by the ebullient John might well push a musician or singer from obscurity to national prominence. He was—and still is today—an unselfish, altruistic man of great integrity. Among his more recent discoveries have been Bob Dylan and Aretha Franklin.

George Frazier was from Harvard, a slender, dynamic, dogmatic, young man who had Hammond's knack for writing sensationally, frequently taking an unpopular stance in the manner of syndicated columnist Westbrook Pegler. I was appalled by his overuse of the first person, however. When his copy left my desk for the linotypes it was filled with heavily penciled excisions of the pronoun "I" and, in retrospect, I can sympathize with Frazier's occasional complaints that I had butchered his work.

Tall, urbane George did all right after those distant days when a *Beat* check for $20 was so important to his career. He became entertainment editor of *Life* magazine, and by the 1970s his column in the *Boston Globe* had become one of that newspaper's strongest features. In 1973, Frazier began a twice-weekly commentary on Boston's WNAC-TV. Clearly he was one of America's topflight writers. He died in 1974.

There were others. Warren Scholl, Helen Oakley, Marshall Stearns, Charles Edward Smith, Paul Eduard Miller, George Avakian, Frederic Ramsey, William Russell, Leonard Feather, Charles Emge and, from France, Hugues Panassie and Charles Delaunay—they were the pioneer jazz scriveners and historians who did the first research, the dirty, exploratory chores which give today's writers the background and references they need in their work.

❈   ❈   ❈

Buried at the bottom of a routine column from Los Angeles in the morning's mail I found a two-line item asserting that the former Casa Loma trumpet and trombone virtuoso Sonny Dunham had bravely splashed his way a quarter mile out into the choppy Pacific ocean to rescue his personal manager, Carlos Gastel, from drowning.

I smelled a publicity plant (publicist Barney McDevitt in Hollywood had an uncanny sense of what kind of "news" might make national headlines) but, on the other hand, Dunham was a truly international class soloist. His heroics deserved more than a two-liner on page 23. I pulled the item out from the column, padded it with background on Dunham and how he had just organized a new orchestra in California, and splashed it on the *Beat's* front page.

A week or so after publication, a big black-haired, bearlike man walked into my office and stuck out his hand.

"I'm Carlos Gastel," he declared. "Barney McDevitt out on the coast suggested I drop off and meet you on my way to New York."

"Are you still burping salt water?" I asked.

He laughed.

"You think that story was a phony," Gastel said, shaking his head and smiling, "but I was dying when Sonny reached me. I had given up. And I was 'specially pissed-off because Dunham owes me a few bucks."

Gastel was to become an important part of my life. He was educated at a private military academy in San Diego and UCLA and had worked for a time as a Spanish-English radio announcer in Agua Caliente, Mexico, long before announcers were called disc jockeys. He moved north to Los Angeles and settled for a job requiring him to clean the underside of Greyhound buses ("with a big, heavy wire brush and a bucket of soapsuds") before he crashed his way into the world of entertainment promoting dances, managing a short-lived orchestra fronted by heavyweight boxer Max Baer, and finally becoming manager of Dunham's struggling band of untried California youngsters.

I took notes on the Dunham aggregation that day in Chicago and ran a small feature. Gastel and I were to meet again frequently. As the best (and best-liked) personal manager in America, handling Stan Kenton, Nat King Cole, Benny Carter, Peggy Lee, Nellie Lutcher, and others in the ensuing quarter of a century, the happy, heavy-drinking Honduran became one of my closest associates and friends.

o   o   o

It occurred to me one Sunday afternoon as I reviewed records at my home that the young Decca company possessed a treasury of inactive jazz singles which might be packaged in album form and reissued profitably. Victor and Columbia were doing it but, to my knowledge, Decca's New York headquarters had no one who could effectively collate the discs and write the booklets which accompanied each package.

I wrote a letter to Jack Kapp, Decca's president. He and his brother Dave

Kapp were Chicagoans who had founded their own company in 1934, shrewdly basing the acceptance of their new product on a three-for-a-dollar price tag. Long employed by Brunswick, the Kapps knew records as few men did then or now. Decca's success was immediate. The Depression had hit its stride by 1934, but Americans rallied to buy the new 35-cent discs by Bing Crosby, the Mills Brothers, Guy Lombardo's band, and others whom the Kapps had persuaded to move from Brunswick to their cheaper blue and gold label. The Kapps almost certainly saved a dying industry with their bold Decca endeavor.

Jack answered me promptly and enthusiastically.

"Submit your ideas as to which records should be coupled and packaged," his letter read. "We will consider your suggestions carefully and advise. For each album idea accepted by Decca you will be paid $35, this fee to include your detailed annotation for the accompanying booklet."

Fair enough, I thought. I pulled out all my Decca jazz singles and a complete catalog of the company's five-year library. It was complicated work; personnel for each performance had to be located and verified, but I soon completed several projects for the reissue series—two albums of boogie-woogie piano music, a Louis Armstrong, an album of clarinetists, a Woody Herman collection, and separate anthologies divided into the best jazz recorded by black and white orchestras.

The Kapps bought them all and put them out within a few months. On my next visit to New York I dropped by their Fifty-seventh Street offices to meet the two brothers. They treated me as if I were someone special. More important, to me, they urged that I conceive additional reissue albums and write the booklet notes.

"Use whatever we have in the catalog," Jack Kapp said. "We believe that albums will dominate an increasing share of the market. Decca would rather sell three to five discs in a package than a single record," he told me. "The profit margin is obviously more attractive."

I repackaged a Count Basie collection, one featuring alto saxophonists, drummers, and assorted Dixieland jazz specialists. The Kapps also approved my outline for a *Kansas City Jazz* album, to be produced live by me in New York.

And so in November 1940, I sat in the booth in Decca's Manhattan studios, for the first time as a producer. The Kapps dropped by merely to wish me well, but Decca producer Bob Stephens sat alongside me—and the one engineer—to offer suggestions and answer any questions I might have. His help was invaluable. I had assembled an outstanding group of musicians from Kansas City, men I had known back in my *Journal-Post* days: the pianist Pete Johnson; blues-shouter Joe Turner; trumpeter Oran (Lips) Page; saxophonists Eddie Barefield, Don Byas, and Don Stovall; guitarist John Collins; bassist Abe Bolar; and drummer A. G. Godley. First we cut an instrumental, a tune based on traditional blues chord structures we called *627 Stomp* in tribute to Kansas City musicians' union Local 627. Then, with Page taking over as leader from Johnson, we waxed *Lafayette* and *South* in the style of the old Bennie Moten orchestra. For the fourth track we made blues-shouting Joe Turner, a one-time Kansas City bartender, the leader and featured performer. His single title choice was an original, *Piney Brown Blues,*, which Joe dedicated to the memory of an old friend in Kansas City who over the years had played benefactor to numerous musicians.

Now we had four well-performed, well-recorded sides in the can. I had concluded my first session as a producer, choosing the performers and the music and supervising the actual recording, and finishing the session within the three hours allotted by the union.

It had been easy. No sweat, as we said in the forties. Now came part two of my first production activities.

Into the studio came a second group headed by the gifted arranger, trombonist, and guitarist Eddie Durham, whose credits included stints with the Moten, Count Basie, and Jimmie Lunceford orchestras. With Durham for my second session were Buster Smith and Willard Brown, alto saxophonists; Lem Johnson, tenor; Joe Keyes, trumpet; Conrad Frederick, piano; Averil Pollard, bass; and Arthur Herbert, drums. We encountered no problems in mastering *Moten Swing* and *I Want a Little Girl*. In fact things went so uneventfully that Bob Stephens left me alone in the studio to manage the date myself.

Afterwards, I remained in New York a week, waiting for Andy Kirk's Clouds of Joy to arrive in Manhattan from an exhausting New England tour of one-nighters. We met at Decca in the same studio, and Mary Lou Williams took over as leader, sitting at the piano. She employed Dick Wilson on tenor sax, Ed Inge on clarinet, Harold (Shorty) Baker on trumpet, Ted Donnelly on trombone, Booker Collins on bass, and Ben Thigpen on drums. Mary Lou's ingenious charts of *Harmony Blues* and *Baby Dear* were our choices for the *Kansas City Jazz* album and they were rehearsed, recorded, and filed on thick wax in two quick hours.

My first sessions had ended. Decca would complete my album by pulling two classics by Count Basie's band (*Doggin' Around* and *Good Morning Blues*) from its archives and by assigning producer Stephens to supervise *Twelfth Street Rag* and *The Count* by the entire Clouds of Joy ensemble.

Back in Chicago, I authored the booklet to accompany the deluxe six-record album and sent my copy off to the Kapps. It was a major project for a major label and I felt proud to have initiated and completed it for the $50 and expenses I was paid.

Kansas City Jazz sold well, and still is available (dubbed off into LP form) more than 30 years later. But my efforts exceeded my expectations in another sense. Dave Kapp issued my *627 Stomp* and *Piney Brown Blues* as a single designed for Negro jukeboxes and it emerged as one of the best-selling singles of 1941, topping the 400,000 mark. Joe Turner still sings *Piney Brown*.

I liked the record business. But I liked being a reporter-editor, too.

◊   ◊   ◊

Easygoing Jimmy Dorsey was never rated the equal of Benny Goodman or Artie Shaw as a clarinetist, nor was he considered an alto saxophonist of the caliber of Johnny Hodges, Benny Carter, or Willie Smith. Yet he was a consummate musician playing either instrument. His band was never less than excellent.

I first met Dorsey in Kansas City in 1937. He, his manager Billy Burton, and trumpeter Clarence (Shorty) Sherock on a night off had enjoyed records and libations at my small Armour Boulevard apartment, and later we formed a hungry quartet which repaired to Kaycee's jumping Eighteenth Street for succulent shortribs and beer at the Kentucky Barbecue. Jimmy was just plain folks; no pretensions, no airs, no ego showing.

In Chicago his band played the Sherman Hotel and the Chicago Theater. Bob Eberly was his big attraction, but soon the modest, quick-to-quip Eberly was sharing the adulation of fans with a dimpled blonde from Ohio, Helen O'Connell. Manager Burton had wrangled a commercial radio show for the Dorsey troupe, sponsored by a cigarette manufacturer (Twenty Grand), and in order to feature both singers extensively within the 30-minute structure, Dorsey conceived the then-unique device of having both Eberly and O'Connell share a song, Bob doing the tune as a slow, pashy ballad followed by Helen's entrance after a short modulation into a faster, brighter tempo. Toots Camarata wrote the charts with uncommon inventiveness and, later, pianist Joe Lippman and arranger Harold Mooney continued the gimmick. Smashes like

First "live" recording session to be produced by Dave Dexter came in 1940 in Decca's New York Studios when Andy Kirk and the pianist in his band, Mary Lou Williams, cut 78 rpm shellac discs for Decca's Kansas City Jazz album. The three pictured here had become friends five years previously in Kansas City. (Otto Hess)

Amapola, Tangerine, Yours, Time Was, and *Green Eyes* resulted from the Camarata duet arrangements and, at long last, Jimmy's band achieved commercial parity with brother Tommy's flashier, more publicized aggregation.

Jimmy's quiet sincerity contrasted with brother Tom's brash, arrogant personality. I quickly adopted the JD troupe as one I wanted to assist in whatever way a tradepaper editor could. His musical product deserved every possible exposure.

I adopted another band at the same time—Woody Herman's.

Little Woody fronted "the band that plays the blues" but it was much more than that. Like Jimmy Dorsey, Woody played exciting clarinet and alto sax. Unlike Jimmy, Woody handled most of the vocals himself. Tom Rockwell's General Artists Corporation booked them both and they followed each other around the land playing the same ballrooms, the same hotel rooms, and the same theaters. They both recorded for the same label, Decca, and they patronized the same New York tailor (Sy Devore) not only for their own sartorial indulgences but for uniforms for their sidemen and singers.

Woody couldn't find the big hit record in those days. He made many fine things, Joe Bishop and Jiggs Noble cleffing most of his charts. *Blues On Parade, Woodchoppers' Ball, Blues Upstairs, Blues Downstairs*—musicians appreciated them but none was a hit with the record-buying public. *Ball* eventually became a winner and is still Woody's most requested instrumental more than 30 years later, but it wasn't until 1946 when he fronted an entirely different outfit—a more modern-sounding, innovative Herman herd—that Woodrow Charles Herman rose to the top of the charts.

I pushed Herman along with Jimmy Dorsey. Every issue of *Down Beat* carried something about the two bands, if not a feature or major news item, then a photograph. I plugged them lavishly in my record review columns. The men who bought bands in 1940 all read *Down Beat.* I suspect the publicity helped.

Chicago's humid summers and bitter, windy winters were motivation enough for any Cook County resident to look elsewhere for a better way of life. But it was not the despicable climate that forced my permanent move to New York.

Every month of my more than two years' effort in Illinois hammered home the indisputable fact that all things musical centered in Manhattan. The big bands were organized and booked there. The most successful singers made Gotham their headquarters. The most prestigious venues were located there. Most records were waxed there. It was Main Stem, the Apple, the Big Time.

My move was instigated by the visit to Chicago of the editor of *Billboard*, the weekly show business publication for which I had served as Kansas City correspondent. Elias E. Sugarman met with me, in almost comical secrecy, to reveal that *Billboard*'s able music editor, M. H. Orodenker, was resigning to return to his home base in Philadelphia. Orodenker had completed a difficult task, building the paper's music section from nothing to the best in the business, better even than weekly *Variety*'s coverage of the industry.

"We want you to take Oro's desk," Sugarman told me. "We will start you at $60 a week and expenses. It's a glorious opportunity for a young man."

I told the eminent New Yorker I would give him a quick answer. I was 24 and far from confident I could do the job. I had visited New York only two times. Yet the proffered salary was tempting and so was the idea of my becoming a part of the music industry's fast-spinning wheel even though my position would be a tiny, untried spoke.

Back in my office, I called Cons. I told him of my *Billboard* offer. He met with me promptly.

"Our New York coverage isn't good," he said. "If you are so enchanted with going there why don't you open an editorial office for *Down Beat*?"

It was a welcome suggestion. I liked the idea, but how could I live in Manhattan on my paycheck?

"We will meet *Billboard*'s offer," the conciliatory Cons declared. "Your salary will be $60 a week."

We shook hands. Ted Toll would take over my Chicago editor's desk. He was more than capable. I would work with our New York advertising boss, Ed Flynn, whom I had known and liked at the University of Missouri. We would need a new office.

Cons wished me well but he wouldn't budge on one of my requests. I not only paid the expenses involved in my moving east; I still was not to enjoy the luxury of a monthly expense account.

Maybe Cons didn't trust me.

I believe that
recording artists admire
each other more than they
indulge in petty rivalries.
You see, we know what
to admire.
—MISCHA ELMAN

ED FLYNN MAINTAINED a small suite for *Down Beat* in the Forrest Hotel on West 49th Street between Broadway and Eighth Avenue, a short block from the old Madison Square Garden. We shared a desk and telephone. We also had his small phonograph and we kept it spinning around the clock with the latest swing music.

It was a mad scene, as frenetic as a Fellini fantasy. Every room in the hotel was occupied by musicians and singers. The bar downstairs was ever-crowded, a newspaperman's Utopia. I began work as New York editor with a ready-made, on-the-spot source for news, features and photos.

Another rich area for copy was the RKO building in Radio City, five blocks to the east. Many of the personal managers and bookers kept offices there and those who did not regularly met in the Gateway ground floor restaurant-bar every noon. Weekdays I sipped soup with the VIPs of the music profession, jotting notes about bandleaders, singers, musicians, and other 1941 newsmakers.

A third site which I covered regularly was Manhattan's West 52nd Street. They called it Swing Alley.

For about a 10-year period, from 1935 through 1945, small clubs like the Onyx, Famous Door, Kelly's Stable, Hickory House, Jimmy Ryan's, and Leon & Eddie's offered the world's finest jazz talent.

It was, for me, tiring work. One had to stick around until three in the morning or later to rap with entertainers during their intermissions. For a man who was in his office at nine and worked a full shift throughout the day, the nocturnal West Five-Two beat meant an 18-hour stint followed by a noisy E train ride home to Jackson Heights, Queens.

It was on one of those late tours of duty in 1941 that I hit Kelly's Stable. Coleman Hawkins was there with his big, golden tenor sax, but it was a little-known man fresh from California who attracted my interest—a tall, black, deadly serious pianist who led the King Cole Trio.

Nathaniel Coles had made a half-dozen sides for a small California label, Davis & Schwegler, and was pacted to cut a series for Decca. He also had recorded with Lionel Hampton in Hollywood. Now Nat was in Manhattan for the first time, a virtual unknown, working intermission sets while the mighty Hawkins and his combo took their rest breaks.

Cole welcomed the visit from a friendly tradepaper man. He had garnered little publicity on his Manhattan gig and he was attracting hardly any attention playing second fiddle to Hawkins at Kelly's. I found him to be all business. "Maybe," he ventured, "our record deal with Decca will start something. Nobody here in the East seems to have heard of us."

Cole sang no solo vocals in those days. His trio's repertoire was built around his excellent pianistics and novelty vocals with Nat, guitarist Oscar Moore, and bassist Wes Prince singing in unison on lightweight fluff like *Hit That Jive, Jack* and *I Like to Riff.*

Unlike most musicians, I found Cole to be unnaturally reserved, incapable of the back-slapping, let-me-buy-you-a-drink exuberance most musicians display on the job. I liked him immediately.

He had changed his name from Coles to Cole. Alabama-born, he had been reared in Chicago as a son of a Baptist preacher. He used no profanity in his conversation; his attitude and outlook were mannerly, reserved, and courteous, but in an undefinable way, distant.

"I think Oscar, Wes, and I will get back to California as fast as we can," he said. "The money's not much out there but at least we feel at home and we have a following. I don't think New York wants us."

Cole played piano no less than magnificently that first night I met him. I couldn't forget his driving, virile, highly inventive technique.

We would meet again later. And I would then find Nat an entirely different person.

○   ○   ○

Greenwich Village had a number of music hot spots, but only two were worth consistent coverage. Barney Josephson's Cafe Society was unlike some of the 52nd Street saloons, honestly operated and comfortably designed with the patrons' satisfaction paramount. It was there that I saw a former chorus girl—a soubrette—in a Harlem club make her debut as a singing single.

Helena Horne had much to learn. Josephson pleaded with the beautiful young girl to stand at the mike and sing naturally but she persisted in trying to emulate white singers, employing their physical mannerisms and vocal inflections. Eventually, she became known for her distinctive personal style under the name of Lena Horne.

Nick's in the Village attracted Dixieland buffs, mostly college kids who were enthralled to hear and talk with Eddie Condon, Pee Wee Russell, George Brunis, Muggsy Spanier, and other high poohbahs of the two-beat cult. I preferred Josephson's place. Count Basie's band, Teddy Wilson's combo, the boogie-woogie piano duo of Pete Johnson and Albert Ammons, Imogene Coca—Barney presented a wide variety of topnotch talent. His able press agent, Ivan Black, also became a valuable news source to me.

° ° °

Harlem was a consistently better site for copy than the Village.

Everyone enjoyed the Apollo Theater's weekly stage shows. The best bands, the best singers, the best dancers, and the most entertaining amateurs all appeared there. A few doors away on West 125th Street was a place called Jim's Bar and Grill, where one could pick up a dozen news squibs while nursing a cold Budweiser. The Hotel Theresa nearby, the Braddock Bar at Eighth and 126th, Murrain's Cabaret at Seventh and 132nd, Small's Paradise at Seventh and 135th (with its fancy four-leaf-clover bar), and the 721 Club at St. Nicholas and 146th—all had appeal.

The jukeboxes were loaded with blues and black jazz. And if you had the time after a Giants game in The Bronx you could be sure of a news bit—or at least an abundance of juicy gossip—at the bar of Bowman's Grill on the hill overlooking the Polo Grounds.

These were all hangouts for pimps and prosties and numbers men as well as musicians. One felt a little gutsy going there. Yet I never once was treated any way but warmly in the nearly three years I walked around Harlem at night, usually alone. I've had more trouble on Hollywood's Vine at high noon than on the many dark Harlem sidestreets I frequented in search of news and musical kicks.

° ° °

Glenn Miller slumped down at my table at the Hotel Pennsylvania's Cafe Rouge early one evening between sets.

"Dexter," he growled, "I've got a beef with you."

"Everyone does," I answered. "What's yours?"

You rapped our new record in your *Beat* review this week," Miller mused. "I don't believe you knew what you were writing about."

"I didn't like all that handclapping on the *Volga Boatmen*," I told him. "That's right off the cob, something Sammy Kaye might do, not Glenn Miller."

Glenn looked at me a moment. He was trying to be tactful.

"Dave, do you know what a canon is, a musical canon?"

"No," I answered. "Should I?"

"A canon," Miller explained gently, "is a complicated device going back to Bach and maybe even farther. One voice begins a melody, then a second voice imitates the first a few beats later. The second voice can be at a different pitch or the same pitch. The first voice is sometimes called the dux; the imitation voice we call the cones. In our arrangement by Bill Finegan we use the handclapping sequence in canon form against the brass. No other band has ever attempted it.

66

"You don't have to like it," Miller added, "but I think you are unfair in calling it corny. Listen a little more carefully the next time we play it."

He got up, returned to the bandstand and kicked off his set. The first tune up was *Volga Boatmen*. I listened as if it were Beethoven's Ninth. It was indeed complicated, and more musical than I had recalled his recorded version being. He was right. I had written about something of which I was ignorant, a legitimate musical device beyond my perception.

Miller returned to my table a half-hour later, smiling. I admitted my ignorance but told him I still didn't like the arrangement. Miller laughed:

"Okay, Dave, it isn't my favorite in the book either. Let's go to Lindy's for some jelly pancakes."

o   o   o

Record sessions occupied as much of my time as I could spare. The Kapps and Bob Stephens welcomed me to anything they scheduled at Decca. My favorite dates were those featuring Jimmy Dorsey and Woody Herman. Watching Helen O'Connell sing a vocal on *Yours* in her Ohio Spanish is unforgettable. Not all sessions are grim.

And then I was invited to a Glenn Miller session at Victor.

He was infinitely more finicky than Dorsey or Herman. He sat in the booth for 30 minutes instructing the engineer on the balance he demanded. He walked out of the booth and into the studio to personally pull the lead clari-

Appearing over a national CBS radio network, Dexter presented Glenn Miller and his tenor sax soloist and singer Gordon "Tex" Beneke with awards for being voted America's avorite bandleader and sideman in 1940. Also starred on the program at that time were the Andrews Sisters. (Ray Levitt)

netist's (Willie Schwartz) chair 16 inches closer to the reed mike. He directed each of the Modernaires precisely where to stand when they were singing.

Glenn thought of everything. He even hired a trombonist, Tom Mack, to be his road manager so that on record dates Tom could stand in Miller's spot with the other 'bones while Glenn listened to the blend from the booth. Then, satisfied that the results were up to his standard, the fastidious Miller rejoined his brass section for the actual recording.

Miller overlooked nothing in maintaining his position as the world's most popular maestro. He merited everything he harvested. Leonard Joy of Victor signed him to a new contract during the summer of 1941 which called for payment of $750 a side ($3,000 per session) against a five percent royalty. No other performer in history had been paid as much.

The record industry in those weeks prior to World War II was booming. From an all-time low of only 6,000,000 sales in 1933, volume had consistently risen to a 1941 mark of 102,000,000, the highest since 1929. Victor, with its Bluebird and Red Seal auxiliary labels; Columbia, including Okeh; and the upstart, less expensive Decca line competed for artists aggressively. *Billboard* reported that Americans were playing nearly 400,000 jukeboxes. Almost every radio station depended on discs for its around-the-clock programming.

I continued to review records for the *Beat*, mailing my copy out to Ted Toll every Sunday night. We started a best-sellers chart and devoted twice as much editorial space to reviews as we had allowed in previous issues. Circulation moved up above 60,000 an issue.

But on the whole my work in New York differed little from what I had done in Chicago. There were just more news, more feature stories, and more photographs for me to handle in Manhattan than in Chicago and I found it trying to make my daily rounds covering my numerous sources. Ed Flynn was a big help. He took notes while selling ad space and frequently came up with a choice, page-one item.

I went over to the Paramount Theater one afternoon to hear a new band fronted by guitar-playing Alvino Rey, recently of the Horace Heidt troupe. Rey was cordial, and suggested I go upstairs to the dressing rooms to meet the four singing King Sisters. One of them, Louise, was his wife.

I walked into a sort of recreation room and was immediately surrounded by four bathrobed, yelling young women who didn't like what they saw.

"You didn't appreciate our last record," one of them screamed. "And we tried so hard to make it good."

I had known the Boswell Sisters, the Andrews Sisters, the Peters Sisters, the Dandridge Sisters, and some of the Little Sisters of the Poor in Kansas City, but never had I encountered anything like the Kings.

Yvonne, the youngest, started crying.

"We rehearse so hard to be professional," she sobbed, clutching at my lapels. "Then you come along and say we're no good."

Another sister began to cry as they clustered around me, all of them jabbering and talking incoherently. Finally, they calmed down and we discussed their records with Rey's band on Victor. I assured the girls they had made some good sides and that their future output—considering their dedication—could only produce truly admirable artistic accomplishments.

Now they all smiled. One of them patted my shoulder. "You're a nice man," Yvonne said. I thanked them for their time and fled for the elevator. As I walked away, they waved friendly goodbyes and implored me to visit them again.

And damned if two of the four weren't crying again.

° ° °

For several months I struggled with a series of lengthy features in which the leaders of the nation's most popular, non-swinging "commercial" orchestras would disclose their varied philosophies of popular music. I chose Meyer Davis, who controlled a number of groups using his name, a favorite at Eastern "400" balls and debutante parties: Sammy Kaye, riding high with his *Daddy* million-seller; Horace Heidt, a cunning, calculating showman who utilized his police dog Lobo and the American flag in his eye-popping stage presentations; Abe Lyman, a one-time taxi driver whose orchestra often sounded as if it were comprised of Yellow Cab employees; and Guy Lombardo. Guy was then the crown prince among the icky, mickey-mouse ensembles, and he remains a regal figure today.

It was not a successful series. They all said the same thing. "Look how much money I gross every year," all but Lombardo boasted. I had met Guy and his brothers Carmen, Leibert, and Victor the previous year at the New York Roosevelt and been more than impressed; despite the razzing they had taken for years in *Down Beat*, they were cordial, courteous, and dignified. I abandoned the series before I could interview them.

Heidt told me he enjoyed and respected the *Beat* and its narrow editorial stance. Kaye boasted that his musicians could play anything in the Basie or Goodman books just as well as the Count or Benny, "but we prefer a more musical, more danceable, product." The truth was—and I told Sammy—his musicians weren't skilled enough to haul Count Basie's baggage. Lyman blew cigar smoke in my face and bragged about his bank account.

They weren't my kind of people, I'm afraid. So it was back to the jazz world and to hell with the corn merchants. I know when I lay an egg at the typewriter.

° ° °

The most sought-after radio plug in Manhattan in 1941 was Martin Block's daily WNEW *Make Believe Ballroom*. Block had copied the format of a KFWB program in Hollywood emceed by Canadian-born Al Jarvis, a red-haired former bank teller with whom Block had worked briefly in his youth. Millions listened to Block's *Ballroom* six days a week. When he pushed a record it quickly became a brisk seller.

A man named Alan Courtney itched to break up Block's monopoly. Courtney toiled as an announcer on WOV, knew bands and singers intimately, and

69

was thoroughly professional in his microphone technique. He asked me to become a regular commentator on his Wednesday evening two-hour segment in which the latest record releases were reviewed. In addition to Dexter, Courtney arranged to have guest bandleaders, singers, and arrangers on each panel.

I received no remuneration, but Courtney was generous with his plugs for *Down Beat*. After about three weeks, mail began to flood WOV, Courtney's ratings doubled, and the Manhattan dailies ran stories about WOV's emergence as a major station in the world's most competitive and lucrative radio market.

Except for Bing Crosby's *Moonlight Cocktail*, most of the records we reviewed I cannot recall today. Bing had been the singer who could do no wrong for me since his neophyte days with Paul Whiteman and Gus Arnheim in California. Crosby had changed the course of popular singing with his jazz-oriented approach: Como, Sinatra, Bennett, Haymes, Eberly, and a jillion other baritones owe at least a portion of their success to The Groaner's path-clearing efforts of the early 1930s.

Crosby's voice faltered on *Moonlight Cocktail*. His assurance and poise were absent. I said so, bluntly, on WOV. It was a jarring moment for me. My remarks jarred others as well. The station's telephone lines were immediately overloaded, some of the listeners charging me with heresy while others applauded my candidness and perceptiveness.

Courtney's ratings zoomed. Mail inundated WOV.

I've never understood how radio listeners hear about something new and different—how they will switch their listening habits overnight and adopt an unpublicized smaller station as their favorite—but it happened to WOV, and Courtney deservedly became a power with his controversial record-reviewing conclaves.

Over at WMCA on Broadway, Bob Bach conceived a recorded jazz quiz show with a panel similar to Courtney's—an orchestra leader, a singer, a big name horn soloist and a regular panel member. He called his creation *Platterbrains* and aired it Friday evenings. *Platterbrains* plainly lacked the appeal of Courtney's less-restricted musical menu but it racked up solid ratings, and as a regular panel member for several months I learned first hand that everyone in the music industry dialed it unfailingly.

And so, for the remainder of my residence in New York, I pondered the aberrational behavior of teenaged girls who waited in the halls and lobbies of WOV and WMCA to scream and shove for autographs of an unpaid ex-Missouri newsman who exited the two studios every Wednesday and Friday evening intent only on finding a seat on the subway home to Queens. But it happened to me, month after month, and it was to occur again after I moved to California during World War II. Who can explain the mental and emotional content of the minds of immature young ladies—and certain young men as well? I won't even try.

° ° °

Ever since I was a cub reporter, I've heard the honorable profession of press agentry denigrated, defiled, and denounced. Most of the hundreds of flacks I've known and worked with were pleasant, hard-working men who were of immense help to me.

David O. Alber was the classiest flack I ever worked with. His offices were in the lofty RCA building in Radio City. He dressed like the Duke of Windsor. He spoke softly. His clients were all top-rank.

Alber's problem was Sammy Kaye, whose overly saccharine orchestra was not highly regarded by readers of our rag or musicians as a whole. Yet Sammy knew the value of publicity in the *Beat* and implored the gentlemanly Alber to get him a break.

Alber called me at the Forrest, explaining his predicament.

"If Sammy makes news, we print it," I told him. "The front cover is his if we get the right attention-grabbing picture."

A week later I had a dozen big, sharp, glossy stills on my desk. Sammy was seated cross-legged on the floor. He wore a turban. He was playing his clarinet. And a cobra—or a darned good imitation of one—was dancing to Sammy's music.

We used it as a *Down Beat* front cover. Then, a couple of days later and within a few minutes, I took two phone calls. One was from Alber, thanking me for helping him please a difficult client. The other came from Kaye, who was irate. "I didn't like that pose," he shouted. "You could have used a better one."

Sammy threatened to sue.

I called Alber. He couldn't believe what Kaye had done. He was speechless.

"Now you know," I told him, "why cornballs like Sammy aren't our kind of people. If it had been Woody or the Count or Charlie Barnet, they'd have sent us the snake and a case of Cutty Sark in appreciation."

Alber is dead, and so are several of his colleagues of 30 years ago. I am indebted to a number of them and so is every veteran tradepaper writer or editor. Arthur Pine not only press-agented several bands, he also managed Gray Gordon's Tic-Toc Rhythm Orchestra. Today he is a successful literary agent. There were men like Jim McCarthy, Milton Karle, Henry Okun, Jack Egan, George B. Evans, Sam Wahl, Irving Hoffman, Les Lieber, Bernie Green, Ira Steiner, and the teams of Garfield-Zimmerman and Hansen-Williams. Ned Williams was particularly effective handling Duke Ellington's press; later he moved to Chicago to work as managing editor of *Down Beat*.

Thousands of people make up the music business. We hear about the singers, composers, lyricists, managers, bookers, record producers, deejays, critics, musicians, editors, writers, and even, in the counterculture of the seventies, the sex-motivated groupies who hang around the rock combos blatantly servicing one musician after another. It seems to me that the anonymous publicists and promotion folk behind the scenes deserve more kudos than they get.

Even Sinatra needed their perspicacity when he left Tommy Dorsey's troupe in 1942 to start a career as a single at the Paramount Theater. George B. Evans paid a covey of teenaged, shrieking females to leap from their seats at each Sinatra performance. Some swooned in the aisles. Without that novel assist from Evans' fertile brain, Francis Albert might not have launched a new era in pop music for at least another two or three weeks.

I used to become indignant
when all those Tommy Dorsey vocalists
would suddenly arise, lock arms and announce,
dear God, that they would never smile
again. Today I would feel sorry
for the poor bastards and try
to brighten their corner.

—GEORGE FRAZIER

If Chicago reminds me of unbearably cold, windy, miserable weather—and it always will—then I remember New York for its lovely early summer days and nights.

The Astor Hotel roof could in no way be faulted as an ideal setting for a dance band. It was in the center of Times Square, and those fortunate enough to rate a booking there were granted heavy full-network airtime. It was, moreover, an exquisite room with its tiny pink table lanterns casting a cheery, subdued glow which women patrons found flattering.

Tommy Dorsey was king at the Astor. He wore white suits, white shoes, white ties, and white shirts while conducting his superb orchestra and a battery of vocalists which at one time or another included Sinatra, Jo Stafford, Connie Haines and the Pied Pipers.

In the TD brass section sat Bunny Berigan. Bunny drank too much. Some nights he couldn't play his book, or the daring, inventive trumpet solos for which he was renowned among musicians. Tommy coddled him and accepted his frailties for five months before he was forced to give the pitiable Berigan his notice. Bunny went out to form his own band—he had filed bankruptcy with a previous one—and died of alcoholism before he could get it off the ground. The Berigan story is, like Holiday's and Bailey's, one of the most tragic I know.

Like millions of others, I thrilled to TD's music, but I never felt comfortable around the band. Tommy could be brusque and haughty, if he even condescended to speak. He kept a string of stooges around him, flunkies and yes-men who regarded themselves as exalted, privileged persons. I concluded that Tommy resented my friendship with his older brother, with whom he had had differences since they were small boys in Pennsylvania.

I swung by the Astor early one balmy evening to check on rumored personnel changes within the band. It was a gala opening night. Tommy showed his musicians a stack of congratulatory wires and there were a couple of the tired old "hope your opening is as big as Sophie Tucker's" gag telegrams from song-pluggers in other cities who gleefully presumed they were the first to use that stale line. I talked with some of the Dorsey musicians and departed.

It was a major error. A few hours later brother Jimmy dropped by to wish Tommy well. He never had the chance. Tommy saw him, seated with music publishers Rocco Vocco and Jack Bregman, and rushed to Jimmy's table. "I didn't mess up your Hotel Pennsylvania opening last month," Tommy yelled. "Why the hell did you come here?"

They argued for a moment. Then Tommy, his face a deep red, and agitated and breathing heavily, lost control. He swung a right, hitting Jimmy in the head. Jimmy shook it off and returned the punch. Jimmy's friends interceded and pulled them apart. Jimmy then strode to an exit, Tommy moving off in another direction.

"Then," Jimmy told me the next day, "I saw my brother approach me while I awaited an elevator. He had circled around, and I was pleased that he wanted to shake hands and maybe even apologize. Instead, he walked up to me and gave me another punch in the nose.

"To tell you the truth, I never have understood my brother. But he's the best damned trombone player in the world and don't you ever forget it."

o   o   o

There were other nice places to go on a warm evening in Manhattan.

Frank Dailey's Meadowbrook played more big names than any place in America. Frank and Vince Dailey ran a first-rate kitchen, they served unwatered drinks, and their dance floor was spacious. Meadowbrook offered more airtime than any spot in the East.

It was about an hour's drive there from Times Square. I owned no car, but music publishers Lou Levy, Mickey Goldsen, Happy Goday, and Al Gallico alternately offered me rides under the Hudson River by tunnel and out into the clear, clean, fresh air of the Jersey countryside along the Pompton Turnpike.

It was at Meadowbrook I met Norma Egstrom.

She was new with the Benny Goodman band, a plumpish blonde from North Dakota who lacked confidence at the mike and who, at first, was tagged as a weak replacement for the Helen Forrests, Martha Tiltons, and Helen Wards who had held the canary's post with Goodman previously. With Goodman, Norma used the name Peggy Lee.

She was on edge, nervous and incapable of singing as well as she knew she could. Benny had hired her only because Mrs. Alice Hammond Goodman, Benny's bride (and the sister of John Hammond), had watched her work as a single at Chicago's plushy Pump Room of the Hotel Ambassador. She insisted that Peggy would be an asset to his band.

"So," said Peggy, "I'm not going back to North Dakota until I've given it my best shot. Benny, thank goodness, is a patient man."

She wasn't impressive that first week at Meadowbrook, either in person or on the air. After meeting her, I concluded she would make some hard-working Dakota farmhand a darned sweet wife. Soon.

°　　　°　　　°

Les Brown seemed to play all summer *every* summer at a place in nearby Armonk known as the Log Cabin. My friend Alan Courtney of WOV had plugged a novelty by Brown's Bombers called *Joltin' Joe DiMaggio*, and Les broke through with a semi-hit disc.

Doris Day had quit the Crosby Dixielanders because one of them, a titan on his instrument, persisted in making amorous advances to the point where the former Miss Kappelhoff couldn't handle him. She then joined Brown. The months passed, and in trombonist Al Jorden she found a man whose honorable intentions she delighted in accepting. They were married in 1941. Doris retired. Like Como, she had had enough.

"Being a mother is my next goal," she told Les as she departed for Cincinnati.

Brown replaced Doris with Betty Bonney, a brunette looker.

The Log Cabin was a rustic outdoor restaurant with a small dance floor. Patrons lolled around gnawing corn on the cob and shouting requests. Brown and his band were paid bare union scale but they broadcast every night and built up a reputation which would pay off on one-night stands and in record royalties.

I didn't care much for *Joltin' Joe DiMaggio*, an inane novelty built around the record-setting 56 consecutive game hitting streak established by the incomparable Yankee centerfielder, but I dug Brown's band. He had style. His ensembles were clean and his soloists excellent.

Miss Bonney's vocals were good and she had all the physical attributes orchestra orioles needed, yet I regretted the early retirement of Doris Day.

She was unique, but the world would never know it.

°　　　°　　　°

The third suburban site for name bands was on Long Island Sound in Westchester County, the Glen Island Casino. Glenn Miller's group played there several summers. After Miller hit, he invested in new orchestras led by his pals Claude Thornhill, the pianist and arranger; Charlie Spivak, a trumpeter with a sublime tone; and Hal McIntyre, for several years Miller's first chair lead alto saxist. All three made the Casino their base.

It was an unbelievably lovely setting. The Casino was constructed by the water's edge. Patrons could see the lights of small craft gliding on the sea a half-mile from the bandstand. The open air and salty atmosphere seemed to make the music sound mellower.

Glen Island had one annoyance—a waiter. My table seemed to attract him regularly. He was a dark-haired, belligerent man who seemed to detest every patron he served. He spoke with a marked German accent.

"I'm getting tired of that bastard's rudeness," Happy Goday said one evening.

"How in hell does he hold his job?" Lou Levy asked. "He has all the warm, loving qualities of a Nazi Stuka pilot."

But when Thornhill's piano went into his rapturous *Snowfall* theme, even the insulting waiter was forgotten. Spivak and McIntyre led competent young bands; Thornhill's aggregation was simply magnificent—one of those unarguably perfect organizations, yet one which somehow never caught the public's fancy.

We made the rounds of the Meadowbrook, Glen Island, and the Log Cabin every two weeks, the publishers pleading with the bandleaders to perform their newest songs while I asked questions, exchanged scam, and absorbed newsy tidbits. There was another night at Meadowbrook I remember vividly. Joe Venuti rarely played the New York area. On this night his jazz fiddle and orchestra opened to a sell-out house.

I revelled in Venuti's hot violin. His band was so-so. Many of us were intrigued with his girl singer.

"She's a hillbilly, part Indian," Venuti advised me during a break. "I hired her in Memphis, but she's sung in Oklahoma and Texas and God knows where else. I think she started in radio when she was a first-grader. Go talk to her. Her name is Kay Starr."

I did. Like Peggy Lee, Kay was overweight. And, like Peggy, her strikingly pretty face overshadowed her obesity. Unlike Peggy, though, Kay sounded sensational, a young girl with a huge voice that, to my ears, was more jazz-oriented than country.

I don't remember what we talked about. She had sung a few nights with Bob Crosby's band and it hadn't worked out.

She wasn't as shy as Peggy Lee. Kay spoke with a husky, Okie-tainted inflection, much like the sound I had grown up with in Missouri.

She went over to Charlie Barnet's band a year or so later and made several exciting records which drew unconditional praise in *Down Beat*. I couldn't forget her sound. And if I had to bet my pants on their futures, I told myself, I would quickly give odds that a slimmed-down Miss Starr would enjoy more success than Miss Lee.

Both would become major stars in time. And I would have at least a whisper in assisting them to stardom, but I didn't know it that night as Levy and Goday drove me back to my Forrest Hotel office.

￮   ￮   ￮

Along about August I spent a day and a night with my Honduran friend Carlos Gastel. Carlos was still managing Sonny Dunham's ragtag crew. We attended Sonny's opening at the Meadowbrook (yep, an imbecilic songplugger in Hollywood sent him the same old Sophie Tucker good wishes telegram) and watched an astonishing 16-year-old tenor sax player, Corky Corcoran, whom

Few big band maestri enjoyed the popularity of the Dorsey Brothers of Pennsylvania. On this broadcast in the 1940s, Dexter is flanked by Tommy (left) and Jimmy, virtuosi of the trombone and alto sax-clarinet respectively. (Kem-Pix)

It was the summer of 1941 at Balboa Beach, California, that Stan Kenton organized his own orchestra. Visiting him, as New York editor of Down Beat *magazine, was the author. To the right of Kenton and Dexter are Carlos Gastel, Kenton's manager; Mrs. Violet Kenton, Stan's first wife; and Jimmie Lunceford, one of the most renowned bandleaders of the Swing Era.*

Dunham had found on the West Coast carrying his horn in a paper bag.

It was probably the most memorable night of Dunham's long career as a trumpeter doubling trombone. Every publisher was there; each tradepaper was represented. Dunham's book was loaded with charts by George Williams carefully tailored to the heavy but ever-swinging Jimmie Lunceford jazz style. Gastel bought drinks for everyone he recognized. It was a triumphal night for all.

I had a call from Gastel the next morning.

"I'm driving back to California, Dex," he declared. "Pack a couple of shirts and go with me. We'll get there in time for Woody Herman's Palladium opening."

I had two weeks' vacation coming, but enjoying it in Hollywood was something I hadn't thought about. Why not?

We rolled away from West 49th Street the following day. I didn't object when Gastel, sweating and nervous at the wheel, insisted on stopping off every hour or so for what he called "a little taste." He preferred Moscow Mules at a time when few Americans had ever heard of vodka.

Gastel again and again talked about his two best friends in California.

"Stan Kenton is going to be the biggest, money-makingest, most famous bandleader ever," he said. "He's got everything—he's a bitch of a pianist, he writes great arrangements, he looks good, and he's hired the best young musicians on the Coast. They'll forget Glenn Miller and the Dorseys when Stan comes East."

Kenton's band was breaking in at the Rendezvous Ballroom in Balboa Beach. Carlos assured me that it would be the first place we went once we attended Herman's Palladium opening.

The second friend who, I gathered, was something of a superman, was Glenn E. Wallichs. "He runs the best record store on the West Coast, and maybe the entire USA," Gastel pronounced as we steered our way through Illinois. "He knows records, he knows all the artists who make records, and he is even thinking about running a record label himself. He's a sweetheart—you've gotta meet the guy."

In Kansas City, we enjoyed a boozeless ham and spuds dinner with my parents. They said they'd never seen anyone like Carlos. It was like feeding a young grizzly. He was a big hit with them, telling nutty stories about his childhood in Honduras and how he lost his savings trying to make a big name bandleader out of dethroned heavyweight champ Max Baer.

Carlos cannily avoided driving through Kansas and Oklahoma. They were dry states. Instead, we rolled north through Wyoming, stopping on the hour for his "little taste" and a check of the records being played on the noisy jukes. We found no Dunham Bluebirds.

Eventually we made Los Angeles. He dropped me off at the Alto Nido, two blocks up the hill from Hollywood and Vine, and I moved in with Woody's hustling little personal manager, Mike Vallon. Herman's opening was a smash.

His band was the best he had ever fronted and he was signed to appear with it in a movie. He insisted I sit at a table which, during the evening, I shared with Bing Crosby, Lana Turner, and Louella Parsons. Louella's capacity for alcohol almost equalled Gastel's.

The next night Gastel and I drove to Balboa, on the Pacific shore.

"Kenton can't be as great as you say," I told him. "I think you are overselling the guy."

"You'll see," he answered.

I did. Kenton was the tallest cat in the music business, a hair under six-five, and a dynamo physically. He leaped about the stand exhorting his unknown musicians, he jogged to the piano to take an occasional solo, and he jumped off the stand at the end of each set to embrace dancers and ask for requests.

I found him fascinating, a truly different breed of man with enthusiasm and personality like no one in the business. His music was unconventional, too, with a noisy, sledgehammer rhythmic attack somewhat reminiscent of Lunceford.

Carlos, Stan, his wife, Violet, and I talked until five in the morning after the Rendezvous Ballroom closed for the night.

"I've played in every smelly theater pit in California," Stan said. "I've worked in trios, quartets, and as an accompanist to bad singers. This band has just *got* to make it big."

Gastel became his manager and Decca's Joe Perry signed Kenton for records.

It was a rewarding vacation. I spent time with Gil Rodin and the Crosby Dixielanders, I roamed around the City of Angels catching singers and bands, Gastel and I took a wild flight in Lunceford's sleek Bellanca monoplane with Jimmie at the stick (I remember swooping down over Forest Lawn cemetery in Glendale while a terrified Gastel pleaded "No, no, Jimmie!"), and there was a lavish party at Glenn Wallichs' popular record store in Hollywood known as Music City where I picked up a dozen news squibs from scores of guests.

Wallichs was much as Gastel had described him. A lightweight physically, he moved about his attractively appointed store shaking hands, serving drinks, and making cheerful dialogue with guests. I fould him to be every bit as impressive as Gastel had assured me he would be.

We didn't know it then, but the personable Wallichs would soon found his own record label in partnership with the singing songwriter Johnny Mercer and Paramount Pictures' production boss Buddy DeSylva. And more than 30 years of my life would be wrapped up in their venture.

A silver DC-3 got me back to New York in time to be at my desk Monday morning. I pecked out three bulging envelopes of copy for the *Beat*. Much of it concerned the Kenton band.

By now I had "adopted" three orchestras. Ethical or not from a journalistic standpoint, big Stan and his Balboans were destined for special treatment in *Down Beat*.

       o   o   o

Count Basie's road manager, Milton K. Ebbins, handed me a test pressing of a leaping Basie instrumental one afternoon at the Forrest.

"Review this when you have a chance," he said, straightfaced. "Eddie Durham composed and arranged it. Basie thinks it's something special."

I placed the disc on a turntable and noticed the title, *Diggin' For Dex.* Jay McShann had cut a *Dexter Blues* on his first Decca session in appreciation of my helping land him a contract with the Kapp brothers, but Basie had no reason to dedicate a side to me. Nor did *Time-Life* and Billy May's crack studio band 30

William "Count" Basie and Dexter check the music of Diggin' for Dex, *which the Basie band recorded in the author's honor. The Count has led one of the world's finest dance bands for 40 years. (Charlie Mihn)*

years later have anything to gain by recording *Diggin' For Dex* in stereophonic sound for their Swing Era series except to acknowledge that Durham once composed at least a minor masterpiece and his chart deserved new recognition.

o   o   o

The bombing of Pearl Harbor sent me out on my rounds the following day, a Monday, to obtain reactions from the tradesters. Most all of them said it was a hell of a note.

I encountered Glenn Miller at the Cafe Rouge that wintry evening. Many tables were empty. Waiters stood around idle. Even the magic Miller name failed to draw diners that night.

Glenn walked over to my table. I got no big hello.

"I wonder," he asked, "if any of us are aware of the enormity of changes in our lives soon to come now that we're at war?"

I had never seen him in so contemplative a mood.

"Dave, you and I, our mothers and dads, the children we may someday have, and even their children will be directly affected by what happened in the Pacific yesterday. America will never again be the way it was at midnight last Saturday. Even the whole world will never be the same."

He tapped on the tablecloth with a fork.

"I don't know exactly what I can contribute to the war effort," Miller continued, "but I am damn well going to find out. There must be something a broken-down old trombone player can do to help."

His sincerity that night—those few moments in which he grasped the tragic significance of a nation in crisis—is still vivid in my mind today. Of the more than 50 persons I contacted that post-Pearl Harbor Monday, Miller showed, by far, the most profound perception of the horror of a world at war. He didn't ask me to stick around and have jelly pancakes that night.

o   o   o

For many years before Benny Goodman came along to forever change the course of popular dance music, pianist Vincent Lopez maintained wide popularity with his orchestra at the New York St. Regis and Taft hotels. Lopez, away from the stand, collected stamps and studied astrology. By 1941 he was writing learned, complicated features in which he predicted coming events with the help of the zodiac. I accepted some of his copy for the *Beat*.

The powerful Hearst newspaper syndicate gave one of Lopez's outbursts nearly a full page when Lopez confidently declared that Adolf Hitler "will meet his Waterloo in Syria." He saw World War II ending in 1944. And, as his big, big special, Lopez assured millions of readers that Japan was America's friend and would become a valuable ally in the event our nation was drawn into the European conflict.

When was all this published in the Hearst papers? In the issues dated December 6, 1941.

80

He was in the Army reserves, so my buddy Ed Flynn packed his things and went off to Fort Bragg as a lieutenant a few weeks after Pearl Harbor. It was never the same again around the office.

About the time Flynn left, J. Edgar Hoover and the FBI announced they had apprehended and jailed a group of German spies working out of Westchester county. One of the men they nailed was a waiter. At Glen Island Casino.

o   o   o

On the coldest night of the year in New York in early 1942, Stan Kenton brought his band into the Roseland Ballroom on Broadway. He packed the place. Publicity had been terrific, and radio jocks Art Ford, Martin Block, Alan Courtney, Paul Brenner, Steve Ellis, and Art Greene plugged the long-awaited Kenton debut in Manhattan.

Kenton showed the crowd everything he had: originality, musicianship, showmanship. Hardly anyone liked his music. The dancers at Roseland are unlike those anywhere else. They wanted rumbas and waltzes. The music publishers were quickly turned off, too. Stan played no pop tunes, only originals and standards. They all complained he was too loud.

I waited, with Gastel, for the musicians to pack up when the ordeal ended. Carlos, Stan, and I walked down the stairs to the sidewalk. The temperature was 10 below zero and dropping as we looked for a taxi. Perspiration rolled down Gastel's face as if it were a hot July afternoon. Stan was in shock, acutely aware that he had flopped in New York.

"Roseland isn't for your kind of music," I consoled him. "In any other spot you would have had the kids screaming."

"I'll book you into the Pennsylvania or the Astor," Gastel, mopping his face with a huge handkerchief, promised.

Kenton stood there shivering, miserable, and despondent. Then he suddenly started laughing. "If all this isn't bad enough," he told us, "you know what else happened tonight? The goddam Japs tossed a couple of shells up on the beach at Santa Barbara and blew up an oil tank.

"Frig it, Carlos. Let's go back to California."

o   o   o

I heard rumbles from Chicago. My bosses Cons and Burrs were at it again. Cons had started a second publication, *Music and Rhythm*, in defiance of his partner's pleas to concentrate on building *Down Beat* into a bigger and better publication. There were other conflicts as well. Mrs. Cons did not like Mrs. Burrs.

World War II wasn't enough for the two families. They had their own battle-ground and I could hear the Illinois gunfire from my office in New York. Something had to give.

1O

From the vantage point of my 58 years—from learning and growing and investigating and searching—I have found only *one* absolute in music, and that is that there is no absolute. Everything in music is relative. Everything in music must be sifted through one's musical mind and personality. That's what music-making is all about.

—JORGE BOLET

CARL CONS SOLD his half-ownership of *Down Beat* to Glenn Burrs for $50,000 and dissolved their partnership in March, 1942. Cons telephoned me from Chicago to announce the change and urge me to stick with him.

"I have exciting plans," he confided, "and you are a big part of them."

He succeeded in obtaining the services and financial participation of John Hammond of Columbia Records in expanding and improving Cons's *Music and Rhythm* monthly magazine. Hammond and I had been friends for four years; he interrogated me at length as to Cons' character, ability, and knowledge of the publishing field.

Within days I was named managing editor of the revamped rag at a salary of $75 a week. Hammond and I worked out of a small but ideally located office on the 24th floor of the RKO building in Radio City. We shared a secretary.

The venture lasted five months.

Music and Rhythm was a readable publication, one of the best pop music monthlies ever. Hammond's editorial contributions were gargantuan—he knew everybody, and he had the courage to write forceful, penetrating stories which attracted national attention in musicians' circles. Yet many internal complications arose.

The bulk of the mag's copy and pictures originated in New York; the dummying and printing was done in Chicago. Cons had difficulty maintaining deadlines. I would send in a photo of Bob Eberly with explanatory captions attached and, in print, the name would be spelled Eberle. It happened with too many names and places. Perhaps Cons was understaffed in Chicago. The August issue ended the venture.

Hammond went into the Army and I expected to be drafted momentarily. The war was not going well; hundreds of thousands of men were being processed, uniformed, and armed.

What to do until my number came up?

Bill Burton asked me to join the Jimmy Dorsey band. They were soon to begin a weekly *Navy Bulletin Board* radio show over the entire Mutual network, sponsored by the U.S. Navy and designed to entice enlistments. Dorsey needed a writer. "You can also help with publicity for the band," said Burton. "We will be in Hollywood several months."

It was a fun job—for awhile. Jimmy's band was at its height, artistically and at the box-office. Bob Eberly and Helen O'Connell were unmatched as singing attractions. Men like Johnny Guarnieri, Babe Russin, Milt Yaner, Buddy Schutz, Billy Oblok, and Nate Kazebier gave Dorsey outstanding musicianship behind his own appealing solo alto sax and clarinet wizardry. The band broke Palladium attendance records (on Saturday nights more than 8,000 people jammed the place) and, in the daylight, we doubled at M-G-M's sprawling Culver City studios making a motion picture, *I Dood It*, which starred Red Skelton and Eleanor Powell.

I enjoyed writing scripts for *Navy Bulletin Board*. Navy officers supplied me with information; it was my task to devise palatable enlistment pleas integrated with music. Dorsey did not read words well. With each program I assigned more dialogue to Eberly and O'Connell. They were persuasive and believable. Mail from listeners accelerated with each Saturday broadcast. They asked for *Tangerine, Green Eyes, Brazil, Amapola*, and later that Autumn, a new Irving Berlin song which appeared to have a fair chance to become a seasonal hit, a pretty ballad sung by Eberly entitled *White Christmas*.

I bagged Jimmy Dorsey excessive space in various publications—with the invaluable counsel of Hollywood publicist Barney McDevitt—through then-noted writers like Ted LeBerthon, Matt Weinstock, Harrison Carroll, Erskine Johnson, Jimmie Fidler, and Louella Parsons. I kept Dorsey's name in the tradepapers, *Billboard, Daily Variety, Hollywood Reporter, Metronome, Orchestra World*, and, of course, *Down Beat*. My old twice-monthly sheet continued to prosper under the aegis of Glen Burrs and Ned Williams and I was pleased to maintain cordial relations with them in Chicago.

Maurice Cohen and Earl Vollmer operated the Palladium on Sunset Boulevard in Hollywood. It was an attractive ballroom, opened in 1940 to replace the old Palomar which was destroyed by a fire of still-unknown origin. Everyone in the music business made the Palladium his nocturnal (and Sunday matinee) headquarters.

An occasional guest for the early dinner session was Glenn Wallichs and his wife Dorothy. His record store two blocks away was still the most successful on the Pacific coast. His new Capitol record label was off and running profitably thanks to hit singles by Johnny Mercer (*Strip Polka*) and the team of Ella Mae Morse and Freddy Slack's orchestra (*Cow-Cow Boogie*).

Wallichs, alone and intimidated by Manhattan's imposing canyons of concrete and glass, had asked me to lend him a hand the previous June when he had arrived in New York with samples of his new label. I was then with *Music and Rhythm* and still regularly participating in Alan Courtney's *11:30 Club* record review sessions on WOV and on Bob Bach's *Platterbrains* jazz program on WMCA. Wallichs, a dynamic, driving young Nebraskan, walked around with me from one station to another with his samples, acknowledging my introductions to jocks and librarians, tradepaper writers, and editors and, at night, to bandleaders, musicians, agents, and flacks. We got along well. Capitol reaped unpurchasable publicity. It was a rewarding week of activity.

Now the Wallichses sat in the Palladium eating dinner.

"Dex," said Glenn. "Come to work for Capitol."

I still lived in New York. Moving 3,000 miles only to be inducted into the Armed Forces would be plainly imprudent.

"Can't do it," I told Wallichs. "I want to be a part of the record industry one of these days but now isn't the time."

"You have a job whenever you want it," he declared.

Back to New York I went in December, but not with Jimmy Dorsey's organization. Carlos Gastel also had approached me at the Palladium a few days after Thanksgiving Day.

"Sonny Dunham needs help on the road," he told me, sipping a drink and wiping perspiration from his brow. "He's booked for the New Yorker Hotel and theaters in Brooklyn, The Bronx, and Passaic through the Christmas holidays and then he heads West again. I have to be with Stan Kenton."

With the thirteen weeks of *Navy Bulletin Board* expiring, I no longer had a radio show to write. I had no interest in working for Dorsey or anyone solely as a publicist. Bill Burton and Dorsey were sympathetic. They were as fond of Gastel as I. Back in frosty New York after another transcontinental DC-3 flight, I reported to Dunham as his new road manager.

It was a mistake. Collecting the band's money from theater owners, seeing that it was banked and the musicians paid, keeping track of the advances to kid saxophone players, arranging transportation of mountains of luggage and Dunham personnel, killing time between stage shows, and assisting Sonny in finding replacement musicians for those who were drafted, who quit us, or were canned—all these chores were to me ugly and distasteful. But there is one happy memory of that period. I met and later married one of Dunham's singers, a brunette, beauteous New Mexican named Mickie Roy. Without prompting from me, a rookie nightlife columnist on the New York *Post*, Earl Wilson, sought her out during our three-week gig at the New Yorker Hotel and fashioned a much-appreciated rave in one of his early columns.

I stuck it out with Dunham seven weeks. New York suddenly seemed gray and dirty and cold. Many of my friends were away at war. I arranged with Gastel for a man to take my place with Dunham's orchestra. I cleaned out my apartment. The temperature at the airport the afternoon I checked in with TWA was 15 below zero; the airline bussed us from the passenger terminal to the TWA hangar. There they revved up the two Pratt-Whitneys indoors, out of the cold. We landed at Burbank at midnight in 70-degree warmth.

On the cab ride to the Hollywood Plaza Hotel early that February morning I knew I would never live in the East again. I say it again now.

o   o   o

There was one hitch in Wallichs' invitation to come and work at Capitol. It was money.

"We are a young outfit, Dex," he apologized when I reported to him. "We are hardly in position to compete with Decca, Columbia, and Victor. I think our offer of $200 a month is fair. The musicians' union won't allow members to make records. We can't get shellac from the Orient. And we have distribution branches only in Los Angeles and Chicago. Accept the job and grow with us."

I had no choice. But I wanted my responsibilities made clear.

"You'll like your work," Wallichs cajoled me. "Handle Capitol's publicity, our advertising, our public relations, and be a sort of assistant to Johnny Mercer in finding and recording talent when the union allows us to go back into the studios again. It's a great opportunity."

I accepted. But I obtained Wallichs' promise that I could augment my paycheck by doing outside work on my own time. Barney McDevitt lined me up with a little "where to go in Los Angeles" magazine, *Key*, which paid me $200 monthly for writing each issue. Thus I was earning $400 a month, more than I had rated with Dorsey or Dunham. But I was working 16-hour daily split shifts, too. Even at 27, six days of all work and little play requires stamina and dedication. I had it; so did the nine other Capitol employees who occupied a partitioned, narrow little office on Vine Street in Hollywood.

Blonde Auriel MacFie operated the small telephone switchboard and served as a smiling, attractive receptionist and typist. She was the first girl hired by Wallichs and Mercer (today she is a prominent editor for a California book publisher). Floyd A. Bittaker was persuaded to leave Columbia Records and direct Capitol's sales thrust. We had one accountant, and in a decrepit old house standing in the rear of a parking lot, several persons were employed in our shipping department.

Wallichs and Mercer had founded the company in April of 1942 with the financial backing—said to be $10,000—of George G. (Buddy) DeSylva, a top-ranking ASCAP songwriter who reigned at Paramount Pictures as executive producer in charge of production. Buddy rarely intruded on us and never interfered with our operation. We visited him at Paramount occasionally, lunching with him in the studio commissary and peeking in on the mammoth sound stages to watch scenes being shot. One of them was *For Whom the Bell Tolls*. I remember it not because I saw Gary Cooper for a few moments, but because I *didn't* see the angelic Ingrid Bergman at work. I also remember the picture for its superior music, composed by Victor Young. It sounds even better today.

Mercer was a successful songwriter, specializing in lyrics. At one time in 1942 four of his songs— *Tangerine, I Remember You, Skylark,* and *Arthur Mur-*

ray Taught Me Dancin' in a Hurry—resided in the nation's Top Ten hit charts.

Johnny was an unassuming, earthy, well-liked, light-hearted man who appreciated good jazz and who knew virtually everyone in the profession. He maintained erratic office hours at Capitol, retiring to the Key Club a block north on Vine every afternoon to gather his thoughts and bend elbows at the bar with his cronies. I found him a tolerant and understanding boss.

Wallichs functioned like he was programmed by a computer. Every morning at 7:30 he entered DuPar's little restaurant for breakfast. At 8 he was at his desk, nattily attired in business suit, white shirt, conservative necktie, and shiny, laced shoes. He used the phone constantly and dictated dozens of letters, bouncing around the premises nervously, aware of the smallest details of Capitol's operation.

I went to work at 9, most mornings, with my pockets crammed with news notes acquired the previous night (or earlier that morning) in some musicians' hangout. I saw no reason to dress like a used-car salesman; my tastes ran to open sports shirts and scuffed, no-lace loafers. Wallichs accepted my informal approach for about a week, then one morning accosted me and criticized my appearance.

"Aw, hell," came Mercer's voice from a back room. "Not everyone dresses like a mortician. Who are we trying to impress?"

Mercer strolled into my office. He was wearing scuffed loafers, an open sport shirt, and unpressed slacks.

"Let's not run Capitol like a factory, Glenn," Mercer said softly. "Each of us is a little different from the others."

I thought of Paul Douglas at the Glenn Miller broadcast. But in deference to Wallichs, I was careful to wear a suit and tie on days when I had business outside the office.

°   °   °

I launched a modest little twice-monthly music mag one month after I joined Capitol. It was called *Capitol News* but I was careful to write about recording artists of all labels. The ads alone carried Cap's sales message.

The first two issues had a press run of 7,500 copies, enough for each dealer to have one. In two months we were printing 10,000 and selling them to dealers for a penny each. In October I changed the frequency to monthly and doubled the number of pages each issue. We raised the price to two cents. Our December issue sold 46,000 copies, more than enough to pay for the cost of publishing. Dealers would drop a copy in the jacket of records they sold, and stack them on counters for distribution to customers. Reviewers, deejays, and military bases were sent thousands of copies. Eventually, circulation reached 800,000 monthly, with readers throughout the world.

We unveiled another promotion that summer of 1943. Wallichs and Bittaker arranged to press up 100 copies of each new release on expensive vinylite compound. The reduction in surface noise was marked, and the disc was unbreakable. I typed and pasted a special label on each record:

THIS ADVANCE PRESSING

EXCLUSIVELY PRODUCED

FOR PETER POTTER

Peter Potter and 99 other radio jocks were, of course, pleased and flattered to receive such personalized treatment. Capitol began to dominate airtime nationally. But how I detested the chore of typing those individual labels!

I found time, somehow, to write for *Metronome* in New York and, on occasion, for *Billboard*. And on Tuesday nights I toted a stack of jazz platters over to KFAC on Wilshire to share the *Lucky Lager* microphone with Don Otis and present a full hour of the best in hot music.

Otis had a large and loyal audience in those days before television.

He called me one afternoon.

"Come over tonight and don't bring any records."

It was a curious summons, I thought, but I got there as requested. Otis introduced me to Leopold Stokowski.

"The maestro is going to play a little jazz tonight," Otis advised me. "He's never done anything like this before in his life."

Stokey flipped through a stack of discs, choosing his favorites. Otis introduced him to *Lucky Lager* listeners and the veteran conductor took over. For 50 minutes he rapped about music and musicians, breaking only to allow Don to spin a disc. I have my original notes from that evening. Among other statements lauding the jazz art, Stokowski said:

"Jazz is an important part of our folk music and folklore. It has few traditions and no limitations, and it will go on forever developing so long as musicians give free reign to their imaginations . . . jazz is unique; there never was anything like it. In this kind of music the U.S.A. is second to no other nation in the whole world."

He played the Original Dixieland Jazz Band, Louis Armstrong, Fletcher Henderson, Duke Ellington, Joe Venuti, Eddie Lang, Jimmie Lunceford, Artie Shaw, Woody Herman, Tommy Dorsey, and Harry James. Time ran out, else he might have plugged others. It was a memorable program. Stokey's attitude helped dilute the pompous, widely published diatribe by the equally renowned conductor, Artur Rodzinski, who during a concert intermission at Camp Kilmer, New Jersey, prattled that "jazz leads to degeneracy and is one of the greatest causes of juvenile delinquency today."

o   o.   o

Night after night, after 12, I dialed Hank the Night Watchman (Bill Kelso) to hear the latest releases on the major labels.

He caught my ear with a ballad, *All For You*, performed on an obscure label by the King Cole Trio. It wasn't like the music Cole had recorded for Decca.

All For You featured a solo voice—Nat's—which was unlike any voice I had ever heard.

So it was something of a coincidence during that period when I stopped in at Music City on a bright May morning to check with a powerful news source, a former drummer named Hughie Claudin, who assisted my boss Wallichs and Ralph Krause in operating Wallichs' disc shop on the West Coast.

"Have you ever heard a record by King Cole called *All For You?*" Claudin asked,

"Sure—a hell of a ballad," I answered. "Best side Nat ever recorded."

"There's a guy named Bob Scherman who wrote the song and produced the disc on his own," Claudin said. "He wants to sell the master to a major company. You interested?"

I was. Claudin gave me a copy and I charged into Wallichs' office. "We've got to grab this and rush it out," I urged.

Wallichs was aware that the musicians' strike was in its tenth month and that Capitol's supply of masters was approaching the danger level. He listened to the disc. "Grab it," he commanded.

Capitol issued *All For You* in August. It sold more than 100,000 copies by year's end. But more significantly, it revealed for the first time the beauty and expressiveness of Nat Cole's charming solo baritone voice. It also opened the Capitol door to Cole; from that time in 1943 until he died in 1965 he sold more singles and albums than any other artist on our label. Without him, I doubt that the company would have thrived and expanded as it did throughout the quarter-century that followed.

He was, for sure, The King.

°   °   °

Pro musicians flocked back to the recording studios shortly before Christmas, 1943. Their union president, James Caesar Petrillo, signed contracts with various labels calling for pay scales to rise to $41.25 for a three-hour session. Record companies, in addition, agreed to pay the union a royalty on every disc sold in the future.

Mercer went to work in earnest. Capitol was at the bottom of its barrel. There were new songs to record, new artists to sign, and those who had started with the company were clamoring for attention. Johnny quickly signed Jo Stafford, who like Sinatra had recently quit Tommy Dorsey's band. He signed the Pied Pipers, a slick singing quartet. He signed Paul Weston, the arranger-conductor who would later marry Miss Stafford. And because Nat Cole's *All For You* had helped tide Capitol over the long period in which records could not be made, Mercer and Wallichs contracted for his services, too.

Carlos Gastel now managed Cole, just as he managed the Dunham, Kenton, and Benny Carter orchestras. I admired Carter as much as anyone in music. I thought he could sell records. I signed him.

Cole and Kenton had bombed on Decca. Dunham was not successful on Bluebird. Carter had failed on Bluebird and Decca. Of Gastel's entire stable,

Dunham was the only artist unwanted by Capitol.

Nat's first record after the strike was a novelty he composed himself and sold, outright, to publisher Irving Mills for $100, *Straighten Up and Fly Right*. It was even more hitty than *All For You* and established Cole's trio as a platter attraction with unlimited potential.

Mercer and I sat in the booth at Chick MacGregor's studios supervising Stan Kenton's first Cap session. It was a bountiful three hours. Kenton came through with *Harlem Folk Dance, Do Nothin' Til You Hear From Me, Eager Beaver*, and his pulsating theme, *Artistry in Rhythm*. All four were hits.

Carter's struggling band was in San Francisco at that time. I took the overnight Southern Pacific north with Glenn and Dorothy Wallichs. We rented a tiny studio and, despite uncountable problems, managed to can *Poinciana, Love For Sale*, and two pops featuring Savannah Churchill as vocalist, *Just a Baby's Prayer at Twilight* and *Hurry, Hurry*.

Coming south on the train, I caught a cold that laid me flat. It developed into pneumonia. I lost 20 pounds in three weeks. It might have been worse had Gastel not insisted I be treated by his physician. For three months after I returned to work I felt exhausted and strung-out.

It was during those months that I was drafted. I passed the preliminary physical easily and they asked which branch of service I preferred. My brother Dick was somewhere in the North Atlantic on the destroyer *De Haven*, patrolling for Nazi subs, so I pleaded for Navy action.

You've got it, buddy," said an ensign. But then my chest x-rays came through.

"You've had it, buddy," the same young officer told me. "Too many lung spots."

Pneumonia, I suppose, did it.

Carter's *Hurry, Hurry* took off like a Ferrari. It wasn't much with white buyers, but every black jukebox spun it just as they had spun my 627 *Stomp* on Decca. To this day it stands as the hottest-selling record Carter ever had.

o   o   o

Writing and publishing *Capitol News* attracted a stream of dropper-inners to my office.

A stocky, balding man named Frank Laine came by frequently. He managed the singing Barries, a sister team which Mercer liked and had made a couple of sides with. Laine urged that I devote more effort to publicity in their behalf. One of the Barries was his sweetie.

"You know, Dexter, I know a little about this business. I used to sing, back in Cleveland. And I just may resume singing again one of these days."

Laine never pushed me, or Mercer, about his chances of making records. He seemed interested only in the Barrie girls. But somehow Berle Adams of Mercury heard about him and rang Laine in on a session Adams was producing mainly to get two sides from Jack Benny's funny aide, Artie (Mister Kitzel) Auerbach. Laine shocked Adams almost as much as he astounded me when he

Supervising a jazz session for Capitol, the author takes five with Coleman Hawkins, Buster Bailey, and Benny Carter. The records were released as the Capitol International Jazzmen. (Charlie Mihn)

Jack Teagarden and (right) Joe Sullivan were two of the prominent jazzmen teamed together by Dexter for Capitol's New American Jazz *album during World War II. Recorded at the C.P. MacGregor Studios in Los Angeles, it was the first of many jazz packages Capitol would market in the next 33 years. (Charlie Mihn)*

popped up with a three-million seller, *That's My Desire.*

I regard my letting Frankie get away as the biggest gaffe of my career. He made millions for the young Mercury company and he still razzes me about my goof. I blew it, but I blew it big.

◦   ◦   ◦

It was Adams who requested my production services in recording a young and unheralded Pittsburgh pianist, Erroll Garner, for the infant Mercury label. We met at C. P. MacGregor's studios.

Garner simply was astounding at the keyboard. He couldn't read music; he didn't have to. I recall that we made four masters, including *Full Moon and Empty Arms,* based on a pretty Rachmaninoff melody, and *If I Loved You,* the hit ballad from the Rodgers-Hammerstein musical *Carousel.* On one of them Garner improvised a daring, flamboyant coda-an ending—that ran for more than a full minute. It was a dazzling exhibition and it stands up today.

Erroll of the impish face was seized on his job at the Suzi-Q Club in Hollywood the night after our session and charged with marijuana possession. He left for Pittsburgh when he was freed. Today he plays formal concerts throughout the world, agented by the Sol Hurok office. And his albums are in demand.

He is one of America's most effective jazz ambassadors.

◦   ◦   ◦

Mercer and Wallichs projected a series of albums—Capitol's first—which would feature Mercer's vocals (everything he recorded in those days sold exceptionally well) backed by the Pied Pipers and Weston's smooth studio orchestra. There also would be Christmas carols by the St. Luke's Church Choristers, Hawaiian music by Harry Owens, and a program of romantic ballads sung by Dennis Day, the tenor who was featured regularly on Jack Benny's broadcasts.

I rushed in with a plea to include a jazz album on the first release. They approved it.

Within a few days I assembled the best jazzmen in California at MacGregor's studio on Western Avenue off Wilshire. Jack Teagarden, Joe Sullivan, Jimmie Noone, Zutty Singleton, Billy May, Artie Shapiro, Dave Barbour, and Dave Matthews produced four exceptional tracks. They used no written charts. Every note was improvised.

It was the last session for the distinguished clarinetist Noone. He died a few weeks later, thinning the ranks of the original New Orleans pioneers.

I had half my album canned. I needed four more tracks. Setting the session date for January 7, 1944, I succeeded in assembling a second all-star group comprising Pete Johnson, Eddie Miller, Barney Bigard, Nick Fatool, Nappy Lamare, Les Robinson, Shorty Sherock, Stan Wrightsman, and Hank Wayland. No weaknesses there.

But I needed a singer. Two vocals and six instrumentals, I felt, would give my *New American Jazz* package balance. Who could do the job?

11

Patience and faith are requisites in our business; most artists do not produce hits their first time out. It wasn't until we had issued three albums by Judy Collins that we could begin to gauge her audience, not until her sixth album did we realize we had a substantial artist and not until her eighth album were we sure we had a gold artist.

—JAC HOLZMAN
Elektra Records President

PEGGY LEE WAS my choice for the session.

She had come to California with Benny Goodman's band. They played the Palladium, and during that engagement she and guitarist Dave Barbour had married. Becoming pregnant in 1943, she and Barbour elected to remain in Hollywood when Goodman's ensemble returned East.

Peggy underwent surgery while carrying her daughter, Nickie Barbour, the only child she ever was to conceive. Nickie was born by Caesarian surgery on Armistice Day. Barbour, unemployed for the first time in a decade, scurried about Los Angeles seeking work.

Peggy was still recuperating when I telephoned her in January.

"It's nice to hear from you," she said, "but I'm retired. I want to devote all my time to my husband and baby. I've had enough singing."

I couldn't budge her. For two days I called around, trying to find someone like Ivie Anderson, Helen Humes, or Lee Wiley to make my session, but no one was available. I called Peggy a second time.

"You don't give up, do you?" she kidded. "Why me?"

I considered her the best singer for the job, I explained, but I didn't tell her that I felt I owed her something.

On her first engagement with Goodman in New Jersey two years earlier she had silently endured the knocks of almost every writer and deejay who watched her. I was one of those who had given her little chance of succeeding with the Swing King and his powerful aggregation. Then, week by week, she improved as she gained confidence. Within a year she was unquestionably one of the best—and prettiest—band singers anywhere.

"What does your session pay?" Peggy asked.

"I can get you $100 for singing two songs," I replied. "You'll be home in two hours."

She showed up on time. Her husband had driven her to the MacGregor studios in a rickety, sputtering, pre-war Ford two-seater. Peggy was chubby, but she was smartly dressed and enthusiastically welcomed by the musicians I had assembled.

I invited Peg into the booth and asked that the old standard *Sugar* lead off the session. It gave Peg 30 or 40 minutes to get the feel of the studio and the musicians. She enjoyed every solo, particularly Eddie Miller's tenor saxing and Pete Johnson's raunchy, two-fisted piano contributions.

And then Peggy officially emerged from retirement, taking over the mike to shout *Ain't Goin' No Place*, a raucous, up-tempo blues that reminded me of her bawdy vocal on the Goodman *Why Don'tcha Do Right* Columbia smash a year or so previously. All of us stood around enjoying a playback and one of the men said aloud what we all were thinking: *"This chick sounds like a drunken old whore with the hots."*

That mood was quickly dispelled with Peggy's second master.

We chose a song from the thirties, *That Old Feeling*, Peggy employing the infrequently heard verse before moving into an ethereal, delicate chorus daintily backed by rhythm and Stan Wrightsman's moody celeste. Her sound had become pure Angel Food.

It was a stunning reading.

"That's it, lady, go on home to your daughter," I yelled from the booth. Peggy appeared pleased as she and Dave walked out the door.

○   ○   ○

Throughout World War II the author volunteered his services as writer, producer, and announcer for the Office of War Information. Programs were reproduced on sixteen-inch discs and flown to war theaters throughout Europe and the South Pacific. Here Dexter is shown supervising Peggy Lee and Garry Moore, both of whom were frequently heard on NBC's Fitch Bandwagon *program in the 1940s.*

New American Jazz sold well, but I was even more gratified that many radio jocks pulled Peggy's *That Old Feeling* from the album and gave it heavy airplay.

The performance garnered enough attention for my buddy Carlos Gastel to persuade Peggy to sign a longterm contract with Capitol. He also became her manager. Like Perry Como and Doris Day earlier, retirement was not for the blonde North Dakotan. She had too much to offer, as she has today.

Capitol's growth in 1944 escalated so rapidly that Mercer and Wallichs accepted the advice of Paul Weston to hire a one-time Dartmouth College trumpeter, James B. Conkling, to assist Mercer with artists and repertoire activities. Weston himself was a Phi Beta Kappa from Dartmouth and his insistence paid off. Conkling became a valued Capitol exec within weeks; Peggy Lee was only one of several artists assigned him.

I spent most of my time writing and editing copy for the *Capitol News*. Wallichs doubled my salary long before my first year with Capitol ended and I no longer had to continue as a writer for *Key* magazine.

I was still responsible for the company's publicity, public relations, and advertising, and I constantly met with singers and musicians under contract in and away from our small offices on Vine Street.

Peggy Lee wasn't like the others.

Perhaps it was traceable to the poor press she reaped when she first joined Benny Goodman, or maybe it was because she was a farm girl who had lost her mother when she was four and who never was close to her father—whatever the reason, the teenaged Peggy lacked confidence and poise.

She had worked as a milkmaid in North Dakota, as a coffee shop waitress, as a carnival barker, and, for a time, she scrubbed floors for a living. Yet, in the school and church choirs in which she sang, she learned that she possessed uncommon talent for music. At 17 she went to California, sang briefly and without success at the Jade Club on Hollywood Boulevard, then ended up back in the Middlewest with the bands of Sev Olsen and Will Osborne. Finally she was booked as a single into the ultra-posh Chicago Ambassador Hotel.

"I had no money," she recalls. "For three days and nights I had nothing to eat. One of the hotel maids learned I was hungry and brought me scraps from room service trays."

Peggy laughs. How did the maid know she was hungry? "I never saw you leave your room," the woman explained to Peggy, "and I didn't see no grub coming in nor any bones going out."

The Ambassador's Ernie Byfield was informed of his singer's predicament.

"My God, girl," Byfield exclaimed, "don't you know you can have anything you want at any time? You simply sign your name to the tabs."

It was during her Ambassador run that Alice Goodman heard Peggy and persuaded husband Benny to give her a trial as a replacement for Helen Forrest.

I'll say this for the Goodmans: they were the only persons on earth who heard something special in Peggy's voice at that time. Her first discs for Columbia—

some of them reissued and still available in the 1970s—confirm that she fell somewhat short of Miss Forrest's indisputable abilities. But each record got better.

Baby Nickie is the parent of three children today and remains close to her glamorous mother. Peggy and Barbour were divorced many years ago. He died of natural causes after Peggy had married again (her other ex-husbands include bandleader Jack Del Rio and actors Brad Dexter and Dewey Martin) but Peggy says Dave was her only true love. Their estrangement remains the most tragic event of her life.

You watch her walk out on the stage at Las Vegas or Miami Beach or New York, and you see one of the truly extraordinary showwomen of our time. The lighting is ingeniously staged, her music is perfectly rehearsed, and Peg is, as always, immaculately gowned and coiffed. She has worked tirelessly to present an ideal performance despite her reliance on the oxygen which she keeps handy in a personalized breathing machine she calls "Charlie." Peggy also battles arthritis of the spine and a crushed vertebra as well, bravely defying constant, sometimes unbearable, pain without complaining. The one-time Norma Egstrom is quite a woman.

Peggy wants to produce motion pictures. She's done everything else. Million-selling records, a Best Supporting Actress nomination (1956) for an Oscar, scoring motion pictures, writing poetry, composing successful songs like *Mañana, It's a Good Day*, and others, appearing in network television specials and—perhaps closest to her heart—succeeding in being a loving mother to her daughter (now Mrs. Richard Foster) and her precious grandchildren: no other performer I know is more versatile, nor more admirable.

I received a query a while back from the Sylvania firm in Chicago asking if I could recommend a "big name star" capable of painting a series of oils which they would reproduce in full color and offer as a premium to persons purchasing their new television sets.

"Tony Bennett has that gift," I told the Sylvania representative. "But for my tastes in art Peggy Lee has even more talent. I'll check her out."

I telephoned Peggy at her Tower Grove Drive residence in Beverly Hills. Luckily, she was not out on the road. I explained what was wanted and admonished her that Sylvania would need the four paintings within three weeks. The line went dead for a moment. Then Peggy's soft, purry voice resumed.

"What," she asked in a near-whisper, "will they pay?"

Sylvania received her four lovely still-lifes three weeks later. It took only a little longer for Peg to get a check for $5,000 in the mail. Everyone was pleased.

°   °   °

Nat Cole angrily burst into my office one day in 1944. He was shouting, waving his arms wildly, and was obviously overwrought emotionally,

95

"That drawing," he yelled, "it's an insult, man. You ought to be as ashamed of it as I am."

It took a few minutes to ascertain precisely what drawing he had in mind. When he made it clear, I obtained a copy and studied the sketch to which he was objecting. It was an advertising streamer promoting his new single, one which we shipped out to be hung in record shops, and the drawing depicted a black angel.

"Looks like an old-fashioned pickaninny," Cole snorted.

I studied the "art" for a moment and agreed it was hardly a Titian.

"Nat," I explained, "we employ an old lady up in the hills of Hollywood to illustrate our promotional and advertising material, some woman Wallichs has favored since he first opened a record shop. I agree it's lousy artwork but no racial slight is implied or intended. It won't happen again."

Cole composed himself, sat down, lighted a cigarette, and we started talking baseball, but offending Nat had wounded me deeply. Wallichs and Mercer were told of the incident and, to their credit, they discontinued Capitol's reliance on the little old lady up in the hills and contracted with a major California advertising agency to handle our growing account on a permanent basis.

Cole was the same sincere, conscientious musician I had pegged him as being back at Kelly's Stable in New York, a man who was genuinely an *artist*. When his new records for Capitol started clicking his manager Gastel had no difficulty booking his trio into the swankiest nightery on Hollywood's Sunset strip, the Trocadero. They even redecorated a comfy side room and named it the King Cole Room. It was packed with fans and fellow musicians every night until 12—wartime restrictions closed every liquor-selling establishment at midnight sharp.

Unless he was traveling, Nat delighted in playing on our Capitol softball team. He was tall, supple, agile, and physically strong. He ran, hit, and threw a ball well. I have a faded, blown-up photograph in my office today—fully four feet wide—which shows a happy Cole posing in a dark blue uniform with other members of our ball team. Gordon MacRae, Andy Russell, Jack Smith, and Stan Kenton also played from time to time; Cole and Russell were superior athletes.

Jim Conkling produced Nat's sessions for a couple of years, a period in which the trio's output consistently paced the industry's sales. Then a new producer, Lee Gillette, was brought in from Chicago to assist Mercer and Conkling. Gillette was a singer, once featured with movie actor Buddy Rogers' short-lived orchestra. Along with responsibilities to supervise the company's country and western stable—men like Tex Ritter, Foy Willing, Wesley Tuttle, Jimmy Wakely, Gube Beaver, Cliffie Stone, and Merle Travis—Gillette now would be directing the recording careers of the Cole trio, the Dinning Sisters, and later, the Pasadena deejay Tennessee Ernie Ford and the orchestras of Jan Garber and Ray Anthony.

On one of my encounters with Nat Cole at Capitol I brashly violated one of my long-standing vows, a resolution to never show a song I had composed to a

Capitol contractee. I hoped Nat wouldn't object; with his fame he was constantly pestered by songwriters and publishers, all of whom swore that theirs was a "sure" hit. I tried a different pitch.

"It isn't much," I said. "A simple melody, a simple lyric, but they aren't like any others you've heard in 20 years and you might find it worth considering." Nat glanced at my crude leadsheet, folded it carefully and placed it in his jacket pocket. He called me a few days later.

"I'm like you, Dave," he confided. "Your tune may not be much but it sure doesn't lay like all the others I've been getting. I'm cutting it tomorrow night."

I sat in the booth throughout the session. When it came time for my *That's a Natural Fact*, Nat asked over the intercom for me to come out into the studio.

"Your first chorus," he said, drawing on a cigarette in a long, slender holder, "makes more sense as the closing chorus. Your last chorus lays better as the opener. Do you mind if I switch them?" He smiled devilishly.

"Do what you like." I told him. "I don't care which comes first so long as you get it on a record. Changing it around to make it a stronger song makes you the co-composer, you know."

Nat made a marvelous master of my tune. I gratefully cut him in for half of the composing royalties. But Conkling chose to release our little gem on December 24, a time when dealers are not buying additional product and—even worse—the radio jocks are playing only Christmas music.

My tune is not remembered as one of the top-selling King Cole Trio singles today. And what meager royalties I received were split 50-50 with Nat. Maybe someone else will someday record it again and get it out on the market at a time other than Christmas Eve.

∘   ∘   ∘

Jazz was selling briskly in the mid-1940s, so much so that more than one hundred labels specializing in that idiom sprang up. Few survived.

I was putting together another all-star session that would feature Coleman Hawkins, Benny Carter, Bill Coleman, John Kirby, Oscar Moore, Buster Bailey, and Max Roach. And because Nat Cole was being castigated by the eastern critics in *Down Beat, Metronome*, and lesser publications for deserting jazz to become a pop singer, I asked Nat if he would join us.

"Say when and where," he answered.

I didn't tell the musicians, but I had also invited a young, busty, big-throated girl singer to participate on two of the four planned masters. She was Kay Starr, a confident, ebullient, part-Cherokee brunette whom I had met when she worked for a time with Joe Venuti. She sang great.

It was a sensationally successful clambake. Nat played scintillating piano and Kay boomed out *If I Could Be with You One Hour Tonight* and *Stormy Weather* as if she owned the copyrights. The musicians applauded her. No critic had the temerity later to knock any of the four sides we captured. They were too beautifully performed.

Nat thanked me when the session ended.

"I love to play piano," he said. "When it comes right down to it, I'd rather play than sing. But you remember, Dave, how far I got when I served up nothing but jazz? I was so discouraged that night you walked into Kelly's Stable that I was ready to shine shoes.

"Now I'm going back and be a singer again. But today was one I'll never forget."

Nor would the capable Miss Starr. The session led to a longterm contract with Capitol and a new and lucrative career.

°   °   °

In Kansas City, I watched a mob of more than 7,000 cheer Cole's combo as he appeared at Municipal Auditorium on a Gastel-produced one-nighter with Benny Carter's solid band.

We went out for ribs after the show. I was feeling like a stranger in my home town. After eight years I didn't recognize anyone. Cole, Carter, and Gastel made good company that night.

Nat spoke that morning of his boyhood in Alabama and of the days when he played piano as accompaniment to the choir and congregation in his father's shabby Baptist church on Chicago's poverty-ridden South Side. He spoke of racial prejudice.

"I've never thought you could make things better by going around poking bigots in the mouth," he said. "The Negro must be educated, and allowed better jobs, better housing, better, more nutritious food. It won't happen this month or next but things improve a little all the time. I have faith."

Cole was a gentle, God-fearing man who adhered to the principles of Christianity imposed upon him by his father. He was sometimes criticized by other blacks for his unwillingness to take the lead among other showfolk in their 400-year fight against racial discrimination. He, instead, played numerous concerts in which all proceeds were given directly to black organizations. Nat did not subscribe to militant philosophies. By just being Nat Cole, a decent, lovable man of integrity, he accomplished more in the still-continuing fight for equality than any organization.

We talked until dawn that morning in Kansas City. Cole and his wife Nadine were soon to be divorced. He deplored his failure as a husband. Later, he married Maria Ellington, a comely Boston singer who had sung briefly with Duke Ellington (no relation). Their marriage appeared ideal. Unlike Nadine, Maria accompanied her famous husband on virtually every trip he made, including treks to South America, Mexico, and Europe.

Back in Hollywood, I had a call from Cole one afternoon. He surprised me by asking if I had any more songs lying around.

"We're looking for something rhythmic, something that might go big in the jukes," he explained. "A bright little novelty is hard to find."

I showed up on the session within hours with typewritten lyrics of a "bright little novelty" I hoped he might accept. There was no music. My words fitted the traditional blues chords every musician knows. I hummed them in my ragged Missouri baritone as Nat studied my typewritten sheet.

"We'll see," he said. "And while we're at it I'll caution you to never audition for a job as a singer."

Nat and his trio canned my simple, inane little *I Think You Get What I Mean* in no more than 20 minutes. He did not ask for co-composership credit. Nor did Conkling release the record during the Christmas holidays.

It was not a best-seller and I believe I know why. *I Think You Get What I Mean* was a poor song, if you get what I mean. Nat never asked to see more of my work and I don't blame him. I never composed any more lyrics.

°   °   °

The Dodgers moved to Los Angeles from Brooklyn in 1958 and their most rabid supporter, I suspect, was Nat Cole. He bought a box seating eight persons even though he was aware that he would be on the road, unable to watch Walter O'Malley's squad play in Chavez Ravine more than three or four times a season.

I became a Giants man the moment they fired big-mouthed Leo Durocher as manager. When they moved from The Bronx to San Francisco I adopted them as my own. O'Malley pulled many capers I found reprehensible. Every year I hope that the Dodgers win enough games to lose the pennant to the Giants on closing day by one percentage point. Some years they've come close.

Nat and I argued our teams' merits and weaknesses a hundred times. He frequently had business to discuss with Lee Gillette, but he always stuck his head in my open door on his way out. Sometimes his way out took 35 minutes.

Came 1951, and the Giants moved a hustling young superstar named Willie Mays up from Minneapolis. Nat met him while Willie was still a rookie outfielder and the two established a long and intimate friendship.

So Cole's devotion to the Dodgers was tinged with admiration and love for Willie. Nat could never get irked when I pleaded the Giants' cause. His man Mays was a Giant.

Then, as it must to all men, death came to Nat Cole in early 1965. He fought the battle with cancer admirably, and there were times when it looked as if he might win. The soft, persuasive, believable voice that so many of us will never forget was stilled forever.

His widow requested the use of Dodger Stadium for a massive memorial concert, receipts from which would go directly—without any deductions—to the Nat Cole Cancer Foundation which Maria Cole established during Nat's illness. Nat had appeared at various Dodger events through the years for no fee. He was almost an annual attraction at the Baseball Writers' Spring Banquet held at the close of spring training at the Palladium. But O'Malley, a multimillionaire, refused Maria Cole's simple request. He said he couldn't throw a benefit for every entertainer who died.

12

You have
to blame
Thomas Alva Edison
for today's rock 'n' roll.
He invented
electricity.

—STAN GETZ

THE TRAGIC AND unbelievable news that Major Glenn Miller was lost and presumed dead after attempting a flight from a British air base to Paris, over the treacherous English Channel, came through a few days before Christmas, 1944.

His loss was incalculable. The band he had organized and conducted for the U.S. Army after he volunteered for service in the spring of 1942—only weeks after I had sat with him in the near-empty Cafe Rouge of the Hotel Pennsylvania the night following Pearl Harbor—was unanimously regarded as the finest, most distinctive musical organization in America's military history.

Helen Miller would not accept Glenn's death. For many years, into the 1960s, she patiently and confidently awaited his return. Finally, she abandoned hope. Now she, too, is dead.

I had enjoyed Miller and his music—*most* of his music—not only in New York but in Chicago, Kansas City, Detroit, and Hollywood. I had "joined" his band and ridden the Miller bus for a day and a night in Michigan. As a newsman, I found him to be direct, honest, and unevasive when I asked him questions. He was a tough, no-nonsense disciplinarian with his sidemen and singers, yet they respected and liked him.

I thought of the several nights when he, his wife, and I had dropped into Lindy's Broadway eatery for a late supper of jelly pancakes, and how Miller would watch Milton Berle hammily shouting and attracting attention to himself at a nearby table with his fellow comedians.

"Don't judge him harshly," Miller said. "He has a congenital speech impediment—an oversized mouth."

Millions of Americans today do not remember Miller and his music. But those older than 45 do, and fondly. They still buy his records. RCA-Victor long ago remastered them carefully for long-play configuration and there are a few jocks still active who loyally spin them on radio stations, mainly FM. I credit Leonard Joy with much of Miller's success. Joy was a Record Man. He assisted in choosing the tunes, getting the proper balances, pushing the exploitation staff to obtain exposure, and goosing the plant bosses to press them up and ship them out expeditiously.

Miller had less than four years to establish his legacy of records. How many discs by the Beatles, the Stones, David Bowie, Alice Cooper, and David Cassidy will be sold 30 years from now? I hope I am still around to collect a few bets with my children on that question.

o   o   o

A collector of blues is incurable. When the legendary Huddie (Leadbelly) Ledbetter arrived in Los Angeles under the auspices of a Communist-front organization in 1944—an arrangement about which I remained ignorant until the war's end—it was my pleasure to record a dozen Leadbelly sides. He sang and played his battered 12-string guitar, then demanded that Paul Mason Howard, who accompanied him to the studio, be allowed to accompany him on a zither. I didn't care to argue with Leadbelly. He had been pardoned from the Louisiana state prison after killing a man. Leadbelly also made a couple of rocky, ragtimey piano solos on the session. Capitol still sells his classic performances in the seventies, remastered and packaged for microgroove turntables.

o   o   o

The company's art director, Lou Schurrer, and I occasionally tired of the record scene. One day, smarting over our ignominious 4-F classification, we took a streetcar to downtown Los Angeles and applied for admission to the Office of Strategic Services. We had heard they were accepting writers and artists to be employed in the European and South Pacific war theaters in creating propaganda and hypoing the morale of American fighting men.

We were not accepted, and much later we learned that the OSS was essentially an espionage organization with an extremely high mortality rate. I resumed my weekly recorded broadcasts for the Office of War Information, a series I began in 1943 under the direction of Martha Wilkerson and Mort Werner in which I interviewed pop music stars and spun their latest hits. It was, of course, a gratis endeavor, and I told myself that every little contribution helped the war effort.

Werner's career didn't end with the OWI. For the last two decades he has been in charge of programming for the mighty NBC television network in New York.

o   o   o

Carlos Gastel got itchy again that summer and implored me to drive to New York with him in his Cadillac convertible. Stan Kenton was going to open at the Pennsylvania Hotel.

This time we had the company of his pretty little sister Chiqui. And riding with us as far as her home town of Albuquerque was my wife, Mickie. Carlos

101

put down the top of his car, gassed up, and headed for New Mexico via Nevada, some 200 miles out of the way.

We got off to a rollicking start. Outside the desert town of Baker, still in California, a tire exploded and we rolled over and over into a ditch. None of was hurt. We thumbed a ride back to Baker and to the same bar which we had left 20 minutes earlier.

The car repaired, we tried for Las Vegas again. There were only two hotels in those days, the Last Frontier and the El Rancho, but they had the same big green crap tables and roulette wheels you see at Caesars Palace and the Tropicana today. Gastel wiped his brow constantly as he sipped his drinks and blew a bundle. Chiqui, Mickie, and I dropped out after the first few minutes of action.

We got to Albuquerque the next afternoon, dropped Mickie off with her parents and started the long, long haul to Manhattan. Carlos stopped every hour or so "to check the jukebox." Each check took a half-hour while he studied the records with a cooling glass of booze.

Somewhere in Illinois, I rebelled. I don't drink the hard stuff; never have in my life. I had gamely tried to keep pace with the thirsty Gastel by nursing beers until they warmed my hands, but I had to do something startling. I bought a lug of shiny red tomatoes, so many tomatoes they would hardly fit into the car's rear seat. Every time Carlos stopped for libations I'd polish up a big red one and start slurping. He was furious with me for this, and I think his sister was ready to chuck me out of the car, but we did make good time from Illinois.

I saved just enough tomatoes to make a spectacular entrance into the Pennsylvania Hotel's plush lobby. When a puzzled, confused bellboy showed me to my room, accepted his gratuity, and left me alone, I stumbled to the immaculate bathroom and threw up all over the place. I never told Gastel, his sister, or my wife.

Kenton's band was his best ever—clean, precise, highly original and eminently danceable to. He had a banner opening night. I rambled about Manhattan meeting newspapermen and radio people, striving to bag all possible exploitation for Kenton. Since it was June Christy's debut in New York as well, she scored tremendously, too. Stan's record sales boomed after a few days of this kind of concentrated promotion. And there were still late-night radio broadcasts to be done. When I telephoned Wallichs in Hollywood to crow over big Stanley's triumph, I felt that the Roseland fiasco had been avenged.

Carlos had other business to transact. He was now representing Peggy Lee, Nat Cole, and Benny Carter as well as Kenton. He and Sonny Dunham had parted. Sonny never quite rang the bell. Later he gave up himself, junking his orchestra and taking a steady, high-paying job in network radio. I liked him and I assume he liked me despite my shortcomings as his seven-week road manager.

There ain't none of us is perfect.

In Hollywood, I persevered with the *Capitol News* and its rocketing popularity, and I conceived a major project for which there was no precedent—a recorded *History of Jazz* featuring as many noted musicians as were available. Mercer, Wallichs, and Conkling bought my plan to record and issue in four albums a panoramic recreation of the music from its early days. Certain giants were unavailable, Ellington, Basie, and Lunceford among them, but by employing their musicians it was possible to realize most of the music necessary.

With Mercer's help I contacted Paul Whiteman. He no longer was the nation's most popular maestro, and he appeared pleased to round up musicians from his first bands in the twenties and have them play the original Bill Challis charts which had helped establish him as an international favorite. *Wang Wang Blues* dates back to 1921; Tommy Gott, Gus Mueller, Mike Pingitore, Buster Johnson, Hank Stern, Hal McDonald, and Ferde Grofe, the distinguished composer, recorded it note-for-note as they had 24 years previously. *San* is from 1927. Whiteman brought in a second group of old-timers to remake it, including Matty Malneck, Perry Botkin, and Elmer Smithers, and mixed them with a dozen young guys to emulate the great PW troupe of 1927 renown.

Between tunes, Whiteman and Grofe stood around with me sipping coffee, and I recorded much of their dialogue on big 16-inch acetates. They recalled the year Whiteman was sponsored by Old Gold cigarettes on a weekly radio show and how they trained from New York to Los Angeles on a special gold-painted train to publicize Old Golds and *The King of Jazz*, a lavish musical film

The self-styled King of Jazz, Paul Whiteman, recorded his original 1921 and 1927 arrangements of Wang Wang Blues *and* San *on a Dexter-supervised 1945 session in Hollywood. Whiteman went even farther—he assembled many of the original members of his orchestra for Dexter's* History of Jazz *album series. (Charlie Mihn)*

they were about to make for Universal in Hollywood.

"That train stopped and started every hour or so all the way across the land," Whiteman laughed. "It may have been the most successful publicity stunt ever attempted. Bing Crosby made that trip, and when we got to Hollywood he was tossed in jail for a crazy drinking escapade and missed making the movie. When he fell in love with Dixie Lee she made him calm down and he's been an exemplary citizen ever since."

Whiteman recalled the days when radio put the record business into a tailspin for several years. And he spoke of the Big Band era.

"I'm disturbed," Whiteman said, "by what I'm hearing these days. Many of our leaders today are forgetting that the big secret is tempo—danceability—and when I hear those sloppy, bad-note bebop trumpet solos I fear that dancers are not accepting them. If enough people turn away to something else then the big bands will die off."

They did. But it was more than bebop solos and charts that swung the axe. World War II decimated the large orchestras with its unquenchable need for men. Gasoline was rationed, making touring difficult. Ballrooms closed. Salaries became prohibitive for all but the top-ranking maestri to afford. And most critical of all, probably, was the rise of the local disc jockey and the resulting decline in live sustaining broadcasts from scores of ballrooms, hotels, and niteries.

Capitol's *History of Jazz* comprised 40 entertaining sides when it was released shortly after the end of the war. Later we reissued it in four 10-inch LPs.

Sales were brisk over a period of 15 years, so much so that I issued it a third time on 12-inch microgroove discs in a revised edition which, most reviewers agreed, was a substantial improvement over the original shellac series.

Almost every notable jazzman participated in the *History of Jazz* anthology. Sales eventually passed the 200,000 level. One of these days I'd like to revise it again, bringing it up to the minute, but any member of a plattery's accounting department will rule that such a project is an unsound financial risk.

Sure. I've heard that song before and so has every other producer with imagination.

*   *   *

The permissive air throughout the 50 states today was not evident 30 years ago in the music business. America's favorite female singers—we referred to them as orioles, thrushes, chirpers, and canaries—all reflected an innocent, almost virginal, purity in their images, an attribute hardly characteristic of singers in the seventies.

America's big names were Dinah Shore, Peggy Lee, Jo Stafford, Helen O'Connell, Helen Forrest, Margaret Whiting, and Martha Tilton, ladylike and soft-spoken all. The overwhelming social revolution engendered by the Beatles' success in 1964 brought with it the bizarre, blatant sexuality of performers like Janis Joplin, Grace Slick, Suzi Quatro, and Bette Midler.

Miss Midler's recent rise to prominence offers a clearly drawn example of the strategy employed by her eager associates in establishing a not overly talented unknown.

Atlantic Records has spent more than $100,000 exploiting her campy act—odd attire, odd makeup, odd physical mannerisms while singing, and a line of patter between songs that is, at best, only occasionally effective.

"You may not like my singing," she tells audiences in night clubs, "but stick around anyway. Pretty soon I shake my tits."

Is it possible for a topflight act to be built around a burlesque show schtick like hers? Does dialogue of that stripe boost the sales of her records? Time will tell. Old Belle Barth did it better at high-priced stag parties years ago.

Kay Starr wasn't like the other singers of the forties. After her two sides with the Capitol Jazzmen were released, her career accelerated. She was only 20, and as unsophisticated as any performer I've ever known. Yet Kay exuded a subtle sensuousness, a physical appeal which came across on discs as emphatically as it did in clubs. Friendly and anxious to be liked and wanted, she had no phony affectations. I went to Boss Conkling requesting that he approve my signing her to a longterm contract.

"I hear she's super, Dex," Conkling told me, removing his ring and jiggling it in one hand. "But what can we do with her? Peggy, Jo, and Margaret are all selling well. We have only so many new songs. We can only promote X number of artists."

I argued that Kay's future loomed as large as any other girl's, and that her Oklahoma-Texas background and varied experience with the Venuti and Barnet bands had given her a fresh approach to songs. "She sings with all the bluesy, gut-grabbing verve of Bessie Smith," I pleaded. "Give her a chance."

Conkling said he would think it over. He was a fair man. In a few days he advised me that because the company would soon launch a new red "Americana" label on which our country, western, jazz, and blues performers would be featured, I could go ahead with Miss Starr.

"But she can't be treated like Peggy, Jo, or Mag Whiting," he warned. "Keep Kay on the blues."

I dug up a batch of old songs—no one at Capitol would let me record any of the new plug tunes submitted by publishers—and assigned arranger-tenor saxist Dave Cavanaugh to sketch the arrangements and lead Kay's accompaniment. "We're on a tight budget," I told Cavanaugh, "but Conkling said to spare no expense with the orchestra except to limit it to eight men."

Kay sang her tail off on that first "Americana" session, and I defiantly slipped in three non-blues along with *Share Croppin' Blues*. I backed her *Share Croppin'* with *I'm the Lonesomest Gal in Town* and in eight weeks it had sold 42,367 copies on 78 rpm shellacs, a highly profitable kickoff for an unknown.

There were 18 Starr sides in all before Conkling in the spring of 1949 took Kay away from me and assigned her to Lee Gillette, who was in position to give her new material like *The Wheel of Fortune* and many other clicks.

I went back to my *Capitol News* chores, as I did for two weeks out of every four, perhaps a bit peevishly. I had brought Nat Cole, the Kenton band, and Peggy Lee to Capitol and they were all chart-busters. In Kay Starr the company had another. Yet I sat on the sidelines writing about them instead of recording their talents.

I figured I deserved better.

                    ○   ○   ○

Jazz sessions became more frequent in the mid-forties. Coleman Hawkins brought his golden French Selmer tenor and combo to a Vine Street Bistro and his presence gave me the chance to produce an entire album—one I had dreamed of recording for many years.

One of the titles, a Hawkins original he titled *Stuffy* in honor of a new disc jockey in town, Gene Norman, surprisingly stepped out and approached the 200,000 mark. Norman used it as a theme on his KFWB nightly show for a beer sponsor and the exploitation, of course, helped sales.

There were problems on one of the Hawkins sessions. His trumpeter, Howard McGhee, spoiled so many takes with fluffs and clinkers that the leader asked him to sit out the session. With Hawkins's approval, I called the veteran trumpeter Red Nichols and pleaded with him to rush over to our studios at Radio Recorders and finish out the date. Nichols got there in 20 minutes.

But when we began to record semi-bebop charts Hawkins had made up for the album, Nichols stumbled around on his horn as ineptly as McGhee had earlier. It wasn't Red's kind of music and I should have known that. We ended up without the sound of a trumpet on one tune. Nichols felt bad, I felt worse, and Hawkins laughed at both of us. But it turned out to be a classy, popular, and profitable album.

                    ○   ○   ○

Wallichs invited me to hire a secretary one morning. I had bitched, mildly, that I needed assistance. He concurred.

I walked over to Music City on my lunch hour to check with Hughie Claudin; he hired and fired people and in his file would be applications for secretarial work. While I was talking with him a little girl walked up and asked if she could be interviewed for a job as a typist, file clerk, secretary, or whatever. Her name was Merrilyn Hammond. She appeared to be about 13 years old.

"Do you know anything about music?" I asked.

"Yes, sir, I do," she said. "I'm a better musician than a typist."

I walked her a half-block south and put her to work.

Merrilyn was older than she appeared to be, but was not yet 20. She learned fast, and constantly demonstrated a loyalty to me that was far beyond what I expected. She became so proficient that the bosses later moved her up to a more creative position in publicity. After 20 years, Merrilyn left Capitol to become a freelance publicist and talent manager.

Johnny Mercer heard her repeatedly playing a lovely instrumental theme from an unreleased 20th Century-Fox dramatic film starring Dana Andrews. The melody was strange, and mysteriously intriguing to Mercer's sensitive ear. After he heard Miss Hammond spin the soundtrack theme for the thirtieth time he borrowed it, took it home, played it several more times, and returned to the office with a remarkable lyric to David Raksin's melody. It was called *Laura*.

Of such flukes are immortal standards born.

☼   ☼   ☼

Don Otis quit radio, so I moved my recorded jazz show over to Gene Norman's KFWB mike. Norman had only one 15-second commercial every 15 minutes and his audience was large. We piqued listeners' interest by playing unre-

On the air at KFWB, Hollywood, are drummer Gene Krupa, Dexter, and singer-leader Vaughn Monroe. Krupa and Monroe died within months of each other in 1974.

(Above) Reviewing new records on a 1946 Al Jarvis radio program in Los Angeles are Bing Crosby, Dexter, Jarvis, and Bob Hope. Seated is the late Ella Logan, who a year later became an internationally known singing star in Finian's Rainbow. (Ray Whitten)

(Right) Artie Shaw shows his Japanese war souvenirs to the author after two years in the South Pacific combat zones as a U.S. Navy bandleader. Shaw's clarinet and orchestra remain vividly in the memories of many as typifying the musical excellence of the Swing Era. (Charlie Mihn)

leased, newly-recorded jazz items which were shipped to me every week from the largest record pressing plant in the world in Scranton. A dozen or more companies in addition to Capitol manufactured discs there; no one could figure how I got unreleased Ellingtons, Basies, Luncefords, and the like on the radio six weeks before they were released.

Norman had the top nighttime rating; Al Jarvis on the same station was the king of the daylight deejays. On Saturdays, Al blocked out a two-hour segment devoted to reviewing the new records in a slightly different format than that devised by Alan Courtney in New York. I was the one panelist who evaluated the eight discs every week, and because I judged as a musican would—aesthetic rather than sales appeal determined my rating of each entry—most of my observations were wildly controversial.

Jarvis presented the greatest names of show business on the panel: one Easter presentation at Earl Carroll's Theater-Restaurant attracted thousands of listeners with Bob Hope, Bing Crosby, and Ella Logan sharing the stage with Jarvis and me. Another week offered Frank Sinatra, Nat Cole, and Benny Goodman. We went from weekend to weekend with the best: Gregory Peck, Red Skelton, Milton Berle, Louis Armstrong, Dinah Shore, Frankie Laine, Paul Whiteman, Duke Ellington, Billie Holiday, Artie Shaw, Freddy Martin, Jimmy and Tommy Dorsey, Peggy Lee, Jo Stafford—the guests were unending.

Only two of them spoke with forked tongues. Armstrong and Ellington liked everything they heard, allotting even the most puerile pop song by the most sophomoric three-tenor hotel orchestra full 100 ratings. Perhaps they didn't want to hurt anyone's feelings.

The Jarvis program ran for years, eventually moving over to KLAC and then to KABC-TV. We lasted only 13 weeks on television. The director said it was entertaining but he didn't know where to direct his three cameras while the records were being played.

I think he might know today.

o   o   o

Artie Shaw came out of the South Pacific 20 pounds underweight and half dead. He headed for his wife Betty's palatial residence in Beverly Hills. She lived with her father and an infant son whom Shaw had never seen. Her father was Jerome Kern.

Shaw rested a day or two and welcomed me for an interview. Like Glenn Miller, Claude Thornhill, Eddy Duchin, and Jimmy Grier, he had enlisted for military service and was assigned to lead a band. Unlike Miller, Shaw was sent to the South Pacific as a chief petty officer. For more than twelve months, he and his musicians saw duty in combat areas.

"Seventeen times," he told me, "we ran to battle stations and shot at Japanese bomber planes. I saw men killed. Our band hitch-hiked from one ship to another at Tulagi, Guadalcanal, Efati, Espiritu Santo, and others in the New Hebrides. The pads fell out of my clarinet and reeds were impossible to find, but we made out even when the guitar and bass men couldn't obtain strings. We had it easy compared to thousands of the fighting men."

Artie laughed when I mentioned Tokyo Rose, the cunning Japanese propagandist who broadcast from Tokyo via shortwave.

"She plays the best American records and everyone tunes her in," he said. "One night she played a Shaw record and announced that my orchestra was playing in the swanky St. Francis Hotel in San Francisco, unworried and unaffected by the war. That got a big roar from the guys on the beat-up old ship we were on."

Shaw apologized for his nervousness. He was not at ease. He showed me a bloodied Japanese flag, a sword, and other souvenirs of the South Pacific, and posed for photographs which later appeared in *Metronome*.

"I need a little rest," he said. "But I'll be back. The war will soon be over. I wonder if the world has learned anything? Or will it all happen again?"

Artie found out.

⚬ ⚬ ⚬

Frankie Laine became the hottest act in show business. I cringed when I heard one of his Mercury records on the radio—which was constantly.

I was writing and handling production of the *Capitol News*, appearing every weekend on Al Jarvis' record-rating program, spinning jazz platters Tuesday nights as a guest with Gene Norman, writing occasional news and features for *Billboard* and *Metronome*, playing on and managing the Capitol baseball and basketball teams, producing records two or three times a month with handpicked jazzmen, and—most rewarding of all—taking over the 2 a.m. feeding and care of my infant son Mike Kenton Dexter, a newcomer in our rented bungalow high up in the hills of Hollywood.

A stickler for office regimentation despite Mercer's less rigid attitude, Boss Wallichs wondered why I came in as late as 10:30 some mornings.

"You should realize it's 1:30 in the afternoon in New York, Dex," he remonstrated.

"But we work in California, don't we, Glenn?"

A less understanding company exec might have justifiably sent me back to a newspaper job. Glenn respected creative people. But they puzzled him until the day he died.

13

There are
only twelve tones.
You must treat them
carefully.

—PAUL HINDEMITH

ONE OF THE MOST popular repeat guests on Al Jarvis's weekend record review show (*Can You Tie That?*) was a diminutive, baby-faced youngster who modestly paraded his exceptional music knowledge with an authority that teenaged girls in our audience found irresistible.

Andre Previn was a refugee, a wealthy refugee, who had fled Nazi Germany shortly before Hitler's panzers and planes crushed Poland. The son of a German attorney and judge, Jacob Priwin, Andre was barely 16 when I first encountered him in Hollywood as a student at Beverly Hills High School. He played piano, he composed and orchestrated superbly, and although he had lived in Germany and France most of his life, he spoke English excellently.

Previn was the darndest teenager I ever met, with the highest intelligence quotient of any of my acquaintances. I watched him record his first piano records for Eddie Laguna's Sunset label. His classical background showed, yet he played surprisingly inventive jazz.

"I try not to be overly influenced by my idols Nat Cole, Art Tatum, and Teddy Wilson," he told me, "but it's almost unavoidable."

Previn knew every record issued, be it jazz, pop, or classical. He was shyly confident at the microphone discussing discs with us, and rating what he heard, on a broad zero to 100 scale. Our evaluations frequently were identical.

He outgrew the Jarvis program, graduated from school, and went to work when he was 17 scoring and composing films at MGM's music department. He moved up to RCA-Victor as a recording artist. He married (Betty Bennett, Dory Langdon) and was later to become twice-divorced as he tired of the plastic Hollywood scene and turned to conducting classical music—an ambition he had secretly sustained since he was a five-year-old in Berlin.

From the Houston Symphony he moved to the London Symphony Orchestra, one of the world's great ensembles. He married actress Mia Farrow, fathered twin sons by her and took over a sturdy brick house—constructed in 1723—on a lovely 20-acre estate in Surrey, about one hour from London. His contract with the London Symphony runs through 1976 and will almost certainly be extended, so tumultuous have British music buffs and the orchestra's musicians responded to his artistry.

I see photographs of Andre today with his long, unkempt hair and black, untrimmed beard, and I think of the soft-spoken, knowledgeable high school kid who at 16 knew more about music than anyone I had ever met. And I recall his describing, a quarter-century later, a strange incident that occurred as he visited his old neighborhood in Berlin for the first time since his family fled the dreadful, deadly anti-Semitic atmosphere imposed by Hitler and his ruthless gang of genocide experts.

Trudging about the city in a snowstorm, Previn came across a streetcorner kiosk upon which are traditionally posted dozens of posters advertising night clubs, motion pictures, and other current entertainment. Andre randomly reached with a gloved hand to wipe the snow from one of the illegible posters and, astonished, read the sales pitch:

FIRST BERLIN APPEARANCE
Tonight Only
ANDRE PREVIN
And The Berlin Philharmonic

It really happened.

           º   º   º

It puzzles me why so many millions of Americans evince so little interest in jazz. The nation's only truly original art form, jazz still appeals to only a limited section of the citizenry. Numerous musicians agree with me that the most chronically tone-deaf slob on the block could be transformed into a raving jazz fanatic if he took just one evening of his life and, with the guidance of a selected stack of records and a patient instructor, assimilated the fine points of the art with an open mind and heart.

I still think it can be accomplished with anyone, given the time and certain discs by Armstrong, Henderson, Ellington, Hines, Basie, Lunceford, Goodman, Holiday, Bailey, Herman, and Kenton. Toss in a Bessie Smith from the twenties and I'd bet on it.

In a youthful effort to broaden the jazz base and disseminate its message to a wider audience, I wrote a book in 1946 called *Jazz Cavalcade*. It comprised 246 pages of text and a dozen or more photographs. It was published in New York by Criterion.

Twice a year I continue to receive small royalty checks, even in the seventies. But I long ago concluded that my *Jazz Cavalcade* accomplished all too little. Today I'm convinced that only television can boost jazz to the level it deserves.

How to get jazz regularly on the tube? I haven't figured that out yet and time, for me, is running out.

           º   º   º

It was on a March of Dimes special live broadcast produced and announced by Frank Bull on KFWB in early 1947 that I first heard an obscure singer-pianist named Nellie Lutcher. She sounded like no other woman, but I didn't know how to contact her, and I gave no more thought to her talents.

But one day a young sax player, Joe Lutcher, sat in my office playing two songs he had composed. The crude little demonstration disc he spun indicated nothing special in his efforts but the female voice was a knockout.

"That's my sister Nellie singing and playing," Joe said.

The rest was a flat-out cinch. She came into our studios, recorded *Hurry On Down, He's a Real Gone Guy,* and two other zany novelties and was out in two hours. *Hurry On Down* became a socko single within hours after it was released; Capitol had another winner.

Ralph Edwards' This Is Your Life *surprised pianist-singer Nellie Lutcher, whose records were a sensation of the post-war years. Dave Dexter explains to Edwards on his NBC television show how he found her and signed her to a contract—at a March of Dimes benefit party in Hollywood. Nellie now is a member of the board of directors of Local 47 of the American Federation of Musicians in Los Angeles. (Gene Howard)*

Jim Conkling had approved my contracting Nellie, but only for our "Americana" specialty label. Lee Gillette experienced the same restriction when he cut *Smoke, Smoke, Smoke that Cigarette* with his big find, Tex Williams. The Williams and Lutcher shellacs were issued by Conkling on the same day and Tex's novelty took off as spectacularly as Nellie's. It was a happy summer.

Nellie had banged around in a deplorable pillar-to-post manner for many years, pluckily supporting a large family by enduring low-pay gigs of every kind. She had grown up in the deep South, near Lake Charles, surviving the vicious racial prejudice of bigoted Louisiana whites with equanimity. I found her then to be the most grateful, the most charmingly cooperative, and one of the most talented performers I knew—and I find her the same in the 1970s.

Nellie is a revered member of the Local 47 American Federation of Musicians board of directors now, a fair and conscientious officer. But ironically, it was the same union which cruelly shortened her career as a top-selling recording artist.

Only months after Nellie zoomed into prominence in 1947, union president James Caesar Petrillo announced that musicians would make no more records after December 31 of that year.

"It won't be a strike," he bellowed. "It will be a refusal to record forever. Making records puts thousands of musicians out of work and we will never go back into the studios again."

It was the second time in six years that the belligerent Petrillo, a hopelessly incompetent trumpet player himself, had issued an edict prohibiting recording.

All through December that year artists rushed in and out of studios attempting to build a backlog of masters. It was difficult, around-the-clock work. Nellie was playing the Sherman Hotel in Chicago that month and I flew back into the bitter Cook County winter to supervise 24 masters by one of Capitol's most valued assets. Nellie was tireless; many of the 24 tracks were things she composed herself during her Chicago engagement. The others were old standards, presented in new and novel Lutcher dress. Remember her *Fine Brown Frame*?

George A. Tasker and Bill Putnam made their excellent studios available. We worked three nights—all night—canning the two dozen sides with Chicagoans Alvin Burroughs and Truck Parham accompanying Nellie's tricky, rhythmic piano and vocal designs. And when the New Year arrived it was those hurriedly-cut masters which we rashly issued one atop another, masters which tended to sound alike by summer. I'll always believe that Nellie might have sustained her popularity had we been in position to make each tune with more care over the years.

She did well anyway, becoming the rage of England on two personal appearances there and, with Carlos Gastel guiding her bookings, working America's most prestigious theaters and cabarets. Today she's a *grande dame* in the most affectionate sense of the term, admired and respected by all who know her in Los Angeles. I value no friendship more than hers.

❅   ❅   ❅

Everyone resented Petrillo's arbitrary, unjustified behavior. President Truman, Congress, and other union chiefs protested.

Petrillo's own subjects called him "Little Mussolini" and many of them came to us to advise that they would happily make any records we required. After months of inactivity, and without acting in concert together, the disc-makers began to choose songs again—and hold recording sessions. They were furtive, of course. Musicians who participated—the best in Hollywood, Chicago, and New York—risked lifetime expulsion from the AFM. Instead of the $41.25 payment required by the expired union agreement of 1943, we paid them in clean, new $50 bills.

I was refused by only one top-rank musician in the many months that we made "illegal" masters. All the others vied to work for us, and for the other labels which angrily defied Petrillo's absurd, one-man edict.

And so Petrillo's refusal to allow musicians to record "forever" became a much-mocked phrase. He sat in his plushy New York offices hearing more and more new records on the air, and reading a constantly-lengthening list of new releases in *Billboard* and *Variety*. He wasn't merely defeated, he was stomped to death by his own musicians. Finally, his negotiators and record executives agreed to new contracts and once again we went about our business in our own studios in sight of all.

Petrillo has not prohibited recording since.

o   o   o

On one of his frequent visits to southern California, Benny Goodman tipped me that his eight-year contract with Columbia was expiring momentarily. He intimated he might be available.

Within hours I arranged a dinner on the Sunset Strip—it was then a much nicer street than now—at which I kibitzed while Benny and Glenn Wallichs sparred and parried in the most adroit Kissinger-Sadat manner. Wallichs ended up guaranteeing Goodman $100,000 in advance against royalties, the most expensive artist acquisition in Capitol's history.

Jim Conkling ably produced BG's records. Benny fronted a trio, a quartet, a quintet, a sextet, a septet, an octet, and a full swing orchestra as the months flew by. Seeking something novel, he reluctantly cut a number of boppish, dissonant arrangements which he personally didn't like but which, he hoped, would re-establish him among the industry's leaders. They didn't.

I persuaded Goodman to participate in a jazz session, strictly as a sideman, along with Benny Carter, Charlie Shavers, Jimmy Rowles, Dave Cavanaugh, Red Norvo, and several other big names of that era. When he arrived, I achieved the impossible when I conned him into singing a duet with Stan Kenton, a lyric designed around stock blues progressions in which Benny and Stan needled each other about their respective swing and progressive jazz viewpoints. It was called *Happy Blues* and they had a barrel of laughs making it. It didn't sell well. Nor did the straight jazz instrumentals we also cut that

(Right) Benny Goodman has long been noted for his devastating "ray" when a musician displeases him, but on this 1947 session the Swing King and Dexter find a light moment. Like the proverbial college professor, Goodman is renowned for his absent-mindedness. But never with a clarinet in his hand. (Gene Lester)

(Below) One of the more memorable jazz sessions in the Dexter career was this, in Hollywood, which found Red Norvo, Red Callender, Jimmy Rowles, Benny Carter, Charlie Shavers, Joe Koch, David Cavanaugh, and Stan Kenton and Benny Goodman recording as vocalists. No hits resulted, Dexter recalls, but there were some laughs. (Otto Rothschild)

afternoon. I thought they were fairly memorable sides; no one else did.

I paid the celebrated maestro-clarinetist $41.25 for his afternoon's work and that included his services as a singer. It had to be the smallest fee he had received since he was a kid in knickerbocker pants playing Chicago bar mitzvahs. Benny accepted the money good-naturedly.

"If this is for my vocal contributions," he mumbled, "I don't deserve it." But he cashed the check.

✿   ✿   ✿

Capitol's industry position in 1948, throughout the second Petrillo ban on recording, was measurably different than it had been in 1942–43. The company now was an internationally recognized major firm, ranking with Decca, RCA-Victor, and Columbia. The original Wallichs-Mercer-DeSylva partnership of six years earlier had been dissolved and stock issued to the public.

In 1947 Capitol grossed $14,500,000 on 230 singles and 24 albums. Personnel in the home executive offices were about to be moved to larger facilities one block up Vine Street, above the Music City record store.

Capitol maintained its own sales branches in 29 cities and planned more. The entire industry was enjoying a boom and our growth rate exceeded our competition's. We never saw DeSylva. His task of running Paramount Pictures was all-consuming and physically debilitating. Nor was Mercer as active as in the firm's early days. Wallichs replaced him as president. Mercer still wrote hit songs but his clout as a recording artist diminished by the month. Many big bands were dying, or dead. Most small bands, the jazz combos, were experimenting and alienating audiences with a hybrid music called bebop. It was an era of change.

There are a number of things I don't understand about the record business. One of them is why old-fashioned, uncomplicated Dixieland jazz sells consistently. I am aware that it is a simple, makes-you-happy music appealing to unsophisticated, unartistic people. But why do 50 versions of *When the Saints Go Marching In* (the poorest of all Dixie standards, I say) continue to move in the marts while classics by Ellington and Basie are pushed onto the delete lists?

I like Dixie for what it is: one can relax, enjoy a drink, and even dance to its archaic beat. It requires no concentration. I've always enjoyed recording Dixie jazz.

Men like Ray Bauduc, Pete Daily, Eddie Miller, Nappy Lamare, Matty Matlock, Red Nichols, Zutty Singleton, Marvin Ash, and many other Los Angeles residents made scores of Dixie masters for Capitol, some of which are still available.

The Dixiecats are a different breed of feline when the little red light glows and the tape starts racing from reel to reel at 15 inches per second. They are unfailingly enthusiastic in their playing and attitude, unlike so many other jazzmen. They even enjoy making a fourth or fifth take to obtain a perfect master. And when it's time to pack up their gear most of them will sit around for hours

117

listening to the results, shouting their approval of a solo and assisting in the splicing of takes.

I dearly love them all, the Dixiecats. They make life easy for the harried, pressured, clock-fighting Record Man. It will never happen, but I'd delight in cutting Dixie sessions three days a week the rest of my life.

°   °   °

The end of the forties saw broader horizons open up for Capitol. Conkling and Wallichs agreed with me that not all talent lived and worked in Hollywood. They approved my plea that I be allowed to hit the road in a quest for fresh, untried artists.

I trained out to Kansas City, visiting my mother and dad and my brother Dick's growing family. I had an edge in that town; it had been my home for 22 years and I was confident some of my old musician friends could prove valuable to Capitol.

Vic Damon's studios were modern and well-equipped but small. I took my pianist pal Jay McShann there and we put together several fine things, employing six or seven musicians and no written charts.

I also teamed McShann and his men with one of my longtime favorite singers, buxom Julia Lee, whom I had first heard while I was a sax-tooting eleventh grader at Northeast High. She had a big, big voice, and she knew every pop tune ever composed. Julia was past her prime, a notch or three below her standards of ten years earlier, but to my ear she still had a future on records.

Damon helped me record a number of Kansas Citians on that expedition to Missouri. Joshua Johnson was almost elderly, yet he sang with touching, heartfelt poignancy, and his heavy, boogie-woogie piano was distinctive and commercial in appeal. Ira (Bus) Moten played piano and sang. He was a cousin of the late Bennie Moten, the bandleader, and though I didn't rate his musicianship on the same level with the others, I succeeded in canning eight masters with him and avoided overtime. I made additional tracks with a young woman, Charlotte Mansfield, and still others with the rough, hard-swinging band of Tommy Douglas.

Julia Lee turned out to be the prize. She came across on shellac like a bitch in heat, and soon I had her in Hollywood recording frequently with her own Sam (Baby) Lovett on drums and aces like Red Norvo, Vic Dickenson, Benny Carter, Henry Bridges, Dave Cavanaugh, Red Callender, and Dave Barbour in her accompanying combo. We billed her as Julia Lee and Her Boy Friends; her *King-Sized Papa, Gotta Gimme What'cha Got, Snatch and Grab It*, and a dozen others attracted little airplay, but hard to find was a jukebox in America without one of her singles in its stack.

Members of the National Press Club present a party every year, the toughest invite in Washington. In 1948, with President Truman as their honored guest, they surprised and pleased him by bringing in Julia Lee to head the entertainment.

(Above) Kansas City reunions in Capitol's Hollywood studios occurred frequently in the closing years of the 1940s. Julia Lee sold hundreds of thousands of records with her sly, sometimes naughty lyrics that offended no one. Dexter, left, poses with Julia Lee's Boy Friends: Vic Dickenson, Sam "Baby" Lovett, Benny Carter, Miss Lee, David Cavanaugh, Jack Marshall, and Billy Hadnott. (Otto Rothschild)

(Left) Julia Lee of Kansas City contributed numerous big-selling singles to Capitol. Dexter recorded her in Missouri and California; she was one of his favorite talents while he was attending high school in Kansas City. She died in 1958 but not before she performed in Washington, D.C., for President Harry Truman. (Charlie Mihn)

Fighting Harry, my gabby barber shop acquaintance of long ago, said he knew Julia's voice and piano well. He sent her a present and thanked her for her music.

Julia fared fine on records for five years, then her popularity waned as times and tastes shifted. She's dead now, but the success she had on discs made her life a little nicer. Mine, too.

°   °   °

New Orleans was next. I had never been to the Crescent City. It was to be unlike any other I visited.

I walked Canal and Royal and Bourbon Streets, enjoying the sights and odors of the Birthplace of Jazz. I ate sugary pecan pralines, drank gallons of chicory-injected coffee, and devoured bowl after bowl of creole gumbo, a thick, spicy, seafoodish soup. I took the Mississippi River paddleboat trip, gawked at the Civil War monuments, and dined at Antoine's. I was a pop-eyed tourist and proud to be.

I made records, too. Sharkey and his Kings of Dixieland were the most popular band in Louisiana in the late forties. We cut eight sides on that first visit. Sharkey (that's the only billing he used though his legal name was Joseph Bonano) wore a perky little brown derby and played spirited trumpet.

He had good sidemen: Monk Hazel, a drummer who blew a hot horn while beating his traps; Santo Pecora, a trombonist who was home again after playing for a decade with several name bands; Chink Martin, a bassist in his 60s, but powerful and right for jazz; and clarinetist Leonard Centobie, who idolized the dead but unforgotten Irving Fazola and Leon Rapollo.

At the Ponchartrain Hotel I found Armand Hug, a stride pianist unknown outside Louisiana but a favorite down in the humid magnolia country. There also was an eccentric man named Sam DeKemel who played jazz on a bugle—no valves—but somehow he played all the good notes with a beat.

And there was the legendary Lizzie Miles, once the toast of Paris, a big black woman with a still-potent, expressive voice. She specialized in blues, naturally. For years she mailed me religious pamphlets, urging me to be saved. The one-way correspondence ended only with her death many years after I first recorded her with Sharkey's band in Station WDSU's studios in the colorful French Quarter.

I liked them all, personally as well as for the music they dispensed so enthusiastically. I made five trips to New Orleans before a change in my job stopped them. Some of those records are still selling in the seventies. They may not have been artistic gems, but they were authentic. I hear one of them now and I can taste gumbo and smell that coal-black Canal Street chicory coffee.

°   °   °

Detroit is as far as you can get from New Orleans in many ways. It is Motown. On a frigid Winter's day it is gray, unhospitable and foreboding. It is

(Above) 'Way down yonder in New Orleans, the author rounded up Sharkey's Kings of Dixieland for a series of jazz albums distributed throughout the world by Capitol. From left: Sharkey Bonano, trumpet; Santo Pecora, trombone; Monk Hazel, drums; Lester Bouchon, clarinet; Dexter; Chink Martin, tuba; and Jeff Riddick, piano. (Art Graphic Center)

(Left) When Frankie "Sugar Chile" Robinson's first records were issued, Dexter was accused of signing and recording a black midget. But the youngster was for real, a 66-pound blues pianist and singer who when he was seven years old performed for President Harry Truman. "Sugar Chile" was nine when he recorded for Dexter, and his Numbers Boogie was a smash. (Otto Rothschild)

the home of the Tigers, the Lions, and the Red Wings. It also is the home of butterballish Frankie (Sugar Chile) Robinson, who back in the late 1940s became a temporary national sensation when he performed for President Truman at the White House. He was then seven years old, born with a freak talent which saw him playing solo piano à la Pete Johnson and Meade Lux Lewis in a solid boogie-woogie groove.

At his first session for Capitol, Robinson weighed 66 pounds. He was 48 inches tall. His pudgy fingers couldn't reach a full octave on the keyboard. I asked him when he started playing piano.

"I was two," he answered in his little-boy soprano. "I played *Tuxedo Junction* on our piano at home.. Then Frankie Carle came to Detroit with his orchestra and put me on the stage at a downtown theater. I even played with Lionel Hampton."

He made a hit on his first try, *Numbers Boogie*. I scrawled the words on the back of a hotel envelope and hummed him a simple melody based on blues chords.

Sugar Chile was a sweet little guy, anxious to make records and amazingly gifted. I remember how he rolled his eyes and laughed aloud when he heard his first playbacks. I asked him if he had any brothers or sisters.

"Oh yes, sir," he answered. "There's Nitty, Brother Lump, Tat, Pretty Big, and Sister Little. And Sugar Chile makes six."

The son of a Detroit ice truck driver, young Robinson came to Hollywood later, waxed more records (including an album of 12 jumping blues), and appeared in M-G-M's *No Leave, No Love* with Van Johnson. His records spread his fame.

He made two tours through England. I inquired about him recently and was told that he now tends bar in Detroit.

Around the office I was constantly asked if Robinson was for real. It got to be a drag. Finally, whenever some wiseacre dug me about Sugar Chile's prodigious musicianship, I had a stock answer: "He's a 33-year-old midget."

I now beg Robinson's forgiveness. All children should be as sweet and natural and as lovable as he was at seven. I hope he saved his money.

° ° °

I suppose I was too absorbed in my own activities as the 1950s arrived to profit from a scene that occurred every afternoon below Capitol's offices at Music City.

Dozens of Hollywood High School kids, the majority of them girls, began dropping in and asking to hear the latest records by Bullmoose Jackson, Earl Bostic, Ivory Joe Hunter, Muddy Waters, Chuck Berry, B.B. King, Fats Domino, and Bobby Bland, all of them completely unknown to Hughie Claudin and Ralph Krause, who managed the spacious self-service store for Glenn Wallichs.

"Who in hell are these singers?" Claudin asked me. "What labels are they on?"

We all found out soon enough. The labels were small independents like King, Chess, Specialty, Imperial, Modern, Aladdin, and Peacock, founded by men who—like me—loved the blues and collected old records.

Unlike me, they had the foresight to take their savings, or borrow financing, and start their own companies. In that early fraternity of gamblers were Syd Nathan, Saul Bihari, Leonard and Phil Chess, Don Robey, Art Rupe, and the Messner Brothers.

It was the start of rock 'n' roll. Certain stations played indie labels exclusively, and their audiences enlarged week by week. The solo singers gave way to four-man vocal groups (the Dominos were early favorites), but not until Elvis Presley came along on Sam Phillips' little Sun label in 1955 did the music break out into the open market and change America's culture.

I simply wasn't aware of the overwhelming revolution in musical preferences until it was well underway. And the one thing I remember like a painful childhood enema is what one of those 16-year-old Hollywood High girls said to me when I asked her in 1950, about which records she preferred.

"I only know Bullmoose Jackson is my kind of music," she told me. "And I know I can't find my music on any of the regular labels. If it's on Decca or Columbia or Capitol I don't want it. They only make music for old folks."

The revolution had begun.

14

I dislike all this talk of stars and superstars. Some of them are not even good entertainers. And I don't like groups and singers from England coming over to the USA and taking huge sums and then knocking America when they get back home. There are some things wrong with America, but I'm damned if we're all wrong.

—PEARL BAILEY

WHATEVER THE HUMAN frailties of Sammy Davis, Jr., he does not lack courage in a personal crisis.

There was the time when Sammy's Maserati, his Rolls-Royce, his Mercedes-Benz, and his Duesenberg, vehicles for which he paid $108,000, were all undergoing repairs and maintenance checks simultaneously in Beverly Hills garages. Sammy stoically refused to panic as many a superstar might have; he maintained his poise amid calamity by democratically choosing to drive a domestic rent-a-car that was no more luxurious then those most of us own.

Sammy had no car when I meet him in Los Angles in 1948; he was working as a singing dancer, alone, at a black nitery in the Central Avenue ghetto. I had heard him on an after-midnight broadcast over a small radio station and was instantly attracted to his unusual sound. Next day I called my old Kansas City drummer friend, Jesse Price, and asked if he could contact Davis for me.

"That little cat's no singer," Price protested. "He's a hoofer, part of an act with his old man and his uncle. You sure you got the right Davis?"

Sammy, excited, called me at Capitol a few hours later. He appeared elated that someone had heard him and was impressed.

Meeting in my office with his father and Sammy's "uncle," Will Mastin (who is not Sammy's uncle, actually, but a longtime friend of Sammy, Sr.), I suggested that we select four songs, decide on the right kind of orchestral accompaniment, and go for a hit single.

"My God," he yelled in disbelief, "I'm starting with a major label—Nat Cole's label."

His father and "uncle" were extremely helpful, siding with me when Sammy and I differed on songs. Often dogmatic even then, young Davis—he was 24—displayed all the confidence and ego that he exhibits today. I hired Dave Cavanaugh to do the arrangements and conduct a mixed black and white orchestra of Hollywood's finest studio musicians.

On February 21, 1949, Capitol released *I Don't Care Who Knows* and *The Way You Look Tonight*, both slow-tempo ballads, on our purple deluxe label. Sammy sang the first title straight while on the revered Jerome Kern-Dorothy Fields standard he tossed in his uncanny imitations of Frankie Laine, Nat Cole, Billy Eckstine, Vaughn Monroe, and his idol, Frank Sinatra.

I worked around the clock for many weeks with our promotion men to obtain strong national airplay, but for all our ingenious exploitation, hardly anyone bought the record.

Sammy wasn't discouraged, nor was I. In April a second single (*You Are My Lucky Star/I Ain't Got Nobody*) also failed to move in the marts.

Inordinately ambitious and ever-eager to cooperate, Sammy hungered for success like no other performer I've ever known. "Occasionally," Sammy told me one afternoon while we sought a hit among scores of old standards submitted by publishers, "we play Las Vegas. There are two sensational gigs there and my dad, my uncle, and I can bag $350 a week at the El Rancho Vegas or the Last Frontier. That's a big, fat hundred bucks each after deductions. But it's a drag for us personally. We have to enter and leave those places by the back door, through the kitchens. We can't live at the hotels. We are not allowed on the casino floors. The only place we can get a meal is at the bus station.

"We've worked there several times, starting in 1944. Now it's five years later and things in Vegas haven't changed a bit—not if you're black."

Cavanaugh and I were quick to hand Sammy a ten or a twenty when he put the touch on us "until pay day." Today, his income exceeds $3 million annually, and recently he became the first black in Nevada history to become part owner of a swanky Vegas Strip hotel. He paid $720,000 for an eight percent interest in the Tropicana. It was also the year in which Richard M. Nixon called him to the White House and appointed him to the National Advisory Council on Economic Opportunity. Sammy sat in the president's box with his third wife, Altovise Davis, at the 1972 Republican National Convention, giving him some solace after being courted, then rudely dropped, by both the John F. Kennedy and Lyndon B. Johnson families in the 1960s.

Sammy had little interest in politics a quarter-century ago in Los Angeles. Sinatra had been kind to him in Las Vegas and a grateful Sammy had quickly established the New Jersey singer as his idol, trying to dress, talk, pursue females, sing, and think like Frank.

○   ○   ○

Davis and Sinatra in recent years have suffered serious criticism as a result of their political stances.

Why the two entertainers would change overnight from militant liberals to aggressive supporters of men like Spiro Agnew, Richard Nixon, and Ronald Reagan has not yet been disclosed. But their offstage activities surely were a factor in the embarrassingly low ratings chalked up by Sammy's quickly cancelled "Follies" NBC-TV series and by the shockingly anemic ratings of Sinatra's post-retirement television "specials" in 1973 and 1974.

Playing personal appearances, both men continue to attract the pseudo–jet set. Sinatra no longer sings well. His intonation is faulty and he struggles to sustain certain notes.

"Somebody should do something about Sinatra," Rex Reed candidly suggested in his New York *Daily News* syndicated column recently. "His public image is uglier than a first-degree burn, his appearance is sloppier than Porky Pig, his manners are more appalling than a subway sandhog's, and his ego is bigger than the Sahara Desert.

"All of which," Reed conceded, "might be tolerable if he could still sing. But the saddest part of all is the hardest part to face about this once-great idol now living on former glory. The grim truth is that Frank Sinatra has had it. His voice has been manhandled beyond recognition, bringing with its parched croak only a painful memory of burned-out yesterdays. Frank Sinatra has become a bore.

"You wouldn't know that from the attention he demands and gets. He insults the press, makes patronizing remarks about women and oppressed minorities, bullies everyone from bellboys to room service waiters, and offers nothing in return in the way of talent or quality entertainment.

"Yet his blindly loyal fans laugh off his sick jokes and tolerate his bad temper and suffer the shoves of his bodyguards, repaying him with applause when he deserves none.

"We should really be ignoring Frank Sinatra to death, but instead we are doing him a disfavor by feeding his colossal ego. By forgiving him everything, we have allowed him to think he rules the world. He's become the Genghis Khan of Tin Pan Alley and, frankly, it's getting nauseating. . . . Frank Sinatra won't go away, leaving us with unblemished memories of what it was like to be the best of everything. He just keeps on proving for posterity he's not really the Tiffany solitaire we thought he was. He's just a Woolworth rhinestone now."

One may or may not agree with the violently opinionated Reed, but he does confirm the obvious—that Sinatra has always phrased, and still phrases, a line, a word, a syllable, more musically than any other vocalist. And that while performing he exudes a potent personal magnetism unequalled by rival artists. For all his foibles, and in the face of his long-standing, petty, and tireless attacks on Rona Barrett, Barbara Walters, the late Dorothy Kilgallen, and the toiling newswomen of Washington and Australia whom he imprudently described as "cheap hookers," Sinatra remains The King. Como, Tony Bennett, and others may sing better technically in 1975 but no man anywhere ranks at Sinatra's level.

Sammy Davis continues to imitate Sinatra, decades after the period in Hollywood when I was the only man outside Sammy's family who believed implicitly in Davis' talents and spent thousands of dollars of my company's funds vainly attempting to establish him as an acceptable recording act.

Sammy's "pal" Sinatra might have helped him in those discouraging, scufflin' days. But he didn't. Sammy did not complain. He repeatedly said he idolized Frank.

"Frank's my man," Sammy told me several times. "Him and I are buddies." Davis preferred sipping Jack Daniel's bourbon only because it was Sinatra's favorite potable.

In the years that followed, Davis for a time turned to acid trips, marijuana, and two bottles of Jack Daniel's every day.[2] Success brought him undreamed of wealth and ever-increasing frustrations. His marriage to Swedish actress Mai Britt led to unbearable emotional turmoil and brutal criticism from many blacks. Yet in the two years that I worked with the multi-talented Davis he was a paragon of cooperative behavior.

We tried every conceivable kind of song—and arrangement—in those distant days when nobody knew him. On one session I even recorded him doing a tap dance. The 20 masters he made were all good musically, but playing them today (some of them are available on a Pickwick "budget" long-playing album) it's obvious that his performances lack the panache—the mysterious, indefinable sound—that produces million-sellers.

A subdued, serious Conkling called me into his office one morning in May, 1950. He removed his gold ring, as usual, and started tossing it up and down in one hand just as George Raft had flipped a coin in the old Warners' *Scarface* film.

"Dex," he said, "we're simply too topheavy with artists. We must cut down. What hits we have are not making the profits we need for the company's expansion because we fail with so many deadbeat artists.

"That kid Davis you've been working with," Conkling went on, "go pay him off. If his contract calls for two, six, or 20 sides still to be made pay him for not making them and wish him well. We'll save money in the long run."

Save money in the long run? That's funny in retrospect. Yet Conkling, at the time, was right. Capitol had not retrieved (and has not today) the many thousands of dollars it invested in Sammy's career on records. So, reluctantly—I recall how embarrassed I felt—I called Sammy at his small hotel room and promised him a check would be forthcoming for the unrecorded masters. It was a difficult chore. I admired and respected him. He had been a pleasure to work with; ever-eager, ever-cooperative. I even apologized for having failed to establish him as a top-rank star on discs.

His father and his "uncle" got on the phone and graciously thanked me for my efforts in young Sammy's behalf.

In New York's Shubert Alley one afternoon a few years later, shortly after he had scored a smash record triumph with *Hey, There* (from *The Pajama Game*) on Decca, I bumped into Davis unexpectedly. He was now Mr. Wonderful of show business. Like Sinatra, he was accompanied by an officious retinue of hangers-on everywhere he went. Sammy had lost his left eye in a calamitous California motor car accident, but his good eye saw me clearly.

He paused for an instant, then turned away and hurried by without a hello. No man cares to remember his failures.

The producer is always the goat. It's his fault that an artist flops on records. Sammy Davis isn't alone in believing that; I know numerous singers and musicians who go through life bitterly blaming an a&r man for their failure to top the pop charts.

Maybe they're right.

◦ ◦ ◦

It was during Sammy's apprenticeship at Capitol that two revolutionary technological advances were adopted by the industry.

The first was tape. The second was the introduction of discs played at 33 and 45 revolutions per minute.

A Danish physicist, Valdemar Poulsen, in 1898 conceived the principle of recording on steel wire, and demonstrated its practicability. But wire had serious limitations. Its frequency response stopped at 4000 Hz, coercivity varied from 25 to 35 (compared to 150–200 today), and its bulky two-inch width was awkward to handle. In 1928, Germany's Fritz Pfleumer obtained a German patent involving the coating of lightweight paper tape with magnetizable, pulverized iron particles. By 1934, Pfleumer's invention—an extension of Poulsen's early efforts—was demonstrated at the Berlin Radio Fair. The first recording of music was achieved two years later when German engineers taped a concert of the London Philharmonic Orchestra conducted by Sir Thomas Beecham at Ludwigshaven am Rhein.

Throughout World War II, Germany utilized the new system extensively. Remember the reports that there were "several" Adolf Hitlers broadcasting in different areas of the Third Reich simultaneously? They were, of course, taped Hitler speeches, shrewdly spliced and edited, a ploy which the Nazis also used skillfully in interrogating prisoners of war. Some of them were heard making statements which, in truth, they never made at all.

America's military was still struggling with the less efficient wire, but 23-year-old Marvin Camras, a student at the Illinois Institute of Technology, and Dr. Joseph S. Begun, a German who had fled to Cleveland before the War, were diligently experimenting with tape and gaining on Germany's pre-eminence in the field.

With the War's end, wire was abandoned and tape prevailed. The best of the early tape recorders was produced by the Ampex firm of California, and by 1948 all of Capitol's masters were being made on new Ampex consoles installed at Radio Recorders studios in Hollywood. The improvement in sound was unmistakable. No longer did we wait for an engineer to lift off a fragile 16-inch acetate (lacquer) disc from a spinning turntable when a trumpeter clinked. On tape, it was possible to record over the error later, then splice the two acceptable takes into one perfect master.

Tape is even more efficient today, and is used by every label everywhere in the world.

The death of the old 78 rpm shellac record came suddenly, only months after recording on tape became common, when Columbia Records introduced the long-playing, microgroove disc perfected by Columbia University's Dr. Peter C. Goldmark, who later was to develop color television and the video cassette. The LP record was not new. RCA-Victor had attempted to market a 33 disc fifteen years earlier and EMI in England also had produced and sold a similar product, but neither was perfected. Dr. Goldmark's disc brought an entirely new and thrilling sound spectrum to the industry. In 1975, 91 out of every 100 records sold were long-playing discs, which most of us call albums.

RCA-Victor technicians working under the guidance of Dr. Harry Olson emerged almost at the same time in 1948 with their unique 45 rpm disc. Its odd "doughnut hole" center required a special phonograph, as did the Goldmark record. Then followed a two-year industry war in which Columbia and RCA strove to popularize their radically different products.

Millions were spent by the two industry giants. Rapidly, record sales dropped in all 48 states. Buyers were mystified reading the communiques of the 33 versus 45 "war." They were sure of but one thing: the phonographs they owned had suddenly become obsolete. Which way to go? ·

We at Capitol hesitated only momentarily. Both RCA and Columbia were urging us to adopt their respective systems. Boss Wallichs was the first man in the industry to install new pressing equipment in Capitol's Scranton and Los Angeles plants that would press *both* modes, and so for about a year we issued discs on all three speeds. By 1951, no more 78 rpm shellacs were being manufactured, and our competition had followed Capitol's policy in offering both new-type discs to the public. Sales climbed. Another industry crisis had passed.

❁   ❁   ❁

I was rapping with Conkling one afternoon in his office when he said something startling.

"If you hear any wild, unfounded rumors about my leaving Capitol to take a job back East," he confided, "I want you to know they are true."

Soon he was in New York with a rival label, Columbia. The job he accepted was the presidency of that distinguished firm, a profitable arm of the Columbia Broadcasting System.

Wallichs replaced him with our expert in the field of children's discs, Alan W. Livingston, a reticent University of Pennsylvania grad who was working as a whiskey salesman when he joined Capitol in the mid-1940s. He collaborated efficiently with the sales chief, a slender, dedicated, innovating, Illinois hustler named Hal Cook, infield star of the company's softball team.

Wallichs also accepted the resignation of Lou Busch, a skilled pianist and arranger, and the husband of Margaret Whiting, who had worked under Conkling as an a&r producer and who had recorded under the name of Joe (Fingers) Carr successfully. To replace Busch, Wallichs moved a one-time drummer in a U.S. Coast Guard band, Voyle Gilmore, into a producer's slot from his position as Los Angeles branch sales chief.

Wallichs advised me of these important in-house personnel switches with his usual enthusiasm. Then he pointed a finger at me from across his desk:

"You, Dexter, must now make up your mind where you're going. Do you want to continue as a writer and editor fiddling around as a producer on the side or do you want to concentrate exclusively on finding talent, recording it, and becoming a fulltime, dedicated member of our reconstructed a&r department under Livingston?"

I waited just long enough to gulp.

"Find another writer-editor," I replied.

And so I began signing singers and musicians, and for the first time in my eight years at Capitol I was granted access to all the new songs submitted by the major publishers. Gilmore, Lee Gillette, and I were to be handling virtually every pop recording session for the next few years while Ken Nelson supervised the country talent. All of us reported to Livingston; it was he who okayed our signing new artists and determined, with his administrative assistant Francis Scott III, which performers on the Capitol roster merited albums. Only about one of five, in those pioneer days of the LP, did.

My new stable comprised a group of musicians and singers in whom I had unlimited confidence. Gil Rodin brought Bob Crosby's band—reorganized, but with several of the original Crosby sidemen returning—to Capitol with the understanding that Crosby was anxious to go out on the road and build his Bobcats

Playing hosts to music publishers at Capitol Records for many years were the firm's artists and repertoire department producers. From left, Dave Dexter, Voyle Gilmore, Lee Gillette, and Capitol vice-president Alan W. Livingston. Submitting a new song for recording (right) is Don Genson. (Otto Rothschild)

back up to the national popularity plateau they had enjoyed before World War II.

My dimpled friend from Jimmy Dorsey's band, Helen O'Connell, had three daughters to support and two shattered marriages behind her; she was attempting a comeback in Los Angeles as a singer with Frank DeVol's orchestra. I signed her.

With O'Connell set, it seemed only logical to acquire Bob Eberly for a similar resurgence. He and Helen had sold millions of discs for Decca while they worked for Jimmy Dorsey the previous decade. I proposed to record them individually and doing duets together.

June Hutton had succeeded Jo Stafford as the female voice in the Pied Pipers. Now, teaming with her husband Axel Stordahl, a remarkably gifted arranger and conductor, she sought a career as a single. I liked her chances. I was equally sure that stardom on records awaited the beautiful Connie Russell of the Dave Garroway NBC-TV series. She, June, and Axel all joined my cell at Capitol along with O'Connell, Eberly, and the Bob Crosby band.

Yet another musician, unfamiliar to the public and known to me only as a former saxman with Freddie Slack's band and as a singer in Mel Torme's old Mel-Tones vocal combo, was assigned to me by Livingston. His name was Les Baxter.

A year or so previously he had attracted a modicum of attention with a novel *Music Out of the Moon* album comprising original Baxter melodies performed by a small orchestra in which Dr. Samuel Hoffman's theremin was featured. Electrically operated, the theremin produced a shaky, tremulous high frequency sound which I found hard to classify as music.

Baxter was from Texas and had become a Californian after studying at the Detroit Conservatory of Music and Pepperdine College in Los Angeles. Once he agreed never to employ the diabolic-sounding theremin on my sessions, we dug out four songs from the stack submitted by publishers and hit the bull's-eye immediately with a revival of a melodic old ballad, *Because of You*. Tony Bennett on Columbia scored a hit with the same song at the same time.

Then, peculiarly, at almost precise intervals of six months, Baxter's fresh, unique manner of writing for strings and rhythm produced a series of singles that sold well in excess of 500,000 each: *Lonely Wine; Auf Wiedersehen, Sweetheart; Blue Tango; April in Portugal; I Love Paris; Wake the Town and Tell the People; Midnight on the Cliffs; The High and the Mighty; Unchained Melody;* and *The Poor People of Paris.*

Midnight On the Cliffs was a composition of the classical concert pianist Leonard Pennario. Baxter insisted that Pennario be called into our Melrose Avenue studios to perform the solo piano portions. "He will give the record class," said Les, "and besides, he's the only pianist around who can play it."

Pennario did indeed play the work well, but I squirmed and sweated through the long, difficult session as I fought the union clock into overtime.

Les and I, gambling with Capitol's money, brought nearly 50 musicians into the studio to accompany the virtuoso-composer. It takes twice as long to balance 50 musicians as it does to arrive at the sound you want with a mere 15 or 20 musicians seated around the numerous microphones. Yet, for all my worries that night, things turned out fine. *Midnight on the Cliffs* was scored throughout a winning motion picture co-starring Doris Day and Louis Jourdan. Eventually we recouped the costs of the session and turned a small profit as well.

Les and I endured fiery, profane personal conflicts from time to time. His friend Frank Loesser published a theme to run through a cheap prison movie starring Elroy (Crazy Legs) Hirsch of the Los Angeles Rams. Les brought the original untitled manuscript in to me, demonstrated it at the piano, and appeared excited that Loesser had promised to show the theme to no one else.

"Jeez, Les," I argued, "it's just another tune, from a Grade C flicker with a football player as its only cast name. Why waste a side on a nothin' theme that doesn't even have a title?"

Baxter became vocal—and mean. He insisted the untitled tune had hit possibilities. "I've laid a lot of eggs with songs you assigned me," he argued. "Let me bomb out just once with something I picked."

Fair enough. We made the prison theme. I even titled it *Unchained Melody*. Les rushed out to play a test laquer for Loesser, who approved the title but grumbled that a strong solo vocal instead of the close-harmony group singing that Baxter had used would make a considerably more saleable disc.

Unchained Melody became an overnight smash. I had misjudged its appeal. But Les had misjudged his pal Loesser, too.

He, we learned, had raced with Baxter's test disc over to Decca and helped our competitor rush out a "cover" version of the song by the blind black baritone, Al Hibbler.

Our version of *Unchained Melody* narrowly missed selling a million copies. So did Hibbler's on Decca. But had the Hibbler "cover" never been recorded Baxter's would have easily topped 1,500,000 copies, and Les and I wouldn't have written off Frank Loesser as a friend.

The situation was reversed with *The Poor People of Paris*. I found the song on my first visit to Paris in 1955, when it was known as *La Goulante du Pauvre Jean*. Edith Piaf had recorded it with Rene Rouzaud lyrics, in French, but for the North American market I preferred the sprightly Marguerite Monnot melody to stand on its own merits. Baxter savored neither the words nor music.

"It's too ricky-tick," he scoffed. "What can I do with a mickey-mouse melody like that?"

Les agreed to record it after I compromised, allowing him to record two of his original compositions on the same session, and to his credit he conceived a bright and thoroughly irresistible arrangement of the French song sparked by a whistling passage which most auditors credited as the hook or gimmick that boosted sales to well over one million singles in less than a month. Before Capitol issued the disc I obtained permission from Julian and Jean Aberbach of Hill & Range Music to substitute my title for the French original.

"I can't believe a thing like that can sell a million," Les said later. He sent me an exquisite gold record in appreciation.

Million-selling discs were few and far between in the mid-1950s. Today there are several every month.

Working with a musician of Baxter's caliber, as I look back, more than justifies the stresses, tensions, and pressures to which a producer is constantly subjected. We survived our occasional fiery disputes, respected each other's backgrounds and goals, and collaborated enthusiastically in producing good music month after month over a period of 10 years. Les made me a better record producer.

He is still active, scoring for motion pictures in Hollywood. Last time I saw him, he was rolling down Vine Street in his silent Silver Cloud. That's a Rolls-Royce. With a $28,000 price tag.

                    o   o   o

Bob Crosby became involved as emcee of a 15-minute television music series beamed coast to coast—Giselle MacKenzie, the Canadian canary, also was featured— so his plans to take the Crosby dance band out on the road were aborted.

That left me in an untenable position with Capitol. Unless Crosby and his popular sidemen played throughout the nation, exposing their unique Dixieland-styled jazz to record buyers, there was little hope that their records would move.

We made about 20 tracks in the year or so we attempted a Crosby band revival. Some were artistic gems, featuring the tenor sax of Eddie Miller, Charlie Teagarden's trumpet, Matty Matlock's clarinet, and Stanley Wrightsman at the piano. But we never got near the charts. By mutual agreement we cancelled future sessions. Crosby eventually moved to Hawaii, retiring from show business.

Helen O'Connell and Bob Eberly tried hard as they sang their way along the comeback trail on session after session. Both epitomized class. They knew their songs, they were amenable to Harold Mooney's bright arranging ideas, they cooperated with me while I was inside and outside the booth, and, at the mike, they showed charisma and talent.

Helen did well. She had no records in the Top Ten but several sold big. Some of her discs that didn't move were beautiful renditions which deserved better. Certainly she sang better as a single than she had sung while a member of the Jimmy Dorsey troupe 10 years previously. Helen was more mature, more confident, and it showed.

Her best-selling singles were those in which I teamed her with Giselle.MacKenzie. Voyle and I found several novelties in the stack of songs submitted to Capitol by publishers; the idea of teaming two girls was unconventional. *Water Can't Quench the Fire of Love, A Crazy Waltz,* and *Give Me the Name, Age, Height and Size* were three of the six duets Gilmore and I taped with the Ohio blonde and the Quebec brunette. The tunes are forgotten today, but in the early

1950s many thousands of jukes carried them profitably.

The MacKenzie pairing a moderate success, I went to Lee Gillette. "O'Connell likes country music," I conned him. "Will you work with me in recording Helen with Tennessee Ernie Ford?"

Gillette opened a pack of Fizrin. I knew that Ford was hotter on discs than O'Connell and that teaming her with him could only be to Helen's benefit. Gillette, gulping his medication, knew it too.

"Ernie might go for it," Gillette opined. "And then he might not. He doesn't need O'Connell. But we'll see."

We all got together one afternoon in a studio. Ernie seemed pleased. Cliffie Stone led the band. He was Ernie's manager. He also played fine string bass. Helen was out of her element with Nashville tunes like *Hey, Good Lookin'* and *Cold, Cold Heart.* The six or seven Stone musicians were country boys whom she had never seen before.

Ernie decided to use his Bristol accent. He has three distinct speech patterns. One is pure, sophisticated city. Another has a slight rural sound. The third we called his Bristol, from his home town in the hills of Tennessee, which he lays on every word, every syllable, in a hokey, exaggerated manner much as actor Ken Curtis did year after year playing the role of Festus in *Gunsmoke.*

Phony accent or no, Ford and O'Connell taped two extremely pleasing sides. Their single got up on the charts for a few weeks. Ernie declined a second session with Helen. He felt more down home, he said, dueting with Oklahoma-born Kay Starr. Gillette and I didn't push it. With Kay, Ernie had a two-sided smash coupling of *I'll Never Be Free* and *Ain't Nobody's Business But My Own.*

Bob Eberly and Helen O'Connell attempted comebacks on discs in the 1950s, about a decade after their remarkable success as singers with Jimmy Dorsey's band. But they weren't successful. Bob and Helen remain active in the mid-1970s, however, in night-clubs and on television.

I strived, desperately, for a big one with Helen. I put her with Les Baxter, with Bob Eberly, and with another country star, Skeets McDonald. And I tried her with Dean Martin and, singing solo, with Stone's country group.

One novelty from the Stone session, *Slowpoke*, sold nearly a half-million. I even brought in an Hawaiian combo with ukuleles and steel guitars on one of her last sessions.

But she never quite made it. Doris Day ruled the charts and Helen failed to dislodge her. Yet, 30 years after her heyday with Dorsey and 20 years after her Capitol comeback attempt, the still-ravishing O'Connell works the best clubs in the land and is frequently seen on network television, the most attractive grandmother in show biz.

Perhaps she yet will make a hit record.

Bob Eberly's comeback fared less well than Helen's. He still hit the low notes solidly and he expressed emotion as movingly as he had with Dorsey ten years earlier. Harold Mooney's charts were first rate. But the hits were not to come.

Capitol is a California firm. Eberly lived in New Jersey. I found it difficult finding songs for him that could be recorded quickly enough to beat competition. Maybe the songs Eb and I taped were weak. He didn't happen, as they say, and I regret our failure. He was a prince to work with—once we got together.

Nor did Connie Russell and June Hutton enter the charmed circle of gold-record artists. I've analyzed their output many times. Both girls had everything. Twenty years later, I wish I could try again with them.

○   ○   ○

There is a prominent film composer in Hollywood these days named Allen D. Allen. He splits his time working with computers as a research scientist. He's a member of the American Physics Society, the American Association For the Advancement of Science, and the Institute of Electronic Engineers.

Recently, after long experimentation, Allen announced there was "absolutely no mathematical or scientific formulae" for determining what makes a hit record.

He spent months correlating hundreds of hit melodies, feeding a complex IBM 1130 computer facts about chord structures, tempo, time signatures, instrumentation, lyrics, equalization, and other elements common to pop discs.

The computer contributed no answer. There obviously is no specific formula for a hit. "People either buy a new record," Allen concluded, "or they don't."

Shucks, some of us knew that long before World War II. The old axiom "it's got to be in the groove" still stands and always will. The grooves either contain a hit sound or they don't. Most don't.

○   ○   ○

Sammy Davis, Jr., need rent cars no more. He recently added to his vehicle stable a modern-day Stutz Blackhawk with a $33,000 price tag.

He had it *flown* to him in Las Vegas by cargo plane.

15

The record situation today is horrible. I don't think it's because the public's taste has declined—it's just that people are so trusting. Americans are accustomed to getting the cream in everything else, why shouldn't they assume they're getting it in music too? So they swallow whatever's been fed them on radio and in the jukes.

—DUKE ELLINGTON (1952)

MY MEMORY IS hazy as to whether we were riding in a cab along the Outer Drive or on Michigan Boulevard, but I shan't forget what Duke Ellington said after a recording session late one night in Chicago.

"Are you aware," he gently asked as he stared out the left rear window of the taxi, "that I have undoubtedly screwed more women than any man on earth?"

The Duke was in no way boasting; more likely he was merely reminiscing in tempo as we headed for an early morning supper on the city's North Side. It was just conversation. He talked earnestly about his early days in music, first in his home bailiwick of the District of Columbia, then in New York, where, after failing in 1922—when he was 23 years old—he returned a year later to join forces with banjoist Elmer Snowden and secure his first engagement at a cabaret called Barron Wilkins' in uptown Manhattan.

"The young ladies then were truly lovely," he said. "I loved them madly. And I find the ladies today equally charming."

Duke was constantly surrounded by the ultimate in feminine pulchritude, a luscious legion of adoring females of all races, all configurations, and varying mentalities. Yet music came first with him.

He made records as far back as 1925—on the long-forgotten Perfect label—and he savored recalling the excitement of those primitive sessions a half-century ago.

"We were simply thrilled to get into a studio," he said. "You see, in those days only a few bands and singers were given the chance."

The feeling wore off with the years. Nothing excited his sidemen the last 20 years of Duke's life. On a session, every session, they appeared indifferent and casual. Call a record date for 10 o'clock and at that time you'll see a half-dozen men slouched in their chairs, reading comic books or a newspaper. One by one, the others tardily arrive. Some futz with their mouthpieces. Duke is at the keyboard striking odd chords and mulling which tunes should go on record. An hour later he kicks them off with a chair or two still vacant. What emanates from the wildly disorganized, chaotic setting is the most glorious sound outside the world of classical music.

I was fortunate on my first Ellington session in Hollywood.

The first tune we tackled was untitled, a new Duke melody which required about two hours to master. Several of his men were missing parts but somehow they faked it through and we got an acceptable master without a tape splice. The next day, in Capitol's Melrose studios, Ellington entered the booth and ventured a suggestion.

"That first thing we did yesterday, the pretty ballad," he began. "We need a title, don't we?"

"We do if we're going to release it," I answered.

"It's like satin," said Duke. "Sensual, sexy. I think it's pure satin doll."

And so *Satin Doll* it was, and as it turned out, *Satin Doll* stands as the only melody Duke taped for Capitol in nearly three years that became a distinguished, easily-recognizable standard hit to rank with his earlier classics of

Producing Duke Ellington's orchestra for Capitol, the first master Ellington cut under Dexter's supervision was the now-famous Satin Doll. *The late pianist, composer, and arranger was proud of his prowess with a legion of adoring females but rarely discussed his conquests. (Charlie Mihn)*

Mood Indigo, Sophisticated Lady, Solitude, Don't Get Around Much Anymore, and *Take the A Train* renown.

The 1953–55 years hardly comprised one of Ellington's most creative periods. Johnny Hodges and Lawrence Brown were on one of their temporary leaves of absence and their virtuosic solos were missing. Jimmy Hamilton's clarinet, Ray Nance's trumpet and violin, and Paul Gonsalves' tenor sax constituted Ellington's main solo thrust. They weren't enough, outstanding soloists though they were. Duke seemed incapable of coming up with fresh material once we locked *Satin Doll* in the can. Session after session produced only rearranged versions of his old warhorses. He and his men were a road band, and planning songs, booking studios, and setting up publicity and promotional campaigns became more than difficult for me. In his brief term with Capitol, I recorded his music in New York, Chicago, and San Francisco as well as in Hollywood.

Ellington surprised me one afternoon as he telephoned from a hotel room in Massachusetts:

"Let's record."

"When will the band be in California?" I inquired.

"I don't think we are booked out there for another six months. Must we wait that long?"

Then came the surprise.

"I want a hit, Dave. Other bands make hits. I want to hear Ellington records in the jukeboxes, and on the radio, and playing over the p.a. systems in shops and markets."

This was Ellington speaking, the man who unfailingly placed esthetics far above commercial success. It was like Pierre Boulez demanding to record a Tina Turner tune.

We got together at the time of the mambo craze. Perez Prado and Perry Como were riding high with mambo-styled smashes. Duke said he wanted to tackle a mambo too.

He showed enthusiasm for a novelty, *The Bunny Hop.* High school kids were dancing to a Ray Anthony record, and on his one-nighters Ellington had heard numerous requests for it. He quickly instructed his gifted amanuensis, Billy Strayhorn, to arrange it Ellington style. We recorded *The Bunny Hop* in April of 1954. I've never known anyone—even rabid Ellington buffs—who bought a copy.

But Duke persevered. Five months later, taping in San Francisco, he not only insisted on making a second mambo built around *St. Louis Blues* but a *Tyrolean Tango* as well. They fared no better than *The Bunny Hop.*

Now came an avalanche of invective from the featherbrained music critics, all of it directed at Dexter and Capitol. We were charged with sabotaging the Ellington band, lowering Duke's standards to something worse than mediocrity, and throwing the exalted Ellington to the pigs in pursuit of the almighty dollar.

Yet it was Duke's choice. And if those holier-than-thou critics and jazz "authorities" had even a superficial knowledge of the recording industry they would concede that every artist, no matter how high his standards, must pop with a hit from time to time to justify the expense of making records. A critic writes for a certain financial remuneration. *Down Beat* and the lesser jazz publications would abruptly cease publishing if their advertising revenue ended. I'll accept their critical raps when they work for no pay, and no ad lineage.

I once reviewed jazz records for a living. I'm the guy who, in *Down Beat* in the 1940s, got overly cute in reviewing a tune titled *The Sphinx* cut by Teddy Powell's orchestra on Decca. My pompous judgment of the performance: "*Sphinx* stinks."

I stopped criticizing records 25 years ago. Jumping down from my self-made altar is one of my few complete successes in my life in music.

Something of Ellington rubs off on all who associate with him. His was a potent, stimulating personality. Impeccably dressed—never quite like all the others—he commanded awe wherever he went. On his only tour of the Soviet Union, in which he and his sidemen gave 22 concerts in five cities in four weeks, Russian musicians—and possibly some of his feminine admirers as well—followed him as if he were a contemporary Pied Piper. From Leningrad to Minsk to Kiev to Rostov-on-Don to Moscow, Duke's fans grew in number at every curtain.

From Duke Ellington's orchestra, Dexter produced records featuring cornetist Rex Stewart and saxophonists Al Sears and Harry Carney. These sessions were held in Hollywood's Radio Recorders a decade before the circular Capitol Tower was built. (Charlie Mihn)

"We were carried off to visit local music clubs and composer societies in all five cities," Mercer Ellington, Duke's son and road manager, recounted at tour's end. "We were deluged with invitations to orchestra rehearsals and pop music sessions. And we were literally smothered with flowers and embraces and trailed constantly by Russian newspeople."

Adulation like that was also experienced by the Ellington troupe in the Orient, but never at home. For all his idolatry by America's musicians, few nonprofessionals bought his records. President and Mrs. Richard Nixon played host at the White House to Ellington on Duke's seventieth birthday anniversary but, it was learned later, they had no Duke discs in their White House collection.

Yet the unperturbable Ellington continued to compose, to travel, to enjoy his daily beefsteak, and to savor his deeply personal pleasures away from the piano and bandstand. There are learned, scholarly persons around today who assert that the one American whose original music will still be played constantly in the 21st century will be Charles Ives, or George Gershwin, or Richard Rodgers. None of the scholars is right. I say Ellington's works will outlive all the others.

The Duke is likely to be remembered for more than his *Satin Doll* during his alliance with Capitol. His LP of a dozen piano solos (with Wendell Marshall on string bass and Butch Ballard at the drums) was a winner, not only in America but in Europe and the Orient as well. Duke required several weeks of fervent Dexter persuasion—he has never considered himself a giant at the keyboard—before he agreed to perform as a soloist. Capitol reissued the album in 1972 and I suspect it will evade deletion through the rest of the decade.

In May of 1955, Ellington began a session with an original instrumental he slyly called *Discontented Blues*. I got the message.

It was his final session for Capitol. We parted as pals.

"It's time to move on," said Duke, "but I love you madly."

From that time he and his sterling ensemble wandered from label to label producing superior music in the main but inevitably finding their efforts leading to a dead-end street as continuation options went unrenewed.

He deserved better. Duke was the closest thing to genius I've ever worked with, and a delight to know. Not in my lifetime will there be another his equal. I refer not only to his musicianship—consider the world's uncountable Ellington-adoring females as well.

⚬   ⚬   ⚬

I'll say this for Gordon MacRae: of all the artists I've worked with, he had the wife I'm least likely to forget.

She sat in the booth with me—uninvited—on MacRae's numerous sessions telling John Kraus and John Palladino, the engineers, how to balance Gordie's voice with Van Alexander's orchestra. She took over my intercom mike to advise MacRae of lyrical nuances she considered important. She protested that an arrangement was too long, or too short, and she was quick to criticize the songs MacRae and I had elected to record.

"I've seen it all," I told Kraus one midnight following a MacRae taping. "We've got a housewife who knows more about entertainment than all the rest of us combined."

The housewife, as it turned out, *did* know more than we. A few years later Sheila MacRae was featured on CBS-TV with Jackie Gleason and Art Carney every Saturday night, playing Gleason's wife in the entertaining *Honeymooners* sketches. When Gleason went off the tube she earned top dollar working as a single in America's best niteries.

MacRae never enjoyed a 21-karat hit in some 20 years of trying, but many motion picture fans liked him and he was strong enough, on discs, to attain more than moderate success with both singles and albums. He started at Warner Brothers in B productions and worked up to major-budget musicals like *Oklahoma!* and *Carousel* at 20th Century–Fox, an impressive rise for a young man who got his start working as an NBC pageboy in Radio City and as a member of Horace Heidt's brigade of singers.

Gordie had the finest male voice I ever recorded, the finest *physically*. A range that was the broadest, plus pure intonation, clear enunciation, and uncommon control. He had everything but a God-given knack for creating intimacy and believability, the two unteachable elements every woman must hear. I know now why his Shiela sat in the booth. It's plain that she tried to tutor her handsome husband. In motion pictures, and on the concert stage, a ballsy sound is enough. On a record it takes more. Sheila did her damndest to evoke intimacy and believability in Gordie's great pipes. She failed. I failed.

◦   ◦   ◦

Lee Gillette turned out consistent successes by Nat Cole, Tennessee Ernie Ford, Nelson Riddle, and Kay Starr. Voyle Gilmore was off to a blazing start producing Frank Sinatra's new dics, songs which I had located before the intemperate and intransigent Hoboken baritone roared his refusal to work with me. Les Paul and his wife, Mary Ford, made their own Capitol records in makeshift, semi-professional studios at their modest home, and a dozen soared to the heights and proved as popular in Europe as here. To this day, I'm told, the Paul-Ford version of *Vaya Con Dios* remains the biggest seller in Holland's history.

Everything was coming up roses for Capitol in the early 1950s. We enjoyed lavish company conventions at Lake Placid in the lovely Adirondacks of upstate New York, at Estes Park in the Colorado Rockies, and at Pebble Beach in northern California. In 1951, we released 620 singles and 93 albums to gross $13,400,000, more than our fair share of the market. Wallichs extended distribution outlets as far as Japan, Australia, and New Zealand. William Steinberg and the Pittsburgh Symphony were signed to the artists roster. We opened our first recording studios in New York.

But there was a sad note as well. Johnny Mercer disappeared. There were no farewell parties, no ceremonies, no nothing. The founder and former president who had accomplished so much in Capitol's behalf in its early days simply

Tennessee Ernie Ford, little Molly Bee, Dexter and his colleague at Capitol, Lee Gillette, cooperated in producing poppish country hits in the 1950s. More recently—in 1974— Ford toured the Soviet Union and was featured internationally in Russia on television. Miss Bee today is a glamorous single act and the singing star of Granite Records. (Otto Rothschild)

walked away from our Sunset-and-Vine executive offices and never came back.

Buddy DeSylva had died of a heart attack in 1950. Now Johnny was gone. Only Wallichs, of the three company founders, remained. The loss of the versatile Mercer was difficult for me to accept.

He was an inspirational boss who never, to my knowledge, pulled rank with employees. I'll make that even stronger—Mercer would be a powerful asset to Capitol, or any record company, today. He knows everyone in the profession of popular music. He still composes hit lyrics. And he's well liked by everybody.

"Capitol got too big," he told me later. "It wasn't fun anymore."

◦   ◦   ◦

Woody Herman has been touring with his orchestra since 1936. Only Ellington, Guy Lombardo, and Count Basie have toured longer.

He owns a home in the hills above Hollywood's Sunset Strip, a structure which he and his wife, Charlotte, purchased from Lauren Bacall and Humphrey Bogart about a year after Bogey and the actress were married. That was 29 years ago. The house and pool are enveloped by tall, fragrant eucalyptus trees. It is an idyllic setting.

"Yes," Woody says. "I've enjoyed the place less than 30 weeks in 29 years. But it's comforting to know it's there."

Herman's stature in the record business is unmistakable—and deserved. He plays exciting alto and soprano saxophones, a fine clarinet, and sings entertainingly. Most of all, he leads a precise, constantly exciting ensemble comprised of young, ambitious musicians who play electric piano, electric bass, and the conventional reeds and brass in the contemporary, 1970s manner.

Woody heeds the pop music of today's young generation more than his colleagues from the old days do. He's 62 now.

"You must reach the kid audience," he told me recently, "or you are stagnating. I'd toss in the towel if I didn't have a pipeline, an empathy, with the youngsters."

He felt that way in 1954–55, when I was producing his record output for Capitol. We never argued about which repertoire should be recorded. He had an arranger named Ralph Burns who was so gifted, and so capable of bringing out the best of the Herman musicianship, that anything Woody showed me with Burns' Local 802 stamp automatically was scheduled for the upcoming session.

Herman is a little guy with an innate humility equalled by few of his peers. He possesses a built-in ability to take young, untried musicians and integrate them into one of the best dance bands ever. He is blessed with a rare and caustic sense of humor and in my opinion he reigns as the best-dressed man in music year after year.

It was at the New York Paramount Theater years ago that two of Woody's youthful sidemen brought in a monkey to break up the monotony of four shows

Woody Herman, who as a child worked as a dancer in Milwaukee, has been leading his orchestra just short of 40 years. A few years back he "assisted" Dexter in writing a review of a Herman record.

a day. They called her Hazel. Woody went along with the lark, advising scores of songpluggers to take their songs to his newly-hired "secretary" in a rehearsal room. There, of course, they encountered the frisky little simian darting about in a room covered with tattered, stained sheet music.

"One of the music men fooled us," Woody laughs. "He left a stack of copies of his song, an old standard, with Hazel. It was *Yes, We Have No Bananas*."

Seeking something in the way of new music which might provide Herman and his herd with a chart-making hit, I got the first copy of a well-written, hum-able Paul Webster–Sammy Fain ballad which was to be featured throughout a powerful William Holden–Jennifer Jones 20th Century–Fox Technicolor drama being filmed in Hong Kong, *Love Is a Many-Splendored Thing*. Woody liked it, as did I, and the tasty Ralph Burns arrangement featured Herman's solo alto sax.

The record came off just the way we wanted it. Capitol rushed it out to the radio jockeys. That was our error. We started out exploitation push a couple of months too soon—long before the picture went into national exhibition. When it did, the Four Aces timed their Decca version more expertly and reaped a millionseller. But I'll always think Woody's was a better version.

I had an idea for a tune one day in New York as Herman and I set up a series of sessions.

"There hasn't been a boogie-woogie thing out in years," I told him. "Maybe it would be a big new thing to the kids if you made a modern, swinging, big-band version."

"Let's try," Woody agreed.

I sat down with George (Fox) Williams, a freelance arranger whom I had known for 15 years, back to his days with the struggling Sonny Dunham band. I hummed a simple boogie figure and indicated where the brass punctuations and the solo drum passages should fall. Williams patiently took notes, accepting my elementary instructions with undisguised amusement.

I suspect that even Herman was astonished when on the session a few days later Williams passed out the parts and rehearsed the Herd on an instrumental we titled *Skinned*. The Fox had charted a minor classic from my crude outline, with Chuck Flores featured on drums. Then he had taken the same basic theme, expanded it and produced a three-minute sequel which he called *Skinned Again*. We issued it, nothing much happened, but a year later we got one of 1956's hottest-selling extended play albums when I coupled *Skinned* and *Skinned Again* with a sensational drum exhibition by Buddy Rich with Herman's Herd, a performance which ran 4:58 minutes and found particular appeal in the nation's jukes.

Woody's bands are superbly disciplined, well rehearsed and enthusiastic on sessions. The leader, a Milwaukean who was working as a dancer-singer in vaudeville when he was nine and who later played in the orchestras of Tom Gerun and Isham Jones, stands in my dog-eared notebook as one of the "nicest" of all artists I've worked with. How he keeps rolling decade after decade on the highways, driving from one brief gig to another, is a secret only Woody can reveal. One wonders if he will ever hang up his reeds and enjoy the home he has visited so infrequently.

Woody has only one fear. He recently told his red-haired wife Charlotte that under no circumstance would there ever be a Woody Herman "ghost" band using his name after his demise, a practice that started with Glenn Miller and continued with Tommy and Jimmy Dorsey following their deaths.

"I'll come back and exorcise that Herman ghost," Woody threatened.

o   o   o

Several years back, when there were far more nightclubs in flower than to-day, a man with the unlikely name of Leo DeLyon captivated me with his odd act. He played the piano, sang, and made funny noises, some of which ema-nated from his ears and nose as well as his mouth.

I met with Leo. He turned out to be a one-time dance band pianist. He also was a capable arranger.

"I make every musical sound known to man," he said immodestly. He screwed up his face, puffed out a cheek and startled me by sounding exactly like an alto sax. Then he shut his eyes, jiggled his jaws and delivered an uncanny imitation of a trombone.

He was a truly funny man, and inordinately likable. I decided to record him as the world's only one-man band.

First, he carefully wrote out a complete chart—a legitimate arrangement scored for four saxophones, three trumpets, three trombones, piano, bass, guitar and drums. He conceived a four-bar intro to a standard song, the title of which I have mercifully forgotten. The first chorus was for saxophones, in harmony, with occasional brass punctuations, then an artful modulation into another key, then a second chorus with trombones taking the lead, and on out with full en-semble *tutti*. It was a nifty creation, something Hank Mancini might envy.

In the studio, he sang the rhythm parts first, adding guitar, piano, and drum parts to the original bass track. We kept the big Ampex recorder spinning most of the night as the sweating, hard-working DeLyon doggedly reproduced each instrument. Stops and starts, an unexpected hiccup, a sneeze—frustrations abounded. And with each instrument poor Leo's facial expressions became more distorted.

"Your're beginning to look like I flogged you," I commented over the inter-com after six hours. "Do you want to call it a night?"

"No, no, Dave," he yelled from the studio. "I'll be okay once I become a trombone."

DeLyon's musicianship was no less than astonishing. He was blending a trumpet playing sixteenth notes an octave above a tenor sax playing whole notes, and he varied the bass beats from two to four in a measure. I wondered how his chart might sound in the hands of Stan Kenton's men.

Leo came in the booth and we played back what we had after eight hours. He was about one-third through the ordeal. Our master track contained four rhythm, first trumpet, and lead alto sax.

"I don't want to offend you, Leo," I told him, "but I'm glad you're not recording Beethoven's Ninth."

He laughed and no sound came out. His voice was gone. Crushed, he sat in a chair listening to a playback of the six combined "instruments" and noticed, as did I, that even though he hadn't yet completed half the project the master tape disclosed major intonation problems.

Leo DeLyon is a true pro, a top-drawer musician and a gentleman. He leaned over and stopped the tape machine, finally.

"That's enough," he croaked. "It's out of tune. It won't work. Throw away the tape."

"And all these years I thought I possessed perfect pitch."

☼ ☼ ☼

The Cheers will not be listed among the most prominent duos when the history of rock 'n' roll is written, but they played a major role in the idiom's early days B.P.—Before Presley.

Alan Livingston assigned them to my stable in 1954 after he had purchased their romping master of *Bazoom (I Need Your Lovin')* a novelty which racked up surprisingly strong sales without promotion. The Cheers were a UCLA student and a USC student, Bert Convy and Gil Garfield, two ambitious amateur singers using the financial backing of Garfield's father, one of the most renowned real estate agents in Southern California.

"We have a sure hit," Garfield assured me. "It's called *Blueberries*. You gotta let us make it on the first session."

I did. We made it five or six times, then decided it wasn't quite right.

Two months later Bert and Gil returned to the studio. They had rehearsed the song hundreds of times and worked closely with arranger Buddy Bregman to achieve the exact orchestral background they felt the tune required. This time we got a good take.

Nobody bought *Blueberries* that year.

Once again, Bert and Gil got me on the phone and with teenaged enthusiasm asked that I set up another session. "More blueberries on the menu?" I asked Garfield. "No, no," he responded. "This one's like nothing you ever heard. Trust me."

They not only brought in a song called *Black Denim Trousers and Motorcycle Boots*, they brought two equally youthful boys with them to the studio.

"Mr. Dexter," said Garfield, "I want you to meet the writers of our next hit, Jerry Leiber and Mike Stoller."

I acknowledged the introduction perfunctorily and sat back in my booth chair while the musicians rehearsed the song with the two kid singers. It was just as they had promised—like nothing I've ever heard. Leiber and Stoller, unlike other songwriters who visited our sessions from time to time, were leaping about the studio shouting directions to the musicians, loudly coaching Convy and Garfield, and shoving our microphones about.

We spent a lot of time on *Black Denim Trousers and Motorcycle Boots*. The union allows only three hours in which to record four songs. I believe we spent more than two hours on the Leiber-Stoller novelty alone.

The two young writers were everywhere, in and out of my booth, in and out of the studio, issuing crisp directions to us all but in a courteous, confident manner. I was amused by their authority, their cocksure ideas and their ability to get what they sought in the way of sounds. Maybe I was seeing myself nearly 15 years previously in Decca's New York studios putting together jazz masters with Andy Kirk, Mary Lou Williams, and their Clouds of Joy orchestra.

Eventually Convy, Garfield, Stoller and Leiber okayed a master. I complimented them on a most unusual, catchy performance. "But," I advised them with a straight face, "we may not release it."

"Why not?" they all screamed in hysterical unison.

"The title is too damned long to fit on a label," I cracked. They liked that.

BDTAMB was issued in late 1955 and sold big. It had a different beat, a different sound, a raucous, compelling mood which attracted instant attention from the nation's radio deejays.

It was probably the world's first rock vocal duet. But more significantly, it boosted the incredible careers of Leiber and Stoller who later composed songs and produced Number One chart-toppers by the Coasters, the Dixie Cups, the Shangri-Las, and other rock groups and who also wrote many of Elvis Presley's biggest smashes. They are millionaires today.

Convy and Garfield never followed up on their winning single. We did one last session in 1956. None of the four titles we taped sold. Convy turned to acting. Garfield went into his father's real estate business. I see the handsome Convy occasionally on television and I recently read that Garfield "hated" real estate and now operates a clothing boutique in Hollywood. I'll remember them as pleasant young men. And I'll remember Leiber and Stoller as two hustling, far-sighted guys who were smarter than I in recognizing the music of the future. They deserve their rewards.

16

Stereophonic
reproduction of music
on records and tape is only
a gimmick with no sound
musical validity, and will
eventually wind up
a fiasco.

—STAN KENTON (1959)

LEE GILLETTE, VOYLE Gilmore and I were shuffling through new songs one day in 1955. Alan Livingston joined us and calmly announced that Capitol Records had been sold. The consideration involved was $8.5 million.

"As of today," he asserted, "Electric & Musical Industries of England owns 71 percent of the stock, and full control."

We blinked in disbelief.

"EMI operates the Columbia, Parlophone, and His Master's Voice labels in the United Kingdom," Livingston went on. "They also manufacture a number of items like electric irons, bicycles, hi-fi speakers, and God knows what else. EMI has its own record companies in about 30 nations throughout the world. They've coveted an American company for a long time."

Gilmore finally said what we all were thinking:

"Do we still work here?"

Livingston assured us that no changes in personnel were contemplated by the new owners, and that Glenn Wallichs would continue to boss us all and retain Capitol's presidency.

"It can be a most advantageous arrangement," said Livingston, a little feebly. "They'll be selling our records soon in places we've never heard of."

Capitol that year was on its way to record sales of $21,308,633 and its best earnings ever. We were soon to move into our new building, the circular, 13-story Tower on Vine Street. Nat Cole, Frank Sinatra, Kay Starr, Jackie Gleason, Stan Kenton, Les Baxter, Billy May, Nelson Riddle, and a strong country & western roster were dominating the charts from week to week. EMI had taken over at a propitious time.

I walked around for a week or so pondering the new ownership, and the ramifications of our being owned by the British. If they were contemplating opening new markets for Capitol's product, then obviously we would be opening a vast new market—the largest in the world—to EMI.

"Somebody here in Hollywood will be named to head up the international a&r chair," I told my wife, who by then had mothered our three children. "I'd like to be that man."

Livingston listened to me the next day. He asked me to firm up a memo in which I would enumerate my knowledge of British artists. It was easy. For 15 years I had read the London *Melody Maker* music newspaper every week. My knowledge of British bands and singers was at least a tad better than anyone else's at Capitol.

"You've got the job," Livingston told me after he had checked it out with Wallichs and Lloyd W. Dunn, our national merchandising boss. We agreed that I would give up all my American artists, Les Baxter excepted, and that I might still sign a performer or an act if ever I ran across something I was aching to handle.

A few weeks later, the first of the EMI execs arrived in Hollywood.

Charles Thomas was a skinny, elderly man, an utterly delightful World War I airplane pilot who had crashed in combat and narrowly avoided death. Charlie was the best possible representative our British owners could have sent on that first look-see; since he was one of the men with whom I would be working in the future, I walked around the old building introducing him to everyone.

At dinner, we talked of sports. He was a rugby and cricket buff, and we chummily tried to sort out the differences in playing baseball and cricket over chilled white German wine. I went home that night ecstatic about my new work.

In August, Lloyd Dunn and I flew to London to meet the EMI management corps. We visited their factories and plants in Hayes, out in Middlesex, and I spent several days in the crowded, old-fashioned Great Castle Street offices of a&r men Norrie Paramor, Walter Ridley, Ray Martin, and George Martin, the men who chose the artists and songs heard on EMI's Columbia, HMV, and Parlophone labels.

After about 12 minutes, it was evident that the differences in concepts between EMI and Capitol far exceeded the 6,000-mile stretch that separated the two corporations physically.

"We note that you produce only 12-inch LPs," one of the EMI men said. "Over here that size couldn't possibly sell. We prefer the smaller 10-inch disc."

"You'll change your mind," I replied. "We, too, started with 10-inchers but the demand was for six songs on a side. You'll be *forced* to offer a larger, better LP. It doesn't cost any more to press, you know."

The man laughed. My argument left him unconvinced. But a couple of years later the entire British record industry abandoned the 10-inch discs and adopted the larger ones, just as American firms had done five years earlier.

EMI's talent roster was large. They had hundreds of singers and bands on their three labels. Most of them, however, were of the pre-war school. Their music was, by American standards, dated, tired, and obsolete.

The best music I found on that first trip to England was that of the Columbia producer Paramor, a pianist who had conducted a large, string-heavy orchestra not dissimilar to Percy Faith's and Les Baxter's. Paramor did his own arranging. He employed a high soprano, Patricia Clark, to pop in and sing four bars of a song—just enough to spice up the 33 Paramor strings. It was a legitimate, provocative gimmick. I reckoned it might be acceptable in America.

I also asked that tapes of other artists be shipped to me in Hollywood although I had little confidence that they would sell well. Russ Conway's piano, Eddie Calvert's trumpet, Reginald Dixon's organ, Alma Cogan, Eve Boswell, Michael Holliday, Ruby Murray, Brendan O'Dowda, Jimmy Shand—these were EMI's blockbusters at the time. Only Miss Murray's Irish songs proved moveable in the American market.

I suspect the Dunn-Dexter visit proved beneficial to EMI. Paramor, Ridley, and the two unrelated Martins were given more freedom by EMI management to update their talent rosters and modernize their creative procedures.

From London, we hopped the Channel to Paris to meet with our French EMI affiliate, Pathé-Marconi, on Rue Lord Byron. Geoffrey Capstick served as my amiable a&r contact there. He was British, but had lived in France since

In England, popular arranger, composer, and conductor Norrie Paramor (left) and irish singer Ruby Murray spun samples of Parlophone, His Master's Voice, and British Columbia records for the author. Miss Murray's first album for Capitol was released in the U.S. about 90 days later. Paramor's series of "mood" albums were top sellers for a decade. He's now a British Broadcasting Corporation executive.

World War I and had no desire to return to his homeland.

We listened to hundreds of French singles and LPs. Edith Piaf's things were obviously of value in North America. So were albums by Charles Trenet, Yves Montand, and Georges Guetary, all of whom were well-known in the States. But the *artiste* I most preferred was Franck Pourcel, a violinist who arranged, composed, and conducted with marvelous inventiveness and taste. His records were not top-sellers in France, yet I had every confidence that his sophisticated, sleek approach to non-rock music would find a strong reception back home. Capstick appeared surprised but pleased. He asked his assistant, Colette Credoz, to arrange to have tapes air-expressed to Hollywood.

It was on that Parisian visit that Dunn and I constantly heard a French melody, *La Goulante du Pauvre Jean*, everywhere we went. It was a tricky little melody and before we planed out for Cologne I obtained a copy of the song, stashed it away in my bag, and vowed that Les Baxter would some day tape it for Capitol. He did, as I have recounted several pages back. In North America it rocketed to Number One almost overnight in 1956 under my title of *Poor People of Paris*.

The Germans, I found, were technically superior to the Americans, British, and French in recording equipment. They achieved sounds in Cologne which I envied, but I ordered only a small number of tapes. Vocals in German, I assumed, would not have wide appeal in the decade following World War II.

I was wrong by plenty.

One good thing came out of that first meeting with German Electrola officials. I had been impressed with a number of 45 rpm singles which featured Bavarian oom-pah bands with mixed choruses shouting rousing old beer-drinking songs. They were mostly low-fidelity pre-war masters but they had spirit and a contagious, inescapable charm. Later I hooked them together, adjusted the equalization, ran the new, revised tape through filters and put them out in an LP I titled *German Beer-Drinking Music*, a plebeian tag, I admit, but one which reflected the music's appeal directly if unartistically.

The album still sells in the 1970s. It has topped the 150,000 mark. Rival labels have tried to imitate it. The German EMI Electrola people were as astonished as I.

Dunn kept busy with vital conferences pertaining to sales, exchange of graphic art materials, pressing fees, and countless other details involved in an international exchange of masters. He left the selection of foreign repertoire to me. I found it all excitingly challenging. Trying to guess which artists would be successful at home gave my new work a competitive element. It was a new field. With EMI's immense facilities Capitol now possessed a surging, overflowing reservoir of music which no other American label enjoyed.

Dunn and I covered Vienna, Zurich, Rome, Barcelona, Copenhagen, and Stockholm. For three weeks I listened to an indescribable variety of artists and songs performed in numerous languages. In Sweden, Lloyd and I split. He had to get back to Hollywood. I went on to Amsterdam.

The first thing I noticed in Holland was the music of the gigantic barrel-organs on the streets. They produced weird music, a cross between a circus caliope, a harpsichord, and an accordion. Gerry Oord, the aggressive, obliging EMI representative, proved to be the most hospitable man on the entire trip. I found Dutch food to be the best in Europe. I found the streets to be the cleanest. I marveled at the rich Amstel beer. And with apologies to my associates in the other countries, it appeared to me that the Dutch hustled about with more enthusiasm and zest for living than any other people on the Continent.

My barrel-organ LP sold well when I got it out the following year. It trailed *German Beer-Drinking Music* in sales but it was a major winner all the same. Capitol still presses and moves several hundred every year.

Launching our new "Capitol of the World" series of imported albums and singles was like founding a new record company. Back in Hollywood I hired a new secretary, Italian-born Annabella Carta, who was fluent in that language and in three others as well. She also knew music.

Capitol's fast-growing forces moved up Vine Street and into the new Tower in the spring of 1956. It was a festive occasion. Station KTLA televised the event as gigantic portable spotlights sent their brilliant beams into the Hollywood sky. Glenn Wallichs proudly presided downstairs in the two largest recording studios, and EMI's balding chairman, Sir Joseph Lockwood, appeared to jubilantly represent our British owners. Thirty artists participated. The booze and champagne flowed and food was specially catered. I stood around watching the drunks fall down and wistfully concluded that things at Capitol, now 14 years old and growing, would never be the same.

Another era had indeed begun.

It was a productive era, one of increasingly prosperous growth and expansion. Capitol was now issuing classical music on a scale comparable to RCA-Victor and Columbia: the Angel line was unquestionably the most complete and star-studded in the world. We were acquiring motion picture soundtracks and original Broadway show casts. We dominated the country and western field. Our jazz, blues, polka, childrens', Hawaiian, and comedy catalogs were as strong as any in the industry.

Livingston strengthened the a&r division, bringing in as producers Bill Miller and John Palladino from the engineering department and Dave Cavanaugh, the tenor saxist, arranger, and conductor, who had served Capitol well for several years in New York. Then Livingston abruptly resigned his veep post.

"I've always hankered to get into motion picture production," he said. "NBC is soon to begin making movies for television and they've made me an offer I can't ignore." He was a good executive, attuned to the needs of those who toiled under his authority. It was he who had pushed through a generous retirement plan for Capitol employees, fully financed by Capitol from its annual earnings. Livingston was also an experienced, capable contract negotiator, the best Capitol ever employed.

I missed him in the years that followed.

○   ○   ○

Gilmore's tactful handling of Frank Sinatra had helped Frank roar back from oblivion and become bigger than ever. In films, on television, and—above all—on records Sinatra reigned as king. His albums sold, his singles sold, and his extended play discs moved not only domestically but throughout the world.

Gilmore and I were rapping when Lee Gillette approached us one afternoon with a song in his hand.

"Here's an old tune you'll both recall," he said, showing more animation than usual around the office. He popped a Fizrin into his mouth.

"It's called *Melody of Love*. Billy Vaughn on Dot has an instrumental that's breaking nationally. I think we should team Ray Anthony's band with Frank Sinatra and fracture Vaughn's version."

"Frank isn't eager to split his royalty with another artist," Gilmore said, cautiously. "But I suppose it's worth checking out."

Sinatra agreed to the incongruous pairing of man and musicians. He insisted, however, that the second tune to be recorded as a backing for *Melody of Love* be one that his publishing firm controlled. His stipulation prevailed, of course. A studio was booked. Gilmore then flew to New York on other business while one of Anthony's staff wrote the two arrangements.

Came the day of the session. A frantic Gilmore telephoned from New York asking me to sit in as Sinatra's producer. Voyle was tied up and couldn't get back to the West Coast in time.

"Look out for Sinatra's interests, Dex," Gilmore pleaded.

"Gillette will be in the booth doing everything he can to assist Anthony and his musicians. Be damned sure the arrangements don't call for just a vocal chorus—they should be built around Frank."

I sat in the booth when Sinatra arrived with a smaller entourage than I had expected to see; two songpluggers, an anonymous male pal, and a distinctly ordinary-looking woman in her twenties.

I walked out into the studio hesitantly. Sinatra had refused to work with me after I had crawled out on a limb and implored Alan Livingston to sign him. He had said nasty, derogatory things about me—forgetting all the years of my writing rave reviews and features along with an occasional rap—and I wondered if he would accept me as his producer for one night.

He had his hat on, his collar open, and he was gabbing with Anthony. He saw me approach.

"Nice to see you," he said softly, sticking his hand out. I exchanged pleasantries while I explained Gilmore's absence.

"Okay with me," he responded. "Let's get started."

Sinatra was all business. So were Anthony and his sidemen, none of whom had recorded with a star of such dazzling magnitude.

In the booth, Gillette and I shared the intercom mike. *Melody of Love* is a waltz, a dull waltz, and we encountered no problems. *I'm Gonna Live Till I Die* was, as we say so indelicately in the trade, a fast-moving ballbreaker. Frank handled it well. The band blew in tune. Anthony and Sinatra were compatible.

I asked Frank three times during the session to try another take, blaming "errors in the booth." Actually, I thought he could sustain certain notes a little longer if he had another crack at them. He complied, willingly.

It was over in less than three hours. Gillette and I worked for two more making judicious splices to obtain the best possible results. Sinatra gave us a cheery " 'bye now" as he and his friends strode out the door.

I never recorded him again. I haven't seen Frank offstage in years. But I sometimes wonder if his incredible comeback would have happened at all had he not fluffed off my services as his producer. Gilmore did a masterful job with the mercurial New Jersey baritone. Handling Sinatra is like defusing a ticking bomb. I look back now and I'm grateful that the job went to someone else.

❁   ❁   ❁

In 1956 I took off for South America, meeting with our Mexican affiliate on the way to Peru, Chile, Argentina, Brazil, and Venezuela. The Latins, I observed, were no more like the British or Europeans than a puck is like a basketball. For all their differences, I liked them all. On that trip I arranged to import albums by Lucho Gatica, the most popular Spanish-speaking singer in the world, and tangos from Argentina, sambas from Brazil, mariachi rancheros and bullring pasodobles from Mexico, along with folksongs and genuinely ethnic music from other areas. Rio de Janeiro was a dismal disappointment. From the air, peering through the window of a prop-driven DC-7, the city was a jewel at night with its graceful mountains and lovely shoreline. In the daylight I walked along world-renowned Copacabana beach watching children cut their bare feet on broken glass, nails, and bottle caps. The streets were filthy; the traffic disorganized and impenetratable. I've never returned.

Would South American music sell well in the United States?

No, I learned. But Mexican music does.

With Miss Carta's invaluable assistance—we worked many nights until nine or later—I produced about 40 Capitol of the World albums and even more singles that first year. Marvin Schwartz delivered attractive, full-color front covers from the transparencies I obtained, gratis, from the international airlines and tourist bureaus in Los Angeles and New York. Pan-American Airways, in particular, supplied Capitol with dozens of gorgeous, artistic color photos, for which I ran a small credit line on the albums' back covers. I also wrote the annotation for the liners.

Someone in Cap's cost control offices patted me on the back in a Tower elevator one day in 1957.

"Has anyone told you that your series of imported albums shows the highest profit margin of any of our company's products?" he asked. "There's only two of you handling it all—front and back cover art, liner notes, the works. And there's no recording costs involved. It's the damndest money-maker we've ever had."

°   °   °

Stereophonic sound followed microgroove discs in America in about a decade, but it was a British technician, A. D. Blumlein of the English Columbia firm, who deserves homage for conceiving the revolutionary dual sound system. He applied for a patent in London in 1931; it was granted in 1933. Blumlein knew exactly what would be involved in perfecting the magical "sound in 3D" process: new microphones, new recording procedures, new manufacturing techniques, and even new compounds to be used in pressing stereo discs—the old shellac formula would, he said, be far too coarse and noisy for optimum sound achievement.

Bell Telephone began its experiments with stereo in 1933 in America, but Blumlein's contributions are those essentially in use today. Not until 1954, however, did stereo reach the public, and then it was, at first, offered only on tape. British Decca's Arthur Haddy, meanwhile, secretly devised a system whereby two independent channels might efficiently be recorded within a single groove of a disc; it wasn't until 1957 that the American Westrex engineers announced they had succeeded in perfecting a system for recording and reproducing stereo discs (from two-track tape masters) with a single stylus. Westrex demonstrated its sensational record in Los Angeles in September, 1957, and Capitol's Ed Uecke attended the event. He returned to the Tower the following day to advise President Wallichs of the intricate technical aspects involved.

British Decca chairman Ted Lewis was then forced to abandon the secrecy of his company's activities in the stereo field, and by intelligently and unselfishly sharing their knowledge, British Decca and American Westrex agreed on a stereo system which would avert another 33 vs. 45 upheaval within the industry such as had occurred 10 years earlier when both RCA-Victor and Columbia, in America, refused to consider any but their own innovations.

Wallichs and Uecke quickly obtained the required equipment and by 1958 Capitol was recording and issuing albums in stereophonic form. So were several hundred other American firms.

The superiority of stereo sound was and is unquestionable. The old crystal type styli quickly became obsolete as ceramic and magnetic pickups appeared. Americans rushed to acquire new turntables, new amplifiers, and new twin speakers. Another revolution in sound had begun.

°   °   °

Stereo came to Capitol shortly after I made a second trip to Europe in 1957 a tiring jaunt that took me—and my wife Mickie—as far as Athens. Again I met EMI personnel with whom I had only exchanged correspondence. EMI was slowly replacing its 70-year-old executives with younger blood, and its records were improving.

Capitol's sales that year soared to $41,498,000, another all-time high. President Wallichs took pride in the astounding profits picture.

"It's a little different from our $200,000 gross that first year," he chortled. We were lunching at the Brown Derby's American Room, all the a&r men and I. Wallichs liked to get us together for a pep talk once a month.

"Gentlemen," he addressed us as we prepared to break, "you may think I am overambitious, overoptimistic, and maybe even out of my skull, but I see a year coming soon when Capitol will top the $100,000,000 plateau in sales.

"It's there awaiting us. Let's reach for it."

It took 10 years. But each of those 10 years was highly profitable. Capitol's rise as a power was discussed and analyzed in depth by *Fortune, The Wall Street Journal, Business Week, The New York Times*, and numerous other influential, widely read publications of international repute.

My imported music sold well in albums, but singles didn't move. Capitol's sales chief complained that I was releasing "too damned many British dogs." Then came Laurie London.

London was a teenaged singer with a broad Jamaican accent. His hand-clapping version of an old spiritual, *He's Got the Whole World in His Hands*, was produced in England by Norman Newell and it ran up the charts in a few days. I cabled Newell for the tape and got it out fast. Capitol had its first million seller from England within four weeks.

I took no credit for its success. It was a smash in England and all I did was convert it to Capitol's purple label and let it fly. But Ron Goodwin's *Swingin' Sweethearts* was different. It meant nothing in England. I heard it in a Goodwin album I was preparing for American issue. It clicked right off.

Franck Pourcel's million-seller *Only You* was also pulled from an album. As a single, it unleashed an American trend to orchestrating string sections an octave higher than they had been previously. Fifteen years later, *Only You* is the only French record in history that has topped the 1,000,000 mark in America. Pourcel's LPs sold well, too, through most of those years. He's no longer on Capitol, but the beautiful masters he so consistently produces in Paris for Pathé-Marconi are still being sold in the U.S. on at least two other labels.

Paramor's gorgeous strings and the ghostly, ethereal voice of Patricia Clark also scored instantaneously. Their *In London . . . In Love* proved popular enough to rate a sequel, *In London . . . In Love Again*. The first Paramor stereo tapes from London ignited a commotion downstairs in the recording department. To a man, Bill Robinson's staff agreed that the overall sound was superior to American stereo—due, they said, to a different system of microphone placement in the studios.

Jet Flight, The Zodiac Suite, Autumn, London After Dark, Just We Two, and *Strings Staged for Stereo* all matched Pourcel's for mood and musicianship. I still hear them played on FM, sometimes when I'm shopping for tomatoes at the supermarket.

In time, rock 'n' roll took over the market. It became increasingly difficult to sell legitimate music. I issued dozens of British rock singles, month by month. Cliff Richard was the Presley of England, a handsome young singer who dominated the British charts, but over here we couldn't give his singles away. Nor would American deejays grant him air exposure. My biggest disappointment was a group called Freddie and the Dreamers. They had an indefinable but obvious "different" sound, particularly in their platter of *I'm Telling You Now* and *What Have I Done*, but we sold fewer than 1,000 copies and I concluded I knew nothing about rock.

Yet in 1965, several years after I had bombed out with Freddie, Capitol's rock-dominated Tower label released the coupling again and it shot up to Number One in America, the only smash Tower had before Capitol phased it out of business in the late sixties. So I wasn't *totally* ignorant of the new and raucous idiom, after all.

17

With recording, the music of the world becomes
available at any moment—just like an encyclopedia.
We begin to develop a vast tribal encyclopedia of
musics. Music becomes plural. You cannot speak of it
any longer in the singular, or refer to it as the
international language. We know from recordings that
the old pet cliché of the 19th century—music the
universal language—just isn't so.

—MARSHALL McLUHAN

I FLEW AROUND the world in the fall of 1959 seeking exotic music which might
find favor domestically. First to Hawaii, then Wake Island, and on to Tokyo.
Most of the Japanese records featured kotos and samisens. I ordered some of
their best-sellers, reckoning that the Japanese-American population of San
Francisco, Los Angeles, and New York would insure enough sales to attain the
break-even point. And that's just about what they did.

The Japanese Jazz Club gave me a warm welcome at the Imperial Hotel.
Several members clutched copies of my 1946 *Jazz Cavalcade* book, but I didn't
hear any good jazz in my brief stay there. Nat Cole's discs were favorites in
Tokyo. It's a peculiar feeling, hearing him gently reading the lyrics to *Paradise*
and *Too Young* over the hotel's house radio system—a sort of Muzak arrangement.

In Hong Kong I listened to samples of a dozen popular Chinese male and
female singers. It's a large market despite the prevailing poverty which sees
three entire families—perhaps 20 persons in all—living atop a roof, and thousands in the streets. I remember one scene vividly: a man pushed a rickety cart
from which he sold chestnuts, dried fish, and small, cellophane-wrapped pack-
ets of heroin. He did business out in the open in view of everyone. I was told
that there are hundreds of peddlers like him making their daily rounds with
cool impunity.

Singapore is a beautiful city, with an even stronger British atmosphere than
Hong Kong. The EMI boss there preferred to spend the two days I had blocked
out for auditioning records at a comfy hotel bar, imbibing Scotch, while I
nursed Malayan Tiger beer in a setting like something out of a Charlie Chan
flicker. Chinese servants trotted around, bowing and delivering drinks and

speaking pidgin English as if they expected to be swatted by a rolled English umbrella. It was fascinating, but I obtained no music there. Only atmosphere.

It was a relief to glide into Manila, where more than 200 cheering employees of the Mico Company, with which Capitol had a co-op affiliation, awaited me at the airport. All of them wore tee-shirts emblazoned with a big, blue Capitol trademark. Mico president Eusebio Contreras was an older, dignified, courteous gentleman of the old school. He had me measured at once for a pina-cloth *barong tagalog* shirt, handwoven of pineapple fiber, and it was delivered the next afternoon to me at the Manila Hotel in time for a festive party given in my honor at nearby Quezon City. Mr. Contreras and his staff members tendered a soiree replete with chilled San Miguel beer and animated entertainment featuring traditional *tinikling* dancers who hop in and out between long, sturdy bamboo poles. The poles are slapped together and if a dancer isn't exceptionally agile, he or she may well fracture an ankle.

Throughout the Orient, one notices the preponderance of Filipino musicians in almost every orchestra. Most of them strum mandolins. It wasn't my kind of jazz and I discovered no Barney Kessels or Wes Montgomerys there, but it was a pleasant, honest ethnic music and I later released several Filipino *rondalla* LPs in America.

Motion picture stars, the president of the musicians' union, and the management of the EMI Gramophone Co. greet Dave Dexter on his arrival in Singapore. Malayan music is a hard sell in the 50 states, Dexter learned when he returned to California. German records sell better.

En route to India, we experienced equipment malfunction and were forced to lay over in Saigon for several hours.

I sat at an airport restaurant table with a friendly Vietnamese airport official of my age and asked about conditions there since the French had moved out after years of vainly fighting in the rice paddies and villages for a "principle."

"Ah, the stupid French," the man said, shaking his head. "They brought soldiers by the thousands halfway around the world to die and be maimed. They spent billions of francs. And when they pulled out nothing, but nothing, had been decided."

I wonder what my Vietnamese acquaintance would say today, 16 years later. Might he concede that the "stupid" French were smarter than we Americans? With 45,941 dead; 300,635 wounded; 1,811 missing, captured, or interned; and an additional 10,303 men deceased from non-hostile causes in the 1961–73 period in which Americans fought the Viet Cong, who *was* the loser?

Artie Shaw said it all when he wearily asked no one in particular that afternoon 15 years previously at Jerome Kern's house in Beverly Hills:

"I wonder if the world has learned anything?"

○　　　●　　　○　　　　·

The flight to Calcutta was made via BOAC in one of its new British Comet jets. We were at 28,000 feet and an hour east of the overcrowded, unseasonably hot industrial city on the Hooghly River when the captain took the mike and said something like this:

"We are advised that rioting in the streets of Calcutta is in progress. Passengers who plan to deplane there are urged to remain in their seats while we refuel, then continue on to Karachi and return to Calcutta after the rioting ends. Conditions are unsafe—I repeat the word *unsafe*—in Calcutta and passengers who deplane and enter into the city will do so at their own risk."

It was a revolting development. The captain repeated the warning. We set down at dusk and exactly three of us gathered our handbags and started for the air terminal. We were stopped by airline representatives, who asked that we stand by and identify our luggage in the hold. Only ours would be removed.

The drive into town from the airport was hairy. Small fires burned everywhere. Hundreds of persons lay in the streets. I thought they were dead, or dying. "No, no," the taxi driver said, "these are people who live in the streets. They are merely trying to get to sleep now that it's dark."

He dropped me at the Great Eastern Hotel. I had an appointment the following morning with Jimmy George of EMI at the factory at Dum-Dum, a Calcutta suburb where the infamous dum-dum bullet was conceived and manufactured by the British military long, long ago. When I telephoned George from the hotel the next morning, I was told that he would not be in his office that day or any day until the rioting ended.

What to do? Sit in a drab hotel room from Friday night until Monday morning?

I walked out on the street. I could hear shouts, and smoke billowed above the city's buildings. But I saw no violence.

I walked farther, around Dalhousie Square and along the wide Chowringhee with its theaters and ornate shops. On one side of the boulevard was the Maidan, a grassy, vacant field where important rugby matches are played. It was almost a serene, rural setting.

Small pools of blood on the sidewalks puzzled me. There were hundreds of them. And the cattle wandering around, blocking automobile and pedestrian traffic alike. They are sacred animals in India and no one dares protest their behavior. Naked children ran up to me, arms outstretched, begging for coins. Adults lay along the street curbs, most of them emaciated, listless, and physically deformed. I returned to my hotel.

A morning phone call connected me with a Mr. Menon. He appeared unafraid of the strife and welcomed me to EMI India warmly. Within a half-hour he had picked me up at the Great Eastern. In another hour we were in his office playing records.

I asked him about the pools of blood on the sidewalks. They were frightening to contemplate and repulsive to see. He laughed.

"It is not blood," he explained. "It is the juice of the betel nut—pan—which many Indians habitually chew. They expectorate, of course, just as Americans who chew tobacco do. It is shipped here from East Pakistan and is sold for a penny or so, wrapped in betel leaf coated with lime. Those who use it claim it soothes the nerves, aids digestion, and has mysterious, subtle therapeutic values."

Menon smiled. He was younger than I by almost 20 years and fashionably dressed; his English was precise, with a British accent, and he presented a handsome appearance. He asked questions about Capitol and the American record scene.

For every question he raised I sought information about India and its music. It was a delightful session, and he promised to ship me tapes of several prominent Indian performers for issue in our Capitol of the World series of albums.

I never did meet Jimmy George, but Bhaskar Menon was more than a competent substitute.

I tramped all over Calcutta the following day, a Sunday, and read in the English newspaper that the riots had ended with 21 fatalities and scores of injured. Sunday night I flew KLM west to Karachi. It had been a strange and unforgettable visit, one that remains vivid in my mind, for I was to meet the engaging young Menon again in the future. As my boss in Hollywood.

Karachi is about one third as large as Calcutta, and ideally located on the Arabian Sea. EMI dominates the record industry there as it does in India, where no competitive labels are permitted by government edict.

I found no particularly distinctive music in Karachi, though. Just more crimson betel nut pools wherever I went. The EMI people told me, as I had been advised in Manila, that I was the first Capitol representative ever to visit them.

They showed me their pressing plant. It was clean and small. All pressing plants look the same no matter what part of the world one may be visiting. Some are just larger than others.

From Karachi I flew into Jerusalem, a city divided since 1948 into two separate cities by barbed wire and a narrow neutral zone. I was in Jordan, and from my hotel room I could almost have thrown a bagel over into Israel. EMI had no representation in Arab Jerusalem at that time; I dropped in for a day's visit just for the hell of it. From there I would fly into nearby Cairo the next morning.

The historic birthplace of Jesus Christ is a mixture of Moslem Arabs, Circassians, Persian Bahais, Copts, Turcomans, Syrians, White Russians, and a couple of hundred Samaritans who are descended from Biblical times—and can prove it.

I walked until I dropped. The Church of the Holy Sepulchre, perhaps the most venerated shrine in Christendom, where Christ was laid to rest after the Crucifixion; the Garden of Gethsemane, where Jesus was betrayed by Judas; the Via Dolorosa and its 14 stations where Christ walked from the court of Pontius Pilate to the hill of Golgotha; the Mount of Olives; the Tomb of the Virgin Mary; the Dome of the Rock on the site of the original Temple of Solomon; the Wailing Wall, legendary gathering place of Jews; and the Citadel, also known as the Tower of David, a group of towers erected in the 14th century as part of the walls of Jerusalem—I visited them all, a Missouri WASP who forgot the record business and everybody in it on that lovely October day.

At the airport the following morning I was told that no flights to Cairo were available. Back to my hotel I went. There I found an Arab driver who said he would drive me to Bethany and thence to Bethlehem for $10. His battered Plymouth sedan appeared to be a pre-war model but it got me there, and back. Along the way I studied the rocky, dry fields adjacent to the highway, reconstructing the setting of almost 2,000 years ago when a bright star guided three camel-riding travelers to a stable. It had to be a rough journey over that bumpy, desertlike terrain.

I flew to Cairo Wednesday morning, visited the Pyramids, rode an ill-tempered camel, and, at night, enjoyed the most awesome, memorable view of my life from my room high in the Hilton.

Across the Nile, and far out into the desert where Moses once led the believing—the sight was overwhelming. A dragoman drove me about and we talked music. I didn't hear any, except over the radio, and I didn't understand or appreciate what I heard. In the Hilton dining room that night a salon orchestra offered *Smoke Gets in Your Eyes* and *Stardust*.

Istanbul was somewhat like Cairo, crowded with humanity and endowed with numerous sightseeing attractions. From the ancient Topkapi Palace's summer terrace I could see the Golden Horn where the Bosporus and Sea of Marmara converge. EMI's quarters were out in the suburbs, in the village of Yesilkoy. The EMI boss sat me down in his office and played every type of Turkish music, most of it recorded long before tape facilities were available in

Istanbul. Like the music of Egypt and Pakistan, it was difficult to appreciate. I ordered just enough to make up a single LP.

The remainder of the trip was uneventful. Dutch KLM flew me into Zurich and from there I made the rounds of EMI's European posts renewing acquaintances and listening—until my ears were fatigued—to music which might find favor at home. In Paris I asked Geoff Capstick if I might meet with Edith Piaf, who had not been available on my two previous visits to France.

"I'm afraid not," Capstick replied. "Madame Piaf just left for New York. She needs money. Over there she is paid $1,000 a night in cash following her every performance. She works a couple of months and comes home to Paris to spend it.

"A goodly share of that American swag," Capstick added, "goes for alcohol."

Capstick saved the day by arranging luncheon with the gifted Franck Pourcel. we projected plans for a half-dozen orchestral albums to be recorded in 1960–61.

I reserved a full week for meeting with Capitol's EMI bosses and associates in London and Hayes. Sir Joseph Lockwood took me into the chairman's private dining room one noon for a chummy one-on-one luncheon.

"I admire you Americans and your unflagging enthusiasm for your work," he told me. "Capitol's success is the most remarkable story in the world of business in the last quarter-century.

"I do wish we could transmit that aggressiveness and know-how to other companies within the EMI worldwide family."

In London, I sat in on recording sessions with Walter Ridley and Norrie Paramor serving as producers. Everything was being taped in stereo. Producer Ray Martin had quit EMI and moved to New York, where he became a house maestro for RCA Victor. George Martin, who bossed the struggling Parlophone label, took me to see Laurence Olivier in a stage play and indicated that he—Martin—was discouraged with his work and fearful of the future of Parlophone.

"I am a classically trained musician," he said. "Yet all my work involves pop. With rock ruling the charts I just don't know which way to turn."

Martin, of course, is the man who unleashed the Beatles three years later. We were to meet again many times.

With boxes of tapes from all over the world inundating my offices in the Tower, I returned to my desk ready for a long vacation. It was not to be. Our Capitol of the World series required 16-hour work shifts and the scheduling of singles and albums through 1960.

I learned that Edith Piaf had recorded in Capitol's New York studios during her visit there. Test pressings lay on my desk. One of the titles she chose to do, in English, was simply unbelievable: *Black Denim Trousers and Motorcycle Boots*, the same noisy, screaming song that Bert Convy and Gil Garfield had recorded for me several years previously in Hollywood. To me it seemed like mixing a dill pickle with vanilla ice cream. I put it out. It didn't sell. Piaf's followers preferred the little French sparrow in the simple black dress to sing only in her natural Gallic tongue.

○   ○   ○

The best thing about Little League and Pony League baseball for boys nine through 14 is the homogenizing process they undergo. The idea to shape and train them into skilled athletes with possible professional careers in the majors is patently absurd; in the 11 years I devoted to the program as an extra-curricular, on-my-own-time community project in Encino I learned that only one out of 500 boys shows anything extraordinary in the way of skill. Most of them participate because all the other boys do.

Encino is 12 miles west of Hollywood in the sprawling San Fernando Valley, a haven for families with children. There are numerous synagogues, Roman Catholic and Protestant churches, and schools of private and public enroll-ment. Every spring I enlisted the help of newspapers and disc jockeys to spread the word that tryouts for our 18 Little League squads and six Pony teams were to be held on three successive weekends. Between 500 and 600 youngsters turned out every year.

California governor Pat Brown flew down to Los Angeles in 1966 to assist Dexter and other Birmingham High School parents raise funds for a $300,000 outdoor stadium. Ac-tors Dennis Weaver and Dick Van Dyke also worked to make the stadium a reality. Dex-ter served two terms as president of the Birmingham Dads Club and also participated in Pop Warner football and Little League athletic programs. (Herb Carleton)

165

Team managers sat on the sidelines of our five beautiful diamonds, notebooks in hand, rating each boy's performance. Then they drafted the kids they preferred. Thus every team was randomly comprised of Catholic, Jewish, and Protestant youngsters, a democratic blend of race and religion. Each manager then was ordered to have a meeting of the boys' parents, at which some of the WASP, Jewish, and Catholic mothers and dads met one another for the first time—and enjoyed it.

Through my old buddy Carlos Gastel, I met John Wayne, an Encino resident, who generously popped for a $300 sponsorship fee. He truly loves kids. For more than 15 years he has faithfully sent Encino Little League a $300 check every March. One may deplore his political convictions but those of us who know of the countless unpublicized charities he supports will brook no criticism of Wayne as a good and generous human being. Another Encinian, Dennis Weaver, the actor, not only used his checkbook to help, but he managed one of the better teams and assisted us in acquiring sponsors. Billy Eckstine's son developed into a star pitcher by the time he was 14, perhaps the Pony loop's best, yet his singing father declined to assist our program. The big-voiced, strikingly handsome senior Eckstine sometimes parked his Lincoln out beyond the right field fence and refused to come out and mix with his son's fellow players and their parents. I sensed that his boy was embarrassed by his dad's aloofness.

One of our devoted dads was Henry Miller, the theatrical agent, who on several occasions brought Nat Cole to our diamonds for gabfests with the youngsters. I also pinched Nat for $50 ads in our souvenir program every year.

Doris Day and her third husband, Marty Melcher, whom I knew years ago in New York first as a songplugger, then as a road manager for the Andrews Sisters, cheerfully sent $50 checks for advertising support. So did Johnny Cash during the brief time he lived in Encino, but the ultimate achievement in raising funds was selling the boss of General Amusement Corporation, Tom Rockwell, the satisfaction of sponsoring a team for $300. Rockwell lived in New York. Agent Henry Miller helped me with that 3,000-mile transaction.

My sons Mike and Davey benefitted in many ways from Pony and Little League activity, but in my 11 years of managing Duke Wayne's Giants, soliciting funds, writing and planting publicity, laboring on the diamonds with nails, rakes, and paintbrushes, and serving as president of both organizations, I reminisce with a certain pride, aware that more than 2,000 other boys derived similar benefits. Best of all, they struck up friendships which otherwisse almost certainly would never have been realized. Hundreds of their parents made permanent friends in the same program.

And despite our lofty it's-how-you-played-the-game philosophy in Encino, I'm pleased that several of our youngsters grew up and were drafted by major league clubs.

✿   ✿   ✿

As the sixties swept in, how little anyone in or out of the music business realized what overwhelming changes our lives would soon undergo, and what inestimable, unpredictable modifications in the world's pop music culture lay ahead.

It seems so recent. President Dwight D. Eisenhower toured South America and later in that autumn of 1960 his difficult executive position in Washington was won at the polls by a youthful John F. Kennedy. Francis Gary Powers' high-flying U-2 was shot down over Soviet-Afghan territory by a Russian rocket. The fifteenth session of the United Nations General Assembly opened with Premier Nikita S. Khrushchev and Premier Fidel Castro conspicuously absent.

Americans were reading *To Kill a Mockingbird, Born Free,* and *The Rise and Fall of the Third Reich. Advise and Consent, A Taste of Honey, Camelot,* and *The Unsinkable Molly Brown* dominated the Broadway theater. Hit movies included *Can-Can, Exodus, Spartacus, G. I. Blues,* and *The Apartment.* It was the time of unsophisticated songs like *Alley-Oop, The Twist, You Talk Too Much,* and *Itsy Bitsy Teenie Weenie Yellow Polkadot Bikini.*

In the Capitol Tower—known as The Silo to many employees—the year's sales stopped at close of business hours New Year's eve at exactly $46,946,000. But the big jolt as 1960 ended was the return of Alan W. Livingston from NBC. President Wallichs reinstalled him as vice-president in charge of a&r. The soft-speaking University of Pennsylvania grad received an ovation from all of us when he walked into our regular Thursday morning department meeting shortly before Christmas. Someone asked him why he no longer was with NBC's movies-for-television wing. "I found that I liked records better," Livingston answered.

The conclave broke up with all the producers returning to their offices determined to create hits. They could go down into our studios and make the effort with songs and performers of their own choosing. I sat at my desk shuffling imported discs over which I had no artistic control. I regarded mine as the more difficult challenge.

18

I regard all pop music as irrelevant in the sense that people in 200 years won't be listening to what is being written and played today. I think they will be listening to Beethoven. Pop music is just fun. That's one of the reasons I don't take myself seriously. I love music. It's my whole life. But I love it because it is fun. Eighty percent of the music business is a drag. I know it is the music that counts, but I also like it when someone puts on a good show. Ninety percent of my act is music, the heart of it is music, but the 10 percent theatrics is fun. Fun for me and the audience . . . I really have fun touring, particularly in America. I love having parties and making records. If I weren't making records I'd like to work in a record shop.

—ELTON JOHN

ONE OF THE BIGGEST hits of the 1960s was one that was telephoned in from a small town in California.

Let me explain how it happened.

A radio deejay in the Fresno area, aware of the numerous Japanese-Americans in his audience, from time to time programmed a Japanese vocal on his turntable. He played an authentic Tokyo Toshiba master one day and suddenly it was like a second Pearl Harbor. Telephone lines were instantly clogged and mail poured in the following day. He had a freak hit—a monster—on his hands.

I don't recall the jock's name. He couldn't read Japanese and it took a couple of days for him to get a translation of the original title, *Ue O Mui Te Aruko*, which in English comes out something like *I Look Up When I Walk So the Tears Won't Fall.*

He copied the song's title and telephoned me, breathlessly describing the sensation the imported record was creating among the populace.

"It's a cute vocal by a girl," he told me. "And it's a modern orchestra behind her. A vibraphone is featured."

I thanked him profusely and checked my file of Japanese samples, but at the moment none of the Toshiba LPs were by females. I then sent a cable to my Toshiba contact in Tokyo, Mr. K. Ueno. His answer stopped me. The only vocal on that ballad, he reported, was by a young man who doubled as a movie actor and singer in Japan, a 22-year-old named Kyu Sakamoto.

I found the LP and the tune. It sounded nice, a sing-songy, middle-of-the-road performance. Japanese records are the best in the world for absence of surface noise. The compound they use is expensive, and superior to American material. I took the sample record downstairs to the recording crew and they mastered it within two hours.

But I'll say this with uncharacteristic modesty: I figured the chances of Sakamoto's unintelligible vocal becoming a success to be somewhat more than a jillion to one. How many Japanese-Americans are there who might like it as they did up Fresno way?

The song's title was quickly changed to *Sukiyaki*. It is one of the few Japanese words Americans recognize.

It didn't matter, as it turned out. The catchy, wistful sound of Sakamoto was all that mattered. *Sukiyaki* climbed the charts right off, without any special promotion. In about two months the record was certified as gold.

But that isn't the end of it. Kyu Sakamoto's singing spread to England, Germany, Sweden, Holland—all over the world it blazed as a best-seller.

I still don't know what *Sukiyaki* had that others lack. A mood, I suppose. But none of Kyu's follow-up records had it. We tried two or three. Few were sold. I haven't heard his name mentioned in years. He was another of those inexplicable freaks, a one-shotter.

And it all started over the telephone.

∘   ∘   ∘

The Seekers were unknowns from Australia, a vocal group made up of a girl and four boys. They made their way to England, procured a contract with EMI and one day their first record was enclosed with many others in a carton delivered from London to my desk.

I thought *I'll Never Find Another You* was saleable but hardly a smash. Voyle Gilmore gave me an argument. "It's a chart-buster," he insisted. "Get it out quick."

I watched it climb the charts just as Gilmore had predicted it would. I tried a second Seekers single, *A World of Our Own*. It rang the bell too. I felt a little foolish. Couldn't I smell a hit when I held one in my hands?

The Seekers had a couple of flops and then popped with their all-time biggest success, *Georgy Girl*. Then their magic fizzled out. Later they disbanded. A couple of years ago another combination calling themselves the Seekers was organized. The new Seekers produced a hit their first time out, but not for Capitol. Different voices and different songs, yet they scored resoundingly.

Is there any other business as screwed-up and illogical as mine?

∘   ∘   ∘

Bill Morris served for many years as EMI's boss of Brazilian operations. He was British, but, like Geoff Capstick in Paris, preferred living and working elsewhere. On my 1956 visit to Rio I had found him and his wife to be congenial, unpretentious folk. We got along marvelously together.

Along with an LP sample, Morris enclosed a note to me in 1961 in which he asked me to give special attention to a guitarist-singer, Joao Gilberto.

"I must frankly admit that Gilberto does not sell well down here," Morris candidly advised, "but I find his style to be unlike any other, and all the musicians in Brazil are talking about him. If they would only purchase records instead of passing one around and around until the grooves disintegrate I suspect we would have a big hit."

Gilberto sounded different to my ears, too. Not his singing—it was in Portuguese so that didn't matter—but his approach to the guitar was sneaky different, highly rhythmic with a sort of samba beat, and, like Morris, I was impressed.

Capitol issued the album two months later. We got no reaction. None of our salesmen in the field commented on it. No deejay played it. No one bought it. Two years later it was deleted from the Capitol catalog. A bomb.

Then Charlie Byrd's guitar records started selling wildly. Byrd was, of course, on a competitive label. He played beautifully. His appeal, he explained in hundreds of newspaper and magazine interviews and on the air, was based on the authentic bossa nova style from Brazil. A *Time* magazine rave revealed Byrd's unusual character.

"I picked up this bossa nova guitar approach from a Joao Gilberto record," he said. "Gilberto may be one of the best in the world. He deserves the credit."

A man as forthrightly honest as Byrd deserves all the hits he can make. His admission created a precedent; no one in our business ever credits another for his success. And the tagline to this little story?

Bossa nova became the national craze. Capitol reissued my Gilberto LP with a beautiful new front cover that emphasized the "man behind the bossa nova" hysteria. The album was promoted well. Hundreds of deejays were serviced with new copies and in-depth biographical material. Record stores hung Gilberto posters on their walls.

But still it laid an egg.

To this day I detest anything connected with Brazilian music, bossa nova most of all.

°   °   °

A flop comes in numerous guises. Edith Piaf's *Milord* was a smash in France. Everyone in the Capitol Silo said it couldn't miss. The record was one of the few Capitol released in the early sixties that penetrated hundreds of rock radio airings; even the Top 40 jocks loved it and spun it madly.

Jean and Julian Aberbach published the song. They spent thousands exploiting *Milord*, confident it would become the Little Sparrow's biggest of all successes.

But the people who buy records wouldn't buy *Milord*. It lay there.

I play it now and feel sick. It has everything. I know it can be a hit, today or a year from now or even in 1988.

But I know it will never be. What record company, which publisher, would go through all that expense and effort a second time?

Milord . . . a dog that should have gone gold. I can't forget it.

o   o   o

It was pleasurable to work into the Capitol release schedule an occasional personal favorite from EMI's bottomless barrel of available music.

Ray Noble's early 1930s British band with Al Bowlly as singer was perhaps the finest, most musical dance orchestra ever to record. Noble was a dozen years ahead of his colleagues as an arranger, and EMI achieved the most realistic sound imaginable using but one overhead mike and another for Bowlly's vocals.

Nearly 30 years after Noble recorded them in London, I produced a two-record long-player featuring 24 of his prized masters in the *Capitol of the World* series. And I sneaked in LPs of music by Jack Hylton, Freddy Gardner, Fats Waller, Django Reinhardt (with the swinging quintet of the Hot Club of France), Martial Solal and the Double Six, all recorded in London and Paris for EMI.

They were not best-sellers, of course. Yet all but the contemporary jazz pianist Solal were profitable.

Mass sales came easier with German and Italian music. Many Americans enjoy Wolfgang Sauer, Rudolf Schock, Alfons Bauer, Richard Tauber, Marlene Dietrich, and the Vienna Boys Choir. Almost as many buy the Italian Carlo Buti, Sergio Bruni, Renato Carosone, Tito Schipa, and Katyna Ranieri discs.

It's more difficult selling Greek, Swedish, Spanish, Dutch, Swiss, Belgian, Norwegian, Finnish, and Danish performers. I tried them all. Before I concluded my work as director of international a&r for Capitol in 1966. I had built our imported music catalog from nothing to almost 400 LPs, more than 300 of which were profitable. But then none of us expected the fragile bell music of Bali, or aboriginal chants from Australia, or community sings by African Zulus to sell like the Beach Boys. I reckoned that they helped give Capitol the most authoritative, well-rounded ethnic catalog in the world, and my bosses agreed.

o   o   o

Prentice-Hall was in need of a book on jazz to be used by high school and college music students. Their West Coast representative approached me on the matter and suggested that Capitol tie in with the publication of the book with a series of albums. They would be merchandized simultaneously.

I protested that there were already 20 books covering the history of jazz available, including my own *Jazz Cavalcade* published by Criterion in 1946. The P-H man was insistent.

It took about four months of effort, researching and writing and rewriting, until my *The Jazz Story* was completed. I wrote at night, at home. During the sunny hours I sweated out my normal chores in the Tower and worked on a series of four albums which also would be titled *The Jazz Story*.

Jazz is a touchy subject. Everyone who has ever heard a Louis Armstrong or a Duke Ellington record becomes an instantaneous authority on the music. One must be ultra-cautious in putting together an anthology.

From EMI in London I obtained a number of rare, out-of-print masters by Armstrong, Ellington, Fletcher Henderson, Joe Venuti, and other immortals in the field. From Capitol's morgue I acquired greats like Leadbelly, Hawkins, Goodman, Kenton, Carter, Holiday, Hines, and almost everyone I thought the project required. I could not obtain rights to Bessie Smith, Count Basie, or Charlie Parker classics. But by and large the entire panoramic spectrum of American jazz as well represented.

Prentice-Hall coordinated the release date. The jazz critics reacted exactly as I knew they would—as they do whenever anyone creates something they failed to create.

They dynamited my book *and* my four LPs. But the unbiased reviewers outside the jazz world regarded the book as one of the best on the subject.

The book sold exceptionally well, and is still selling. The record set died on the vine. I suppose it deserved to flop. Even I felt it wasn't quite complete without The Empress, The Count, and The Bird.

o   o   o

Annabella Carta quit me to become an interior decorator and she was succeeded by Carol Burke and, later, Ruth Liberman. Without their enthusiasm and devotion I would have been a helpless incompetent in my job.

The success of *Capitol of the World* for five years brought many imitators. One-man record "companies" emulated our front and back covers and sold shoddy, unauthentic music for 99 cents, a price Capitol couldn't meet. Our worldwide repertoire began to pall in appeal; how many albums of flamenco and bullring music from Spain can the market absorb?

So it was with that foreboding cloud on the horizon that we flew to Mexico City in the summer of 1963 for another company convention. There it was learned that President Wallichs would move up to chairman of the board of directors. The new prexy was my boss Livingston.

Employees applauded the change. But who would move up to the vice-presidency of Capitol's a&r division?

There were three of us tabbed as possible veeps. Lee Gillette, Voyle Gilmore and I were senior producers with high company seniority. But I had no chance. Administrative details are not for me; nor was Gillette strong in that vital corporate area. Lee and I both subtley campaigned with Wallichs, Livingston, Lloyd Dunn and any other officer we could corner to pin the v-p stripes on the orderly, even-tempered Gilmore.

I was in Ireland three months later, preparing to return home after a long and difficult tour of Europe in which I acquired more than a dozen attractive albums for American issue, when Gilmore's cable arrived. "It finally happened," he advised. "Wish me success in veep post."

I returned to the Tower invigorated and pleased that one of us would carry on the creative torque which had established Capitol as one of the largest and most progressive firms in the world. Gilmore had achieved a miracle in assisting Sinatra with his comeback (but Frank demanded a different producer, once his success was assured, charging that Gilmore was "too much a company man"). Voyle also had produced a dozen smashes with the Kingston Trio. He had shaped Al Martino, Mickey Katz, Nelson Riddle, Judy Garland (with a strong assist from Francis Scott), Betty Hutton, and a half-dozen other performers into valuable Capitol attractions.

The transition went smoothly. Capitol's sales for that year moved up to $49,189,000, the second most profitable of the company's 20 years. I went back to my auditioning of imported samples, disturbed with the downward curve of my C.O.W. sales graph. It was obvious that my line of singles and albums desperately needed a jolting, hypoing transfusion.

19

The Beatles must find it extremely difficult to accept the fact that their occupation's gone, that they are no longer the absolute monarchs of pop music, the apple(s) of the world's eye, after a glorious reign of close to ten years. And how much harder it must be when they contemplate those who have deposed them: the Mick Jaggers, Alice Coopers, David Bowies, Lou Reeds, Edgar Winters, and Gary Glitters, a vaudeville troupe of trendy transvetites whose sequined surrealism now holds in thrall the pubescent replacements for those of the previous generation who found their thrill in Beatlemania. . . . The Beatles refreshed us with their irreverent impudence and taught us to take ourselves less seriously, they awakened us to the rich actuality and the potent possibility of American popular music, and they even braced, with their frail Liverpudlian shoulders, the sagging English pound. Their sovereign gave them a medal for that—too little, too late. They had already received—no, *earned*—oceans of love, torrents of publicity, a tidal wave of fame, and floods of loverly money. Are there any artists, high or low, before or since, who so completely captured the attention of the world?[3]

—WILLIAM ANDERSON
Editor, Stereo Review

THERE WERE MAYBE 20 records in the carton, all 45 rpm singles air-expressed to my office from EMI headquarters in London.

Samples arrived almost every day from throughout the world. EMI producers hungered for a release of their work in the largest market on earth. At times my office chairs and cabinets—even the floor—were inundated with records cut in more than 25 languages and dialects.

In this well-remembered box from London, however, I encountered a Parlophone debut disc by a Liverpool-based quartet called the Beatles. The name meant nothing to me, nor did the two songs pressed back to back, *Love Me Do* and *P.S. I Love You*. I auditioned every platter in the carton and heard nothing that might smell hitty for Capitol. The Beatles I remembered for only one reason; I regarded the raspy harmonica by John Lennon as particularly distasteful.

Tony Palmer in England accepted my rejection of the entire batch of samples with his usual equanimity and, months later, succeeded in persuading a small Chicago label, Vee-Jay, to press and distribute the same Beatles coupling I had dismissed.

Vee-Jay did a good job. The record garnered wide national airplay. And, although sales were negligible, Vee-Jay executive Randy Wood ordered a second coupling from England, *Please Please Me* and *Ask Me Why*. Again he sought and obtained strong deejay play.

America still did not buy the record. Wood then waived on his rights to the Beatles. EMI expended additional effort, hoping to push the Liverpool musicians into the American charts as they were succeeding in the United Kingdom. In 1963, a third single (*She Loves You — I'll Get You*) was issued, this time on the independent Swan label of Philadelphia operated by Bernie Bennink and Tony Mamarella.

After three months, the platter had sold about 800 copies, all in Philly.

One shot was enough for Swan. "There was no way we could sell those limey kids," said a disappointed Bennink.

Came September and I touched base in London to meet with a half-dozen EMI personnel as a stopover on a European business trek which would take me as far as Helsinki. Tony Palmer maneuvered me into his new Manchester Square office hours after I arrived from Hollywood.

He started playing samples of British music—mostly dull rock—and suddenly Tony reached into a desk drawer and pulled out a lacquer test disc.

"You remember this group, the Beatles?" he asked.

"Sure. Lousy harmonica."

"Not on these new sides," Palmer responded.

"They've died on two labels back home. Why in hell should they die in my arms a third time?"

"Dexter, be a good chap and listen. Everywhere they play in England they're creating riots. Suddenly they are EMI's biggest sellers. Listen to this sound."

I sat down, smug in knowing how I had passed over the Beatles while two of Capitol's rivals had lost money trying to shove them up on the charts. Tony lowered the cartridge to the lacquer.

"Lou Levy in New York is publishing this song and will spend a lot of money promoting it. We suspect we have a smash," said he.

The music exploded. That's the precise word for it—an explosion like a belching, shrieking volcano.

"That's not the Beatles," I shouted above the din.

"The hell it isn't," young Palmer yelled. "Fantastic, huh?"

The song, of course, was *I Want to Hold Your Hand*. Palmer said there was a catch to Capitol's acquiring rights to it and future masters by the group. Their manager Brian Epstein was insisting on a guarantee that the Beatles would be promoted extensively throughout the 50 states.

"Capitol will take full page ads in the three major trade papers," I assured Tony, "and we will send special pressings and biog sheets to all the important radio stations. We'll go all out."

"Mr. Epstein will be advised of your offer," Palmer said with a certain formality peculiar to the British. When I jetted on to Paris the following day for sessions with Pathé-Marconi personnel I was equally pleased that I had obtained American rights to future records by Frank Ifield, whose yodel treatment of *I Remember You* had made the charts in America a few months previously on a competitive label.

In Hollywood later, I approached my bosses with a report on my trip. Suppose they refused to support my promise of tradepaper ads, an expenditure of at least $2,000? The deejay records posed no problem. We automatically serviced 2,000 stations with every new single release and, in addition, sent along biographies of new artists. Yet I was worried. Was Capitol's management aware that the Beatles had flopped on two labels in America?

Alan W. Livingston was now Capitol's president, having moved up from his v-p slot as chief of the a&b division. Lloyd Dunn headed the international and classical department. Voyle Gilmore quarterbacked a&r activities. I was relieved when all three men approved the promotional allocation I had guaranteed Epstein and EMI. I requested Livingston to send a cable promising our good faith and our eagerness to push the Beatles into North American popularity.

"Write it," he said amiably, "and I'll sign and send it out."

He did, within hours. But I noticed on the carbon that he had changed the spelling of Beatles to Beetles, never having read of the foursome. I assume that EMI and Epstein regarded Livingston's gaffe as a transmission error.

I Want to Hold Your Hand was issued December 26, 1963. I coupled it with *I Saw Her Standing There*. By New Year's day orders had exceeded the million mark and were climbing.

New York columnist and television emcee Ed Sullivan frequently took bows and undeserved credit for "popularizing" the Beatles on his top-rated Sunday night CBS-TV variety show, but Sullivan didn't present them until February, seven weeks after the release of *I Want to Hold Your Hand*. By then they were known even to the Zuni Indians in the northern wilds of New Mexico.

The truth is that Jack Paar ran a film about the Beatles on his NBC *Tonight* show, and the news team of David Brinkley and Chet Huntley televised a lengthy interview with the sizzling Lennon-McCartney-Harrison-Starr foursome, on tape, at a time when Capitol desperately needed network exposure. Sullivan's exposure came much later; he was the first, however, to present the Liverpool youngsters live on American television.

Frank Ifield, incidentally, proved a flat-out stiff on Capitol. The charisma he had on records in England evaporated on the western side of the Atlantic.

I Want to Hold Your Hand after eight weeks stood as the most gigantic hit in all the decades of the record business going back to the days of Edison and Berliner. Capitol was forced to use the pressing plants of rival companies to meet the demand. Men like Elvis Presley, Nat King Cole, Frank Sinatra, and Bing Crosby, titans of the industry through the years, had never won such massive, sudden acceptance. Nor has anyone, or any group, since.

Swan reissued their one record—the flop—and it sold 2,000,000 copies before their rights expired and they were forced to turn it over to Capitol. Vee-Jay not only re-released their four Beatles masters but alertly rushed out to a near-hysterical market eight additional masters which EMI had shipped them earlier in hopes that Randy Wood would market a complete, long-playing album. They sold in the millions, too, until Capitol legally retrieved them all and packaged its own *Early Beatles* album in March, 1965.

The first trip to America gave John, Paul, George, and Ringo thrills they lacked the capacity to imagine.

On the big Boeing jet of Pan Am's flight 101 to New York February 7, Harrison complained of illness. He was sure he had the flu. Oddly, there was another George Harrison on the plane, a cynical newsman representing the Liverpool *Echo* who was outspokenly dubious of the Beatles' musicianship. Cynthia Lennon sat next to her husband quietly. It was the only trip she ever made with the group. Yoko Ono was still in John's future.

Epstein, a slight, well-dressed, untalkative young man who was operating a record shop in Liverpool when he took over the management of the group, stared out the Boeing windows trying to avoid several London enterpreneurs who had craftily booked seats on the flight hoping to talk business with him. He managed to avoid them.

"We were all scared daft," Ringo said to me later. "America has everything, we figure. Why would they want us?"

Capitol's full eastern staff greeted the Beatles at Kennedy International, men and women employees all wearing outlandish black Beatle wigs. More than 10,000 others screamed a delirious welcome. A newsman from the *Post* asked, at a press conference in the airport lounge, when the four young men planned to visit a barber shop.

"We had haircuts yesterday," Lennon yelled above the bedlam.

They checked into the Plaza Hotel, complained about the food there, and watched George dose himself with a weedy "medication" just before they were driven to the Sullivan show. The ratings a few days later indicated Sullivan had scored an all-time high viewer mark—more than 73,000,000 watched the Beatles in their first American appearance.

They drew more than 6,000 howling youngsters that week at two different concert appearances promoted by Sid Bernstein of General Artists Corporation in once-staid Carnegie Hall. "I could have sold 100,000 tickets without running an ad," he sighed. Then they were off to Washington for a concert that jammed 20,000 inside the Coliseum, 16,000 more fans than they had ever played to in England.

Miami was next. No concerts, no work. Lennon and McCartney composed *Can't Buy Me Love* on the flight down. The pilot wore a Beatle wig, courtesy of Capitol. Muhammad Ali—then called Cassius Clay—interrupted a training session to greet the troupe. "You cats are the most beautiful," he yelled, "but I'm the greatest and don't you never forget it."

In my office the next afternoon, Beatles producer George Martin curtly ordered my secretary Ruth Liberman to put through a call to the Deauville Hotel in Miami.

"I'll speak to any of the boys you can reach," said Martin, who served as producer of Beatles music for EMI. "But I prefer to converse with Mr. McCartney."

Paul was there. He and Martin exchanged pleasantries. They set a date to meet in London. Then George handed me the phone.

"Hiya, Paul, how's Florida?" I asked.

McCartney sounded enthusiastic. His Mersey accent was difficult to comprehend. We talked for a moment or so and all I recall him saying was that he and his mates were delighted with the equalization improvements Capitol's engineers had devised for their first record. In running the original Beatles tape through our system as an American master was dubbed, we had extended the high frequencies and added slight reverberation to give the single a "hotter" sound.

The Beatles had noticed the improvement and were pleased.

Now I turned to the first Beatles album.

It took me about four weeks to hook together 10 additional songs, arrange with Marvin Schwartz, Capitol's art director, for front and back cover art work and shove *Meet The Beatles* into production. Before 1964 ended, I had produced three additional packages, *The Beatles' Second Album*, *Something New*, and *Beatles '65* with the valued assistance of Schwartz.

But things were anything but euphoric in the Tower. Gilmore was constantly pressured by Livingston to acquire additional masters by the four Liverpudlians. As my immediate superior, Gilmore then squeezed me, and when I couldn't give him immediate satisfaction he contacted England himself, going over the head of Tony Palmer to George Martin and EMI boss Len Wood. There were times when Gilmore failed to get action, so President Livingston himself stepped in and took over. He even went over the heads of Martin and Wood, in London, to the office of the EMI chairman, Sir Joseph Lockwood. That is the way of a major corporation. Every move is pegged to specific levels. Chaos inevitably results.

EMI's attitude toward Capitol changed alarmingly with the success of the Beatles. No longer was the American tail wagging the British dog.

From Lockwood through Wood down into the street level employee at Manchester Square, an undeniable feeling of pride and superiority swept the EMI organization, at least in its relations with Capitol. Letters and daily cables from London insisted that we release certain non-Beatles British masters, music in which I had no confidence. No man in the world knows precisely what will be successful and what will fail on records, but regardless of the Beatles' incredible international popularity the three EMI labels continued to record and issue scores of singles and albums featuring old lady sopranos, 1927-style boy tenors, pathetically old-fashioned dance bands, and God knows how many schoolboy rock combos for which, in my experience, there simply was minimal demand on this side of the Atlantic.

We hit big on several acts. Peter and Gordon proved popular. The Seekers, a vocal group from Australia, made the charts for a couple of years. I waived on Dave Clark's combo, American Epic obtained release rights, and I looked bad as Clark won national acclaim. I also missed with Billy J. Kramer and Gerry and the Pacemakers, both managed by the dapper little Epstein. But then Epstein and EMI had touted a girl named Cilla Black as the next biggest attraction on the horizon. She sang well, I thought, if not distinctively. Ordinarily, I would have declined her masters. But Epstein and producer George Martin as well as the entire EMI organization hyped Miss Black's magic as they had never dared even with the Beatles. She proved a failure on Capitol and no one cared; no one in the Tower reprimanded me for the losses incurred in issuing her singles and an album. Profits from the Beatles covered the debit.

In August of 1964 I braved the searing heat of the Mojave Desert to drive my daughter Janny, then eleven, to Las Vegas for one of the few concerts on the Beatles' first tour of the west. EMI instructed me to check in at the Sahara Hotel, contact the group's press officer Derek Taylor, and meet with Epstein and the Beatles before show time.

Our faces burned by the desert wind and sun, Janny and I pulled into the Sahara parking lot on the Vegas Strip shortly afternoon. Or we intended to pull in. Every space was taken. Baggage was piled ten feet high at the hotel's entrance. Hundreds of men, women, children, dogs, and cats milled around in the 105-degree heat trying to get inside the hotel's entrance.

I somehow shoved and bulldozed my way to the house phones after parking the family Chevy six blocks down the street and leading my daughter through the milling, sweating masses. "Will you please ring the room of Derek Taylor?" I inquired of the operator.

"Are you kidding?" she shouted. She disconnected me.

No one at the desk could help us make contact with the Beatles and their entourage—the harried men behind the counter couldn't hear anything in the melee. We retreated down the road to the Tropicana. Six hours later we sat in on the noisiest, wildest musical performance I've ever—or will ever—witness.

The hysteria of a Beatles live exhibition is indescribable.

I've never been back to the Sahara. And to this day I've never met Derek Taylor, but I am advised by friends in London that he is alive and well, enjoying his position as European boss of American Warner Brothers Records.

The Beatles' first contract to star in a motion picture gave rights to their soundtrack music to Mike Stewart's United Artists label in the U.S.A. Capitol thus watched a competitor sell more than two million albums when *A Hard Day's Night* was released in 1964, but we issued the songs from the film as singles (*If I Fell, And I Love Her, Can't Buy Me Love, I'll Cry Instead*) and each disc sold between one and two million copies. It was a time in the industry when the *Billboard, Cash Box,* and *Variety* charts showed that six of the top ten best-selling singles were by the Beatles. Nothing like that had occurred before, ever.

With the dominance of the Beatles came a marked change of attitude on the part of Manager Epstein and his foursome. No longer could I work felicitously with Marvin Schwartz in designing front and back album covers, choosing the photographs and annotation we thought best. Nor did the bedeviled Epstein allow me a choice of masters to be programmed into album form. Each single, each album, was made to specifications conceived by the Beatles' organization in London. Artwork was mailed to the Capitol Tower from Manchester Square. So were the back cover editorial notes. None, I think, was an improvement over what we in California had been doing.

Communication between Hollywood and London decayed even more by mid-1965.

As Capitol's president, Livingston had been drawn into the Beatles maelstrom unwillingly. Orthodox corporate procedure relies on strict, unvarying delegation of authority from the president's desk down the line. With all other company artists, Gilmore's a&r staff was assigned total responsibility, from selection of songs to be recorded to choice of arrangers, conductors, size and type of accompaniment, and use of studios on through the sound of the finished tape master.

But standard corporate practice was abandoned with the Beatles. After the first year I found it frustrating to repeatedly fail in trying to project future Beatles product. I wrote, cabled, and occasionally telephoned Tony Palmer in London. Palmer was in the same boat as I; his EMI superiors had rushed into the picture to take over the myriad chores connected with getting Beatles singles and albums into the stores. Gilmore's main contact in London was producer George Martin. When they couldn't solve a problem, Livingston took over—reluctantly—and telephoned EMI's top brass. Thus in what today seems like a setting for a Woody Allen film sequence were three separate, uncoordinated operations being frantically attempted day by day over a 6,000-mile circuit.

When the Beatles started their second motion picture, *Help!,* I telephoned young Palmer in London. Would there soon be a soundtrack album? He didn't know, he said. I eventually reached Martin, who not only produced the Beatles records from the booth but sometimes helped sketch their arrangements and played piano on the background tracks behind vocals. Martin had a fast answer.

"No," he said. "We plan no *Help!* album because the boys won't be featuring sufficient songs to fill an LP. and it's a pity, really. United Artists doesn't have the American rights to the package as they did with *A Hard Day's Night."*

So Capitol owned the rights to nothing.

We could issue the songs, of course, as singles. Yet there's a vast difference in two or three hit singles and an album that exceeds one million in sales. Several million dollars difference.

It took at least two months of writing, cabling, and telephoning to acquire two tape reels of the film's soundtrack scraps in my office. There *must* be a way to put together a full album of entertainment from a full-length movie, I told myself. And so I booked one of the studios in the Tower's basement and, working late at night with one of the industry's best sound engineers, John Kraus, we ran through each reel repeatedly on a big Ampex console.

I took notes, a pencil in one hand and a stopwatch in the other. I still have those notes. They indicate there were 36 segments in all, a majority of them extremely brief musical effects and bridges composed by the movie's musical director, Ken Thorne. Much of the music was distorted electronically.

Nor did I have a synopsis of the picture. Someone in England advised me that the story was pegged around Ringo's attempts to escape a murderous gang of Asiatic thugs, with the pursuit of the nosey drummer and his three pals encompassing scenes in the Bahamas, Austria, and England's Salisbury Plain. A ten-armed "Goddess of Kaili" 40 feet tall figured in the plot.

So be it, whatever it was. Working around the seven original songs by Lennon and McCartney (*Help!, The Night Before, You've Got to Hide Your Love Away, I Need You, Another Girl, Ticket to Ride,* and *You're Gonna Lose That Girl*) by adventurous editing and by employing a number of mechanical tricks, I ended up with enough tracks to fill two 12-inch microgroove sides and justify the album's production as a "complete original soundtrack" package.

There were snippets of music which I forced to repeat, like a motion picture loop. I even obliged to accept a dreadfully tired performance of the overture to the third act of Richard Wagner's *Lohengrin* which musical director Thorne had employed for the scenes shot high in the Austrian alps of Obertauern.

One batch of mishmosh I entitled *The Bitter End.* Another mad, up-tempo passage I called *The Chase.* Two earlier hits, *From Me to You* and *A Hard Day's Night,* I spliced together from horrendously distorted tape fragments that sounded like rehearsal warmups and programmed them between the new tunes under the titles of *From Me to You Fantasy* and *Another Hard Day's Night.* The bombastic Wagner bit I retitled *In the Tyrol.* On all the makeshift selections I was careful to credit Thorne as sole composer.

Capitol, thanks to electronics skullduggery, had 12 tracks for an album.

Livingston listened to the finished product the next morning in his Tower office. He was not enthusiastic.

"Is that," he asked, "all there is?"

But he approved issuing the package nonetheless, well aware of the demand for Beatles product. The last time I looked, sales of the bits-and pieces *Help!* album in the United States alone totaled 1,500,000. Another million undoubtedly were sold in Canada, Mexico, and Central America. So an album that might never have existed was responsible for a gross of more than $5 million. It is still selling today.

Success breeds contempt all too often.

Each Beatle changed markedly. Their once-humble producer, George Martin, adopted a lofty executive attitude and condescended to communicate only with Gilmore or Livingston regarding future plans of the four-man act. EMI adamantly insisted that Capitol release a long list of singers and rock groups in which I had shown no interest but they rejected Capitol's plea that more of our artists be promoted and sold throughout the United Kingdom.

In late summer of 1965 Livingston tried to play pacifier. He notified the Beverly Hills police that he was planning a private party at his residence with the Beatles as his special guests. The men in blue responded by the dozens; invitees had to show identification to a phalanx of cops manning their posts a half-mile from Livingston's house.

The booze flowed, the inane small talk of close to 100 guests gradually increased to a roar, and dozens of nicely dressed, courteous little neighborhood boys and girls assembled at nearby residences politely calling for John, Paul, George and Ringo to step outside for a moment. George couldn't; he was in Kansas visiting a sister. John, Paul, and Ringo wouldn't. I asked Lennon why.

"The bloody little bastards," he answered almost viciously, "try to interfere with us constantly, try to deprive us of our privacy. We've had it with 'em, mate."

Actor Jimmy Stewart, Jack Benny, and God knows what other pop-eyed Hollywood luminaries stood around asking the same questions of the three bored Beatles that had been asked them thousands of times from Liverpool to Manila. Ringo stood in the living room sipping deep red burgundy wine, gamely making the best of the type of occasion each Beatle abhors. McCartney was the most popular, at least that night. The most handsome of the group, who plays his bass guitar left-handed, appeared slightly more civil than Lennon but lacked the sincerity and patience of Starr.

"George is a lucky bloke," said McCartney at one point. "He's off somewhere in the plains of Kansas and nobody knows he's there."

Somewhere in time that night my wife and I found ourselves standing along with a slender young actor whose first television series, *I Spy*, was beginning to bring him prominence. We introduced ourselves to Bill Cosby. He didn't acknowledge the introduction. Trying to make small conversation anyway, I was stopped cold when Cosby gave me a death-ray stare and walked away.

"He's even more egotistical than Lennon," my wife said. But Henry Mancini,

Tony Bennett, and other likable, innately modest guests helped make the Livingston bash a success. Outside, by the big blue swimming pool, Mancini showed me the three autographs he had obtained for his children.

"They'll be peeved," he said, wryly. "Harrison's signature is missing."

The contrast in Mancini and the individual Beatles is striking. Hank came out of the Ohio-Pennsylvania mining country, a poor boy, and toiled many years learning his craft. He survived tiring one-night stands as a pianist in dance bands. He worked at Universal Pictures for years in virtual anonymity, composing and scoring music for which others above him on the corporate ladder received credit. Eventually the *Peter Gunn* television series produced by Blake Edwards introduced his uniquely innovative talents to millions; his hit songs *The Days of Wine and Roses, Moon River,* and *Dear Heart* followed. He is a millionaire today, but he's a gifted, deserving millionaire who remains likable and totally unaffected by riches and renown.

Tony Bennett takes a sketch pad with him everywhere. Like Mancini, his background was less than affluent and he sang in scores of drab cafes and niteries for years before he rang the bell with his Columbia discing of *Because of You.*

"The truth is," he said that night at Livingston's house, "I wasn't a very good singer. I had intonation problems, breathing problems, programming problems. But you've got to stick with it, learn, and try to improve. Eventually it all happened for me."

Tony owned fat portfolios filled with astonishingly clever line drawings of people and places and he added a page or two at the Livingston party for the Beatles. But a few years later his entire collection was stolen from a hotel room. He is an excellent, highly emotional, and intensely dramatic singer and he has remained a warm and admirable human being. But like all of us, he endures vexing frustrations. The deluxe "coffee table" art book he worked at for so long will never be published.

о   о   о

George Harrison flew in from Kansas and the Beatles jammed the Hollywood Bowl the following night. I didn't go. Voyle Gilmore thought he could do a better job supervising the taping of the concert than I and he probably was right.

The Beatles to me had become bores.

Their arrogance was monumental. They enjoyed being rude to those who could get close to them to be insulted. They were all too big for their pants.

Capitol's *Beatles at the Hollywood Bowl* album was never issued. Audience noise, imperfections in the music, and a program that depended too heavily on previously-recorded Beatles material forced Gilmore to write off the venture. "It was," he said, "a waste of Capitol's time and money."

In all, I put together nine albums by the Liverpudlians and at least a dozen singles for the American market before EMI dropped its guillotine on my neck. Gilmore called me into his office, cleared his throat a couple of times, and, with difficulty, advised that I was being transferred to a position at Capitol that "urgently requires all your valued experience with songs and artists." The job carried no title, I was pleased to learn. It involved my working with old, deleted records that would be reactivated either by Capitol or its sister label, Pickwick of Long Island. W. H. (Bill) Miller would assume my job as director of international a&r.

"Why?" I asked Gilmore.

"You got a bit strong, a little snippy, in a letter to one of the EMI bosses," he answered. "They ordered a change."

"I wasn't strong enough," I said. "The British bosses think we should release all their stale artists over here but they press up only a few of our Nat Cole, Beach Boys, Peggy Lee, and many other strong artists' things. They demand a one-way street, a one-sided coin."

"They own Capitol," retorted Gilmore.

I couldn't argue that point. But I was taking the lashes for what I still regard as an unfair reason—battling for my company. Gilmore or President Livingston or Chairman Wallichs should have defended my loyalty to Capitol, my attitude, and my job. They did not.

The sun came up the next day as usual. I plunged into my new work, armed with a stack of old catalogs. But I kept a close eye—and both ears—on the Beatles.

The death of their manager, Brian Epstein, in August of 1967 was not only a near-staggering shock to John, Paul, George, and Ringo. It abruptly changed the course of their careers—their lives. Only 32, wealthy and popular, the gentlemanly, impeccably-tailored little manager had indeed provided the brains for the Beatles. But working for them as the fifth Beatle took a fearful toll. He became addicted to sleeping pills and antidepressants and, at the time his body was found in his bed at his residence (Kinsley Hill) in Sussex, police reported they had found 17 bottles of various kinds of tablets, two of them in his briefcase, eight in the bathroom and seven in his bedroom.

A coroner's jury decided Epstein's death was accidental.

The Beatles began to die the day their personable manager was eulogized at a service held at the New London synagogue on Abbey Road in St. John's Wood. For now they were on their own, just as they had been years ago in Liverpool.

The decline was, at first, imperceptible. They produced several more top-selling albums and singles but it became more and more difficult for them to find time to create and rehearse new material. All four deplored the discomforts of touring. John and Cynthia separated; Lennon then met and married Yoko. His differences with McCartney expanded into a bitter estrangement, the core of their conflict centering around the question of who should manage them and their Apple firm in London and New York.

All four men continued to make records individually, as they are doing in 1975, under auspices of the Apple label. Lennon repeatedly recorded with Yoko although she is painfully inept as a performer. McCartney and his wife,

Linda, an American, formed Wings, and while Linda on their discs plainly is no Ella Fitzgerald, she sings better than Mrs. Lennon. Harrison also has made New York his home base, and records regularly, but has lost his wife Patti to British rock guitarist Eric Clapton at this writing. Starr has fared well and enjoyed more publicity than his three colleagues by appearing in motion pictures in straight dramatic roles and pounding out an occasional LP. He now has three children but has long been separated from his wife Maureen.

Capitol has promoted and sold the entire Apple line of albums and they've all proved exceptionally profitable even though the dream is over. At least a quarter of Capitol's album sales today are of individual ex-Beatle product.

But it's not the same. Nor can it ever be again.

A formal dissolution of the four-way partnership was effected in January, 1975, by a British court.

Lennon battles to remain in the United States, to avoid deportation stemming from an old marijuana-possession charge. He and Yoko struggle, between separations, to retain their marriage. He no longer is a leader, an innovator, in the world of pop music.

McCartney, now 33 and a year younger than Lennon, resides with Linda and their three children on an estate in Scotland and appears to be the most content of the four one-time rock idols.

Harrison, also 33, remains a devotee of Eastern religion and music and insists on co-featuring the Indian sitarist Ravi Shankar on virtually every Harrison engagement. George has formed his own record company (Dark Horse) but depresses even his most loyal fans with his melancholy attitude. He is far from happy.

Starr wanders about from coast to coast, stopping off frequently in Nashville, seeking to find tranquility at 35.

Along the way from Liverpool over the 1963–75 period, all four Beatles rashly told their fans to go to hell and leave them alone. Many of those fans have. But it is the wildest, most incredible music story of all time and I'm at least mildly flattered that I played a minuscule part in it.

I'm even more pleased that it's all behind me.

20

I love music passionately.
And because I love it I try to free it
from barren traditions that stifle it.
It is a free art gushing forth,
an open-air art boundless as the elements,
the wind, the sky, the sea.
It must never be shut out and
become an academic art.

—CLAUDE DEBUSSY

ERNEST HEMINGWAY ONCE wrote of his friend Marlene Dietrich: "If she had nothing more than her voice she could break your heart with it. But she has that beautiful body and that timeless loveliness of her face. It makes no difference how she breaks your heart if she is there to mend it."

I listened to Frau Dietrich's sexy voice one afternoon. She telephoned me from nearby Universal studios, where she was making a motion picture. Her call came a week or so after Capitol had issued a Dietrich album which I had acquired in Germany, one in which she sang a dozen songs in German and which I had titled *Wiedersehen Mit Marlene.*

"Mister Dexter," she said, her voice, a dark blue silky sound, "I read that my album is on sale. Send me one hundred copies. I'll need them tomorrow."

She thanked me and that was it. All record companies expect to be tapped for gratis albums by artists, but 100 freebies? I hesitated briefly, then filled out a merchandise requisition and sent it out for processing.

Next day, on the phone, Dietrich again:

"Where are my albums? I told you I needed them this afternoon."

"They're on the way, Miss Dietrich. It takes time. They must be shipped from our warehouse in downtown Los Angeles."

"Very well, but this is important to me." She hung up.

A week elapsed. Again it was the glamorous grandma on the horn.

"Mister Dexter, I need albums. About one hundred will do."

"I can't believe," I responded, "that you haven't yet received the albums I ordered. I'll check on them immediately and I apologize for the delay."

But I had underestimated the lady by plenty.

"Oh, I received the first one hundred copies," she purred. "Now I need another one hundred copies. You see, I have lots of friends."

I stammered a promise that I'd see what I could do. What I did was rush into my boss Livingston's office and explain the situation.

"Well," he said after listening to my problem. "She's not under contract to Capitol and we can't deduct the albums' cost from her royalties. We can't very well charge it to our German affiliate label in Cologne. And we can't drive out to Universal together and demand cash payment. I guess we shouldn't risk offending her, Dex. I'll fill out a requisition and send her the albums under my name."

A month or more went by. Then a call came in from her press agent in Beverly Hills. He wanted "a hundred or so" Dietrich albums to be sent to Marlene in New York.

"We've already sent her about a thousand bucks worth of records for free," I protested. "How long does this gimme act go on?"

"I'll remind you, Mr. Dexter, that we are dealing with Marlene Dietrich, not just a mere singer. She is unique."

"That's for sure," I replied. "I'll call you back."

Again I went to the busy Livingston. He was having a difficult day. I explained the situation. He became testy.

"That's your responsibility," he snapped at me. "Dietrich is your artist, you produced the album and it's your problem to solve."

I strode back to my office, telephoned the Dietrich flack and made a suggestion: his client could damn well buy additional albums in various record shops in New York.

And now it is clear as the years go by that I blew my relationship with The Dazzling Marlene. She never called me again.

o   o   o

A man walked into my office one morning, politely asked if I could spare a few minutes to talk, and introduced himself as John M. Dalton of Missouri.

I gab with everyone. I answer every telephone call. Sometimes I get stuck with an amateur songwriter, or an aspiring singer, or an insurance salesman, but usually my running an open house introduces me to many interesting men and women. And how could I deny a fellow Missourian?

Dalton turned out to be one of my more distinguished visitors. He was the governor of Missouri, elected in 1960 after eight years as the state's attorney general.

He was 16 years older than I, and highly knowledgeable on the subject of music. He said he had a "right nice" record collection back in Jefferson City. His big interest, he said, was sponsoring the Missouri Council On the Arts, and working with the Mizzou' legislature to give the Council recognition. We talked music for 45 minutes.

Later I was advised that the legislature failed to recognize the Missouri Council, but in 1965, after Warren E. Hearnes succeeded Dalton in the gubernatorial chair, the legislature did rally to the Council and approved a bill allocating the funds Dalton had sought so tirelessly.

Bandleader Billy May saw my guest leave my office and asked who the man was. I told him.

"I'd like to hear more about your chat with the governor," said May, "but I haven't the time right now. President Kennedy is double-parked outside waiting to take me to lunch."

                                ◦   ◦   ◦

Even the neighbors are a little funny in California. One of mine, a personable 24-year-old leader of a rock combo named Kim Richard, cooked up a Mother's Day surprise for his mother-in-law. She was the actress Barbara Bates. Kim composed a special song in her honor, hid his band in Barbara's garage, and struck up the music when she motored into the driveway. The reception was so startling that she gunned the engine, drove into the garage, knocked Kim down, and fractured his leg.

                                ◦   ◦   ◦

Dean Martin was never in my stable of artists. During his many years with Capitol, he reported to producer Lee Gillette. Twice, however, my artists were teamed with the Ohio baritone in loose, informal sessions in a party-like atmosphere. Helen O'Connell waxed *We Never Talk Much* and *How Do You Like Your Eggs in the Morning* with the skinny Dino in 1951, and the hardest part of putting the session together was finding a place suitable for Martin to choose the songs and plan the arrangements.

Martin will not step into an elevator. He has a terror of heights. He feels secure only at ground floor level.

So Helen, Lee, and I met with him at Paramount Studios. He was becoming a big man on the lot with his newly-bobbed nose and because of his sock box-office appeal teamed with Jerry Lewis. Dean weighed 40 or 50 pounds less than he does today but didn't croon any better than he does now. He's a personality, not a singer.

I anticipated working with a hard-drinking, profane man who considered himself vocally superior to Sinatra. I found a dead-sober, gentlemanly, genuinely funny guy who gladly accepted whatever suggestions Helen and I made. Martin is well aware that he's not one of the truly talented singers of our time.

Our session went well. The records were light, humorous, and musical, thanks to the emotional chemistry between Helen and Dean. But neither side made the charts.

Four years later we tried the duet coupling again, this time with the French radio and television star Line Renaud. She was big all over Europe. For a time she outsold Piaf. Her English was of course imperfect. Once again the studio ambience was ideal, and a non-drinking Martin quickly made La Belle Renaud, a blonde looker, feel at ease with his breezy and cooperative attitude. Listening to playbacks, Martin edged up to me early in the session and asked *sotto voce*, "what the hell is this chick singing—I can't understand her."

The titles we made included the standard *Two Sleepy People* and a French novelty, *Relax Ay Voo*. It was an unusually happy, no-problem session, but long after Gillette and I sent the musicians home, while we were supervising tape splices in the booth with engineer John Kraus, Martin walked in, lit a cigarette and sat down in a foldaway chair.

"It was a marvelous date," he said. "But I still don't dig a word your French chantootsie sang."

The record, a 45 rpm single, sold well in France.

The reputation that Martin has of being an insatiable alcoholic is as absurd as Jack Benny's parsimony or Cab Calloway's addiction to narcotics. Dean drinks, but moderately. Golf is his passion and the game keeps him in excellent physical condition. He will never die of cirrhosis of the liver.

∘   ∘   ∘

Jerry Lewis was signed by Capitol at the same time as Martin, in 1948. They had impressed Jim Conkling with their zany act at Slapsy Maxie's nitery in Los Angeles. In those days Dino served as a straight man to the unpredictable, explosive Lewis. Jerry would unerringly milk the audience for bonus laughs by interrupting one of Dean's infrequent songs.

Voyle Gilmore produced many of Lewis' sessions, and I sat in on several. Unlike Martin, Jerry would enter the studio noisily, cavort with the assembled musicians and stall around while he learned the songs to be recorded. Gilmore fidgeted in the booth, eyeing the union clock, as Jerry bounced around the studio, took pratfalls, and did his moron act. With Lewis every session went into overtime.

Jerry isn't quite like your nextdoor neighbor, or mine.

He paid $17,000 to have a hearing aid made for his aging dog.

When his 65-foot, $350,000 luxury yacht sank off the California coast, he purchased a 70-foot replacement craft for $450,000 a week later. He designed and built his own radio station, KVFM, at his home, so he could broadcast his favorite records. He takes at least three showers every day. His earnings exceed $3 million annually.

Jerry's friends—his real friends—long ago learned to never compliment him on his clothing. He accepts compliments like no other man, removing the tie you like, or the jacket, or even his shoes, and handing them to you with his compliments.

He's lost his pants doing that.

Jerry made many discs for Capitol. None made the charts. After he left Capitol he insisted on singing straight, at Decca, blind to the blunt truth that he could in no way compete with the Sinatras, Comos, and Bennetts of the 1950–60 period. He sounded like a bad Jolson.

So he stopped making records.

Not so his oldest son, Gary. While his dad was failing on discs, Gary Lewis formed a rock group and sold nearly 2,000,000 singles his first time out. For a year or more Gary was a national hero among teenagers.

One finds irony in the darndest people within our industry.

o   o   o

Dwayne Hickman was the star of the *Dobie Gillis* television show, a consistent Top Ten occupant in the Nielsen ratings. He *was* Dobie Gillis, a teenager with short hair, peg pants, and white buckskin shoes around whom the series revolved. I wondered if he could sing, and I called him.

Hickman expressed interest. "I'm no Frankie Avalon," he confessed, "but I think I'm better than Fabian."

Avalon and Fabian were selling tons of records at the time. I hustled over to Columbia Pictures and after sitting around an hour or more watching a crew shoot three minutes of film, Dwayne—nearly 30 years old and an actor since he was a baby—sat on a prop with me and we plotted his future as a recording artist. I reckoned that his appeal was to youth, and I promised him a contemporary, rock-styled accompanying orchestra. I did not tell him that I had never produced a record like that; my preferences ran to big, swinging orchestras and small jazz combos.

I didn't care to use the same old bored and jaded Hollywood studio musicians who work two and three sessions a day and earn $100,000 a year. I wanted enthusiastic, unspoiled sidemen, and an arranger who could conceive truly innovative sounds in a rock groove behind Hickman's singing.

Dwayne was amenable to recording the songs I gathered from publishers. He seemed confident. We met with a kid arranger who was new in town and dying for a chance with a major label. He noted the musical keys Hickman preferred and a week later came to the Tower's big Studio A loaded with charts.

The musicians were in awe of Hickman. Thirty million viewers followed his every move each week on the tube. Hesitantly, my fledgling arranger-conductor passed out the parts as Dwayne entered the isolated vocalist's booth. I started the union clock and the two tape recorders. We were ready to create a new national singing idol.

What happened next is almost indescribable—I'll simply say it was the most embarrassing incident in all my years in music. The "rock band" on the first down beat instantly became a cacophonous, dissonant, inept group of puzzled, flustered musicians. None of the written notes made sense. My fresh, young, unspoiled arranging find was so fresh, young and unspoiled that he hadn't yet learned to conceive a playable chart.

Hickman, incensed, looked around the studio wildly, shocked by the barnyard babel of sounds. And then, into an open microphone, the idol of teenaged America angrily yelled at me:

"Shit man, I can't hear no friggin' melody."

I charged out of the producer's booth into the studio and rushed the terrified, humiliated kid who had passed himself off as a brilliant new talent who needed

190

only a break. "I guess I should have told you," he sobbed, "I'm just a student. I thought I could handle a session. Now I know I'm not quite ready."

As the musicians, silent, packed their horns, I looked around for Dwayne. He was gone. He wanted no more of me. I could hardly fault him. It was the major *faux pas* of my life. Eventually, I learned that my colleague from our country music department, Ken Nelson, was a devoted Dobie Gillis fan. He agreed to produce Hickman's records. Nelson assembled a first-rate orchestra, worked harmoniously with a placated Hickman, and smoothly achieved everything on several sessions that I had hoped for.

I didn't feel any better, later, when it became obvious that Hickman had no appeal on records. But the likable Hickman was right about one thing; he *did* sing better than Fabian.

Nelson dropped him, of course, but I'm the first to admit that I still owe him considerably more than an apology.

o   o   o

My favorite guitarist in the pop field—and that excludes Andres Segovia, John Williams, Julian Bream, and Chris Parkening—has long been a reserved, modest Burbank musician named George Van Eps.

Nothing ever perturbs him. He's as level, as steady, as a well-wound metronome. He plays an odd seven-string Spanish guitar which he devised himself; even the majority of today's youthful rock guitarists idolize his effortless artistry.

I recorded three albums by Van Eps in the sixties, each an extraordinary package artistically. While we were making the third we were unaware that a freak electrical storm was passing over Hollywood. I sat in the booth entranced with his soft, delicately-phrased pickings. He was alone in the big studio. I had the lights dimmed to enhance the musical mood. It was, in contrast to most sessions, an idyllic setting of serenity.

George was just entering the bridge of *Lover Man* when a bright flash exploded at his microphone. I heard an explosive sound. George leaped up from his stool, threw his arms wide apart, juggled his guitar in the air and let out a shout: "What the hell was that?"

Lightning had struck the top of the Capitol Tower and somehow penetrated the structure, affecting the building's electrical system. Van Eps gulped two cups of coffee, then completed the session.

Just another hazard of the profession.

o   o   o

Tom Rockwell moved up from producing distinguished jazz on the old Okeh label in the 1930s to become one of the giants of the booking world. He headed General Artists Corporation, and on one of his trips west from Radio City he sat in on a Benny Carter session I was producing. He recalled an incident with Louis Armstrong, who in his salad days deceitfully recorded under a pseudonym for companies to which he was not under contract.

"I called him one day and asked him to listen to a trumpet player on Victor, a musician I didn't know, who played sensationally well, very much like Armstrong," Rockwell chuckled. "Louie listened to the entire side and I then asked him if he knew who the soloist was.

" 'No, Mister Rockwell, I got no idea who that cat blowin' so beautiful is, but I ain't never gonna do it no more.' "

The genial Rockwell, seated beside me in the booth, laughed so hard he drowned out Carter's sterling saxophone in the studio. Next day, he returned to New York, became ill, and died.

o   o   o

I needed at least one good track by Armstrong to round out a series of albums I was producing which would feature virtually all the big names of jazz from the Original Dixieland Band of 1919 to the most avant-garde contemporary music. The series embraced 60 performances in five LPs. I titled it *The Jazz Story*.

Louis' manager, Joe Glaser, was not encouraging when I telephoned him in New York. I asked if Armstrong might record one or two songs during his engagement in Las Vegas.

"What will you pay him for one tune?" Glaser asked.

"Oh, maybe $1,000," I answered, hoping my bosses would approve it.

"Dave," said Glaser, "Louis and I have been partners for 35 years. He became a millionaire many years ago and so did I. To tell you the truth, I wouldn't call and get him out of bed for a thousand bucks."

Glaser cooled me good. But I dug around and obtained, from EMI in London, two adequate Armstrong masters for my project without spending a dollar. Yet I don't feel like gloating. When Armstrong died in July, 1971, I recalled along with thousands of others the immensity of his contributions to America and the world. I deeply regret never having recorded his horn and his red beans and rice vocals.

Glaser was right. Louis deserved more than $1,000 an hour.

o   o   o

Sometimes, on sessions, the studio clouds up with smoke from the hard-working musicians and singers as they woodshed their parts, intent on getting the masters made perfectly within the three-hour time limit imposed by the musician's union.

And sometimes—not on every session, but sometimes—that smoke is pure pot and everyone gets a little silly. Marijuana is not the brain-shriveling narcotic we once thought it was. No one gets crazed from it; its effect, as I have noted in being around grass-users for 40 years now, is more like a mild alcoholic high. In the 1930s we called it gage, muggles, weed, or tea, and sometimes maryjane.

I've had more trouble with musicians who took too many pulls from a bottle than I've had with those who spend their fives (the rest periods a producer must give all musicians once an hour while recording) out in the hall or in the men's room sneaking a toke. A drunk is more obnoxious than a pot-happy musician, but the smoker is just as dangerous driving a car or feeding an infant as an alcoholic. Numerous musicians have testified that they perform better when they are not under the influence of liquor or marijuana.

I wouldn't know for sure. I've always felt that it was difficult enough navigating my way through life's daily pitfalls with a clear mind. Resorting to narcotics might make it all the more difficult in a difficult world. I need what few faculties I have, unimpaired by phony stimulants. That's a simple personal belief. Others are entitled to their own.

The old radio comedian and one-time studio trombonist Jerry Colonna topped all the pot smokers and drunks on a Johnny Mercer-Wingy Manone session one night at Capitol years ago. Colonna rode a big gray horse into the studio and refused to dismount until the animal relieved himself among Paul Weston's musicians.

The mess was worse than anything, booze or pot.

"This is the first record I ever made," said Manone to Mercer, "that I know won't sell. It stinks."

21

I heard somebody
one time say that all black
people got rhythm. Bullshit.
Ain't no such thing as that.
You cannot generalize
with people

—RAY CHARLES

THE MOST GIFTED musician I ever recorded was a woman. She played no instrument. Ella Fitzgerald has been singing professionally for 40 years. Like most of the great ones, she started as a dance band vocalist. Chick Webb hired her in the mid-Thirties after she appeared in an amateur contest before an all-black audience in a theater in Harlem.

"I remember it well," Ella recalls. "The song I did was *The Object Of My Affection* and when I sang the line about changing my complexion from 'white to rosy red' the audience freaked out laughing."

She was a frightened teenaged child when Webb, one of the best jazz drummers ever, heard her and put her in front of his hard-swinging orchestra at the Savoy Ballroom. Before he died in 1939 he had become her legal guardian. "He was," Ella says now, "the best friend I ever had."

They had one astonishingly big hit together, *A-Tisket, A-Tasket*, before Webb died of tuberculosis. Ella tried to keep the band together after his death, but after three years it disintegrated and she found herself on her own, at 22.

The Fitzgerald story is unique within show business. She is a truly religious woman, yet she makes no spectacle of her beliefs in public. She doesn't use alcohol in any form. She doesn't smoke. There has never been a hint of scandal in her remarkable career. She is twice-divorced. Her second husband was the bassist Ray Brown. Ella has custody of their son, well-mannered, handsome Raymond Brown, Jr. The last time I was a guest in the luxurious Fitzgerald home in Beverly Hills, young Ray was a student at San Diego State College.

Ella was just about his age when I first met her at Kansas City's Fairyland Park on one of a long and tiring series of one-night stands the Webb orchestra undertook in the summer of 1937. I had most of her blue label Deccas, of course, and even then regarded her as nearly the equal of Billie Holiday and Mildred Bailey. To the white audience she still was unknown—the Webb-Fitzgerald *A-Tisket, A-Tasket* was yet a year into the future. But to many blacks she was a famous name even without a hit disc. I found her backstage on a warm night, a chubby, shy, young woman who provided little conversation as she mopped perspiration from her face and arms. Only by gabbing with Webb was I able to come up with enough copy to turn in an unspectacular little feature for the *Journal-Post*.

Through the decades Ella gained prominence. Norman Granz became her manager and moved her from obscure nightclubs, patronized by blacks in the main, to the opulent, high-paying dinner clubs of the nation's finest hotels. Granz also booked her throughout Europe and the Orient, and via his Verve label improved the Fitzgerald popularity on records. By the sixties she was commanding $10,000 for a guest stint on national television programs.

Granz telephoned me one day in 1966 asking if I might be interested in making a record deal. He had sold his Verve masters to M-G-M and Ella was free to record.

"You are an aggressive, strongly opinionated man," I half-kidded Granz. "If I persuade the Capitol bosses to sign her I would want full and complete control of the songs she does, the accompaniment, the studio sound—the works."

"Of course," said Granz. "You will have all that."

"What kind of front money do you expect?" I inquired.

"Ella works for the usual five percent royalty and an advance against that royalty of $25,000 an album," Granz replied.

I hesitated. "Hell, that's more than Nat Cole gets. Ella doesn't sell that many records, Norman. I don't think my bosses will okay it."

"Try 'em," he said.

I went into the regular Thursday meeting with conflicting emotions. After setting the monthly release and discussing options concerning various artists, the other producers and Voyle Gilmore gave me the floor.

"I'm hot to sign her," I told them, "but the guarantee is out of line. Fitzgerald never has and probably never will top the charts. She's on the road almost constantly and that makes it all the more difficult to select songs—we will have to depend on old standards."

"Dex," said Gilmore, "Ella ought to be profitable for Capitol from her sales outside the USA alone. She's big, maybe the biggest, in Berlin, London, Stockholm, Tokyo and Buenos Aires."

"She's big, but I don't think she sells that many records," I argued.

"Well," said Gilmore, "let's jump off the high springboard and see. Sign her for two years with options."

Everyone in the room except Dubious Dexter slapped backs, lit cigarettes, and expressed enthusiasm. But I was pleased nonetheless. Working with the greatest living femme pop singer was a formidable challenge to contemplate.

First, after contracts are signed, must come the concept. Ella had recorded a thousand or more pop tunes and almost all of them featured big dance band accompaniment. True to his promise, Granz flew to his residence in Switzerland and allowed Ella and me to plan her first album without interference.

We decided on a religious theme. Tennessee Ernie Ford had sold several million packages of simple hymns for Capitol and Mahalia Jackson was a consistent winner for Columbia. Ella threw her house open to me and to Ralph Carmichael, the versatile arranger and conductor, who was—and is now—the most prominent man in the industry with church records. He showed Ella hundreds of songs, most of them in the public domain. Slowly, she looked at them, occasionally setting one aside. She appeared diffident and uninterested, but after a couple of hours she walked to the grand piano in her beautiful living room and began finding her singing key for the titles she preferred.

Discarding the company cost control manual, I hired an immense orchestra and a choir to back the First Lady's debut on Capitol. Ella drove up to the Tower parking lot in her chauffered Mercedes-Benz a full half-hour before union time started. She knew every song letter-perfect. But she showed no enthusiasm as the first of her three session began. Carmichael and I got a cool "hello" as Ella walked into Studio A.

Somewhere along about the second track—I think it might have been her superb version of *Just a Closer Walk with Thee*—Ella abruptly became intensely emotional after listening to a tape playback. She suddenly reached out, kissed Carmichael, then turned and hugged me. Now she was animated, all smiles. And she remained jubilant through the session.

It was a puzzling change in attitude on her part, but a man in the booth must accept the eccentricities of performers and so I thought no more about her cold-to-warm approach. The album was an unqualified artistic triumph, and marked a revolutionary change of direction for the incomparable Fitzgerald voice, but it did not sell well. Of the four Fitzgerald LPs made by Ella for Capitol her *Brighten the Corner* religious package is the only one remaining active in the catalog.

I arranged with Ken Veeder, the director of Capitol's photography studios, for Ella to sit not only for black and white publicity and advertising pictures but classy color portraits as well. And just to show my esteem for her I took a dozen extremely rare and long-unavailable old Chick Webb shellac Deccas with early Fitzgerald vocals from my library, enclosed them in an attractive special album along with a laudatory note, and presented them to her on her first photo session. She looked at the records and set them aside.

"Uh, huh," she said.

A few weeks later I conned Veeder into making up an oversized $100 color print off one of Ella's color negs and drove out to her house to deliver it. A housemaid opened the door. I asked if I might see Ella for a moment. She turned and yelled to someone that "a man named Dexter wants to see you for a minute—can you come to the door?"

"Not today," Ella—or someone—hollered from inside. I then asked the maid to deliver the color portrait to Ella with my fond compliments. I assume she did, but I'll never be sure. Ella never acknowledged the gift. She also is the only artist I ever worked with who failed to send a card at Christmas.

I suppose we all have our idiosyncrasies. I learned first-hand that Ella has hers.

Ella returned home from another road trip several months later and we once again met at her residence. This time we agreed on a Christmas album. She had cut one previously for Verve, a collection of pop tunes. The new ones would be strictly traditional. Again Carmichael showed her a stack of songs. Ella chose things like *Away In a Manger, It Came Upon a Midnight Clear, Joy to the World, The First Nöel,* and nine others. And again she said little, appearing almost displeased with our pre-session planning conclave. Yet on the sessions a few nights later she sang particularly well, again backed by Carmichael's large orchestra and choir. And again, after an hour or so of recording, the warm Fitzgerald smile suddenly appeared and she became effusive in her enthusiasm.

Just as happened on her first album sessions, members of the orchestra and Carmichael chorus impetuously applauded Ella's astounding talent as each playback ended. All the shyness and inborn modesty that I had encountered in Ella far back in 1937 again became apparent; she has never forgotten her dismal days in an orphanage before she sucked in her gut and entered the amateur contest that led to her Webb-sponsored start in show business.

Ella Fitzgerald's Christmas didn't sell profitably, either. Yet it stands as possibly the greatest pop production ever recorded on the holiday theme.

We had now paid $50,000 to the First Lady and spent $30,000 additionally for musicians, choir singers, arrangements, and copying for two commercially unsuccessful albums by Ella. Yet, I wondered as I awaited a caution from my bosses, just what is success in music? The Fitzgerald sound is pure platinum. She hears even the slightest off-pitch sound instantly; no other singer alive has a better ear. She works easily, with enviable professionalism, and her skill eliminates the expensive, tiring overtime sessions which so many singers rely on to complete a project. Her artistry is timeless. Her masters will sound magnificent in the year 2021.

But success is never measured in terms of artistic achievement. Not in today's record business. We were $80,000 in the red with Ella and I began to feel the pressure as I plotted her third album.

She had never sung country music. Few blacks had. But I thought of the blind Ray Charles and the surprising sales he enjoyed with an album of purely Nashville tunes. My old friend from New York, Sid Feller, had adeptly arranged and conducted much of the Charles program and then moved to California. I called him. He was ecstatic at the prospect of working with Ella. Once again, I set up a pre-recording meeting at the Fitzgerald manse.

And once again, Ella listened to Feller and me suspiciously. She shuffled through 30 or more outstanding country songs morosely, but late in the afternoon accepted a dozen and Feller noted her singing keys for each, just as Carmichael had done previously.

The sessions were much like the others. Fitzgerald's inexplicable Jekyll and Hyde behavior was just as before. She knew the songs cold. She sang gloriously.

Feller ran the sessions with authority. After halfway through, as before, the First Lady suddenly displayed an enthusiasm and the frigidity of the big studio melted. No one on planet earth has a more gorgeous smile—or laugh—than Ella.

We called the album *Misty Blue*. It was every bit as musical and as commercial as the Charles LP but sales, again, were disappointing. A year and a half had passed and I was reminded by a hawk-eyed accountant in the Silo that the computerized Fitzgerald tab reflected a serious debit in excess of $100,000.

Now I was down on my own three-yard line on fourth down and time running out. I had no criticism of "Sis," as many of the black musicians called Ella. She had done everything I asked, going along in an attempt to widen her repertoire and broaden her appeal, singing with orchestral and choral accompaniments she had never used before, reporting to each session well before the union clock started, knowing her material intimately, acceding to my frequent requests from the booth for "just one more take" before we moved on to the next song.

But I wasn't pleased with her manager's efforts. Granz, from his base in Switzerland, seemed to me to be in poor position to book Ella on the important television shows that offer invaluable exposure to records. Only rarely did she work the tube, and not once in her Capitol affiliation did she sing one of her album songs in view of millions of television auditors. The Lawrence Welk network hour was just one example. Through Welk's exec producer, Sam Lutz, one of my longtime Encino neighbors, I arranged for Ella to plug two of her album songs and contacted Granz to approve her guest appearance.

"Welk's the lowest pay in the industry," Granz snorted. "I wouldn't book Fitzgerald's ex-husband for that money."

True. Welk was in no position to pay the fat fees Granz sought—and Ella deserved—but his audience was precisely the people who go out and buy the religious, or country, or Christmas songs they see performed on his show. A Welk guest shot was good for 10,000 albums being sold, as Columbia's Anita Bryant had proved.

Capitol's promotion of Fitzgerald merits no praise, either. Rocco Catena's department was deeply involved in exploiting various rock groups in an all-out, pathetically desperate attempt to fill the void of the disbanding Beatles. Fitzgerald meant nothing to them.

I called Ella one afternoon.

"Maybe I've been wrong," I said. "We haven't made it with come-to-church music, or Christmas songs, and it doesn't look as if our Nashville package will ever move."

"What do we try next?" asked Ella.

"Well now," I answered. "Let's make what you do best. To hell with trying to sell to a broad new market. The radio stations are all Top 40 and they won't play anything but rock anyway. Let's go back to jazz."

"You sure that's best?"

"No, I'm not sure," I answered. "But maybe that's what the world expects of Ella Fitzgerald. I'll be out Wednesday afternoon. 'Bye."

It was do or die. I drove the freeways like a zombie, probing every possible path to take with her. And somewhere between the Woodman and Haskell off-ramps on the crowded Ventura pavement I conceived an album of medleys—great old songs strung together—with Ella to be backed by a small, handpicked combo of internationally renowned jazzmen who would improvise as we segued from one tune to another.

Benny Carter was my man. And Ella.'s. He dug the idea. I sounded out three or four major publishers in order to get "rates" on each song used. A two-cent mechanical usage fee for each song is payable on every record sold and if we were to record 30 or 40 songs the cost would be prohibitive. With the help of Eddie MacHarg and Hy Kanter, the prestigious catalog of Robbins-Feist-Miller ("The Big Three") was quickly made available for our unique experiment, at a fee which even Capitol's nervous accountants would accept.

Recording medleys of songs wasn't new. The dance orchestras of Guy Lombardo, Freddy Martin, Russ Morgan, and others had done it several times on long-playing records. But no singer had ever attempted it. Ella would be first.

We met at her place again, and she quietly thumbed through scores of memory-provoking standards, some of which she had recorded for Decca two and three decades previously. Now I was accustomed to her apathy, but still puzzled. Carter is as well liked in the music world as any man who ever lived. He is an alto sax virtuoso, a brilliant arranger, a first rate conductor, and invariably amiable, cooperative, and eager to please both artist and producer. But the First Lady was no more pleasant to him than she had been to Carmichael and Feller. Finally we left. Ella had reluctantly okayed 30 songs, to be broken up by me into six tracks featuring five vocals in each segment.

Benny and I collaborated in choosing the musicians. We brought in Harry (Sweets) Edison, the ex-Count Basie trumpet; Georgie Auld, of Benny Goodman and Bunny Berigan fame, tenor sax; Jimmy Jones, piano and celeste; John Collins, once of the King Cole Trio, guitar; Panama Francis and Louie Bellson, alternating as drummers; and a promising youngster playing Fender bass, Bob West: an eminently compatible group.

Ella arrived in her Mercedes-Benz as always, 40 minutes ahead of time. She adjusted her big horn-rimmed glasses and took her place in the booth silently, just as if she were walking to a guillotine. For an hour and ten minutes we battled to get an acceptable stereo balance, engineer Rex Updegraft handling the big console and Gene Hicks operating the complicated Ampex stereo tape recorders.

And then it all began to jell. *No Regrets, I've Got a Feeling You're Fooling, Don't Blame Me* (soloed by Auld and Collins to give Ella a moment's rest), *Deep Purple, Rain,* and *You're a Sweetheart.* We had one of six difficult medleys canned.

"Hey there Jimmy," Ella yelled as she bounced out of the isolation cell, "that modulation after *Rain* is real, real nice." She was beaming. "I'm beginning to dig this medley idea," she shouted to me in the booth.

Each medley came easier as Carter sketched rough, pencilled charts. Kay

Kyser's fine old theme *Thinking of You, On Green Dolphin Street, Taking a Chance on Love, I Cried For You, Once In a While, I Got It Bad, My Mother's Eyes, Maybe, Elmer's Tune, Just Friends* . . . Ella sang them all, each a sparkling gem. It required three three-hour sessions to complete the album. In the booth, transfixed by the matchless Fitzgerald artistry, I made not a single tape splice. And at last, as Carter and the musicians packed their horns and drove away into the California night, Ella gathered her sheet music, folded her glasses, picked up her big leather purse, and walked up to me in the darkened studio.

"You know, Dave, I owe someone an apology. I thought this whole medley idea was just terrible, somethin' awful, when we started three nights ago. Now I say it's the finest album I ever recorded."

And with her soft apology came a big, warm hug and a heartfelt cheek-kiss. Off went the First Lady into the darkness of the Capitol Tower's rear parking lot.

We released the album under the title of *Thirty By Ella* and it didn't sell even 30,000 copies. It should have topped 300,000. I had employed only a small combo behind her, because of her debit status, but even so there are men in every record company—men who don't know a piccolo from a pizza pie—who are paid to rise up and protest when a contractee's ledger reads out in the red.

Gilmore, sympathetic and tactful, "suggested" that I not even bring up Ella's name when her option came up. He had no choice. Nor did I. And so the First Lady made no more of her remarkable records for Capitol. I failed with her. I'm the man who lost a hundred big ones for my company after trying two years to boost the Fitzgerald name up where it belongs—alongside Sinatra, Streisand, and the few other titans of song.

The truth is, Ella will never have hit records. Nor will many other capable artists. The nation's radio stations do not broadcast them. With programming slanted to the children of high-school age and younger, there exists a ludicrous, reprehensible boycott of true musical talent.

⁕   ⁕   ⁕

After a year or so away from Capitol, Ella was signed by Warner Brothers for records. Someone over there assigned her some Beatles songs and other "contemporary" tunes. "Ella is at Warner's, where she belongs" was the triumphant theme of their ad campaign, which also took a sly swing at the religious and country masters she had cut at Capitol.

Her Warner's album sold even poorer than her weakest Capitol package. But she will record again. There's always someone around who recognizes talent and who is willing to spend a bundle trying to popularize it. I wish Ella luck. She earns $250,000 every year singing throughout the world and she deserves every dime of it.

But I'll never solve her odd, enigmatic personality. Maybe that's a part of genius. Yet it seems to me that, be he an orphan or millionaire (Ella is both), somewhere along the line everyone should learn to say thanks for small favors. Like Sammy Davis, the First Lady never did.

22

There's no question that music and records are the
most powerful branches of show business . . . a
successful record is heard in one day by 60 million
people in the U.S.A. . . . I have had, over the last six
years, more hits than any other artist in the world,
including the Beatles and Simon and Garfunkle. And
more records sold than any other artist. I consider
myself one of the best songwriters in the world today.
People don't know it yet, but they will, maybe five
years from now. . . . You'll look back later and say the
Beatles did this and Neil Diamond did that, and I don't
know who's going to come out ahead.

—NEIL DIAMOND (1972)

DENNIS DALE McLAIN stomped his big foot on the accelerator of his flaming
red Pontiac. He deftly wheeled the car from Detroit's Livernois on-ramp to the
crowded freeway, gunned the engine, and turned to me.

"I say any idiot can throw a baseball," he remarked. "When it's all said and
done some day in the future I hope they will remember me as an outstanding
musician, not as a ballplayer."

He was 24 then, in 1968. He weighed 199 pounds, all muscle. Newspaper,
magazine, television, and radio newsmen followed him everywhere as he rang
up new pitching records for the Detroit Tigers. Not since Lefty Grove achieved
a 31-4 mark in 1931 had an American League hurler proved as effective.

"My dad died young," said Denny, as we headed for the stadium, "but he did
a lot for me. For one thing he constantly played records around our house in
Chicago. He was crazy about music. It rubbed off on me."

We had agreed on a recording contract while he was on the road with the
Tigers in nearby Anaheim, home of the struggling California Angels. I had
flown to Motown to make Denny's first discs. He played electric organ. Now
the time had come to roll tape.

Denny chose his own musicians. We gathered at Ralph Terrana's small but
hospitable Tera Shirma studios.

I won't say that the powerfully built Cy Young award-winner was a pain in the neck on our sessions—that would be understatement. I will say that he was a pain in the ass. I had sent him some 25 songs which I had obtained from reputable publishers, songs which the pubs assured me would be promoted with advertising and radio exploitation. McLain ignored them all. He would, he archly advised me in the studio, choose his own material for his debut as a recording star.

It took a lot of time to put it together. We had a tenor sax, a trumpet doubling fluegelhorn, a string bass, and McLain's manager, Eddie Demetrak, at the drums. McLain sat at the powerful Hammond X-77 organ, an oversized new instrument which fed into six massive speakers and weighed 606 pounds. The Hammond people had given it to Denny as part of a nationwide advertising project.

I sat in an upstairs booth, looking down on the proceedings with increasing agitation as the union clock spun faster and faster. McLain insisted on making tunes like *The Look of Love, Don't Give Up, This Guy's In Love with You, For Me,* and *By the Time I Get to Phoenix,* things which had previously sold a million or more by artists like Petula Clark, Herb Alpert's Tijuana Brass, Dionne Warwicke, Glen Campbell, and Steve Lawrence. After a couple of ulcer-inducing hours of amateur night at the Tivoli I deserted the booth, charged into the studio and implored McLain to record a tune or two which might have, percentage wise, at least a fighting chance to make the charts.

"Get the hell back in your cage," he roared. I burned.

"I don't tell you how to pitch to Yastrzemski," I shouted. "Don't you tell me how to make records."

I thought for a moment that he might swing on me, so intense was his manner. I outweighed him by 50 pounds in those days before I dieted off 80, but my poundage was blubber. He was in shape, and could challenge anyone in baseball with impunity. Denny wasn't a man to provoke.

We made the tunes he demanded.

At session's end, McLain resumed his nice guy posture with me. "I think we've got some pretty damned good music on tape," he said. He arranged to pick me up at my hotel and drive to the stadium that evening for a crucial game with the Cleveland Indians. I watched him hit long flies to the outfielders in the pre-game warmup, and as the umpires walked out to get things started Denny suddenly wheeled from his position near home plate and heaved a baseball high into the box where I was seated. Some 50,000 excited, pennant-hungry spectators must have wondered what the hell was going on as I reached up and snared the ball while Denny doffed his cap and turned to the dugout.

We completed the LP the next afternoon. I selected two of the tunes for a 45 rpm single which Capitol would immediately issue while the pennant race was still hot. Denny appeared slightly more civilized as he pumped the Hammond through *Lonely is the Name, Hurdy Gurdy Man, On a Clear Day, Nice 'n' Easy, Cherish,* and other tired old hits.

The session ended, Denny's attitude and demeanor mellowed.

"I didn't mean to give you a bad time," he said. "It's just that music is so damned important to me, and I must do it my way or I wouldn't have any enthusiasm or inspiration."

He took the mound that night and whipped the Indians 13–1 following a heavy shower which delayed the game's start nearly an hour. The triumph gave him his twenty-third victory of the season. He wound up with the world champion Tigers boasting a brilliant 31–6 record following his sixth game victory over the Cardinals in the 1968 World Series. Not in 37 years had a pitcher achieved that perfection.

I returned to Hollywood, produced the album quickly and was gratified to watch more than 60,000 copies move as World Series play commenced. That's a remarkable sale for an untried performer. We later made a second album while Denny was performing at the Riviera Hotel in Las Vegas in baseball's off-season, but although it was musically superior to the first, its sales were negligible. Denny's fans had turned to football, I guess.

By the time spring training rolled around in 1969 dealers throughout the land had returned 20,000 of McLain's debut LP to Capitol. So once again I was placed in the dreaded position of notifying an artist that his option would not be picked up, and that he was free to negotiate a recording contract with another company. I did it by letter. I wished the emotional Denny well, assuring him that I hoped to see one of his future discs atop the charts and hoping he again would win 31 games for the Tigers.

He never answered my letter.

I now look back at those nightmarish McLain sessions with amusement.

He knew it all, just as he did on the diamond. He knew more about music, more about recording, more about show business than anyone. He typified the big-headed public athletic hero with a loud mouth. Impossible to work with, egotistical, and overconfident, McLain gave me many hours of sheer hell.

Yet I derived no pleasure in watching him fall from the mighty Tigers to the Oakland A's, the lowly Texas Rangers, and the Atlanta Braves, with stints in the minors mixed in. I'd like to see Denny come roaring back and appear in another World Series. For all his imperfections, he has likeable traits and I find it impossible to forget him. Perhaps he will record again. I hope so. But for some other producer.

I go to ball games now and I sometimes think of what McLain told me as we lunched at the Detroit Sheraton during the stretch run of the 1968 American League pennant race: "My grandfather died young. My dad died young. I will die young. I haven't much time to make my mark. I just hope they'll remember me as a musician, not as an unbeatable right-hander with more than his share of personal eccentricities."

          o   o   o

At a time when Mitch Miller's simple "singalong" albums were the hottest sellers in the industry, I arranged with California executives of Anheuser-Busch to take over their comfy rathskeller at their spacious, busy plant in Van Nuys and make a long-player of a community sing which we would promote and sell under the title of *A Night in a Brewery* with generous credit to the brewers of Budweiser and Michelob suds.

It required some doing; I hired a 10-piece band, featuring a tuba and banjo; arranged for Hollywood conductor Ralph Carmichael to be there to lead the group singing; and solicited the help of my secretary Ruth Liberman to copy the lyrics of a dozen well-known pop song standards and mimeograph 300 copies for use by the "artists" involved. With the help of fellow producer Bill Miller, who once was in charge of Capitol's recording department, we set up the facilities of a portable recording van at the rear entrance of the rathskeller, a van equipped with two Ampex tape recorders, stereophonic speakers, and the like.

Now all I needed was the singers.

Mrs. Liberman helped me invite 30 or 40 Capitol employees, emphasizing that they were welcome to bring their wives, husbands, or whomever. About a half-dozen "whomevers" showed up along with the others. I then filled the room to capacity by welcoming scores of parents of my Encino Little League boys, men and women who had never witnessed a recording session. It rurned out to be a particularly compatible mix of beer-swigging, pretzel-gobbling mothers and fathers, in the main.

We started off with the rousing *Beer Barrel Polka*, allowing George Bruns to cavort on his tuba along with the uninhibited group singing. Nappy Lamare's rhythmic banjo (he was guitarist in Bob Crosby's Dixieland band for a decade) abetted the mood as musicians and singers alike quaffed foamy brew in prodigious quantities. We moved into ancient goodies like *Carolina Moon, Love Letters in the Sand, I Don't Know Why,* and *You Always Hurt the One You Love,* taking occasional breaks to allow everyone in the room to relieve their overtaxed bladders.

In between each medley of songs we inserted a shouted fanfare like the ones I had enjoyed at the famed *Oktoberfest* in Munich. Big John the bartender survived an exhausting night refilling the steins as eager hands pushed empties at his face for over four hectic hours. Along about midway I began to think Capitol might have acquired another monster, a big-selling LP to equal or even surpass the freakish *German Beer-Drinking Music* I had put together after my first trip to Cologne in 1955. Certainly we had captured the same high-spirited alcoholic, party-like mood.

By the time we got to the closing tune, *Bye Bye Blues* (the theme song of the Mills Brothers since the early 1930s), the floor was littered with broken pretzels, stray peanuts, pulverized potato chips, and liquids of varying colors, and over in a far corner of the rathskeller one tired old Little League dad lay flat on his back, an empty stein overturned on his chest.

I learned something that night as the free brew flowed. Women outdrink men by at least two to one. They also sing better.

We tipsied our way out the Anheuser-Busch exits sometime after midnight. Our singing guests were still lined up awaiting use of the rest-room facilities, Indian file. But it was a laughing, *happy* line.

In the editing rooms of the Tower the following afternoon I spliced all the best takes together, intercutting the jubilant fanfares. The stereo effects were marvelous. The ebullient Carmichael had coaxed wild, delighted sounds from the imbibing husbands and wives; Billy Liebert's pickup band had performed with abandon and an undeniable beerhall spirit. I had a hell of an album.

It didn't sell well. Capitol promotion nabob Rocky Catena had not attended the alcoholic bash at the brewery and evinced little interest in its sales potential. *A Night in a Brewery* therefore was never released—it just sort of dribbled out to the market. I saw no advertising and no reviews. But the project came off with a modest profit anyway. Anheuser-Busch purchased several thousand copies for use as a sales stimulant with its powerful network of sales personnel throughout North America.

So my calculated sales risk wasn't a financial flop. But another *German Beer-Drinking Music* triumph it was not.

Shortly after our mad, wet session at the Van Nuys brewery, Gussie Busch and the top Anheuser-Busch management in St. Louis ordered the California rathskeller to be closed permanently. They even razed the building, preferring the area it had occupied to become part of a sprawling outdoor park—Busch Gardens—replete with exotic wild birds, animals, and a Disney-like monorail trolley calculated to attract children.

I'm fairly sure our recording beer bust had a lot to do with their decision.

o   o   o

It was long after midnight. The tortuous combination of heat and high humidity made the Texas darkness oppressive. I ambled across the well-manicured grass of America's Manned Spacecraft Center staring up at the moon, a golden melon in the heavens. Was it possible that two men were actually up there, sleeping in their little spindly legged lunar module *Eagle* after bounding about the lunar surface for two hours and 14 minutes like a pair of exuberant, inquisitive, kangaroos?

It was true. Like the 528 million men, women, and children who watched Neil Armstrong and Edwin (Buzz) Aldrin on television sets throughout the world on that sizzling July night in 1969, I too had seen it happen with my own eyes a few hours earlier. And in the big National Aeronautics and Space Administration auditorium in Building One of NASA's headquarters in the suburbs of Houston, where 693 American and 402 foreign members of the news media had assembled for the Sunday evening touchdown on the moon, I leaped to my feet and cheered along with the 1,094 others as Commander Armstrong's voice came through the speakers distinctly, "Houston, Tranquility base. The *Eagle* has landed."

There were only three of us at the Center on that historic occasion with one assignment in mind—to produce record albums. Oddly, all of us were in competition, yet we were employed by the same firm. Mickey Kapp was contracted to *Time-Life* in New York, a commitment he had made before he moved to California to become business manager of Capitol's a&r department. Peter Klein represented the Capitol Record Club, which had recently been sold to the Longines Symphonette Society in Larchmont, N.Y. I represented Capitol Records as a senior producer. All three of us had contrasting concepts of the packages we proposed to deliver to our bosses on tape. Kapp kept to himself. Klein and I amicably assisted each other throughout the tiring July 16–24 work shift.

It was difficult work. I slept when the astronauts slept, fearful of missing dialogue between ground and space that might be vital to the mission's success and my record album. John E. McLeaish and Jack Riley, NASA's veteran public information officers, had devised a foolproof system. Whenever we heard anything over the speaker system that we wanted, we filled out a simple form, turned it in to them and, within an hour or so, Big Bill Johnson's tape crew had dubbed it off and delivered it to our assigned desks in Building One.

We listened to many hours of ground-space conversation day and night, dialogue not heard outside NASA's air-conditioned, comfortable Building One. McLeaish, Riley, and their staff—and I can't forget Jeanne (Chi Chi) Carlin—delivered mimeographed transcripts of all radio communications with Armstrong, Aldrin, and command module pilot Michael Collins to us every 15 minutes. Thus it was a simple chore to mark and order the portions we required for our albums.

Everyone remembers Armstrong's first words as he stepped onto the "fine and powdery" lunar soil from the 16-ton Grumman lunar module:

"That's one small step for man, one giant leap for mankind."

His declaration was marred by annoying static. It was also flawed, Armstrong said later, because he had *intended* to say:

"That's one small step for *a* man, one giant leap for mankind."

It was one of very few imperfections experienced through the entire eight-day expedition. A thousand or more years from now the triumphs and disappointments of the 1970s may be long forgotten, but the achievements of Apollo Eleven's courageous and resourceful crew will be known by every schoolchild.

When Armstrong, Aldrin, and Collins splashed down in the South Pacific in their overloaded *Columbia* command module, a violent human explosion erupted at the Manned Spacecraft Center and at motels, restaurants, and bars along NASA Boulevard. It was been traditional since the 1961 Alan Shepherd Mercury Three flight that men light cigars and hug the nearest women on splashdown. It's equally traditional that everyone drinks himself into oblivion; most of the newsmen with whom I had been associated for eight nervous days and nights decided not to defy precedent.

They leapt into swimming pools fully clothed, men and women alike. And in the two nearby motel bars where I went for cold beer with tape bossman Bill Johnson, I was not allowed to pay.

I bundled eight large reels of tape together with adhesives and carried them in my arms on the flight back to Hollywood. Speed in producing the album was essential. Nothing is as dead as yesterday's new events.

Capitol had arranged for the eminently qualified and capable long-time "Voice of Apollo," Paul Haney, to narrate my Apollo Eleven script. But he had been in England describing the mission over Independent Television Ltd., for British and Russian audiences. Thus I had to wait for his return to Houston and then for his script-reading to be recorded there and flown to me in Hollywood. That took more than a week.

Once his tape arrived, I worked two 18-hour shifts with engineers Jay Ranellucci and Rex Updegraft mixing the thousands of tape-feet of NASA ground-space dialogue with Haney's voice tracks and sound effects. It required four Ampex machines. Then we mastered the final tape in Hollywood and shipped it off to our pressing plant in Scranton 2,500 miles to the east, where printed album jackets designed by Marvin Schwartz from graphics I had brought back from Houston awaited the newly-pressed LPs. My assignment was finished.

But it wasn't. Robert Dempster of Capitol's Special Markets division in the Tower called me and suggested I revise my Capitol *We Have Landed on the Moon* album and immediately produce a second LP which, he said confidently, his department could sell in highly profitable quantities to banks, grocery chains, and petroleum companies.

Back to the studios. I changed the introduction, inserting the late President John F. Kennedy's address to Congress from May 25, 1961: "I believe this nation should commit itself to achieving the goal, before this decade is out, of landing a man on the moon and returning him safely to earth."

I deleted some of the material, but I retained portions of the pre-liftoff countdown at Cape Kennedy, the launch from pad 39-A, the voices of Armstrong, Aldrin, and Collins and the ever-cool dialogue of the flight control chiefs from "the trench" at Houston. I included President Nixon's telephone call to the moon-walkers and the splashdown excitement in the South Pacific. Both my records, I thought, came off well.

Yet we were disastrously late in getting them out on the market. Nor had I anticipated another peril, the cheapie disc selling for 99 cents, produced strictly from the CBS, NBC, and ABC network coverage of the event for television. More than a dozen were issued; half of them were released prior to Capitol's. It seemed to me almost like unfair competition. I do not include the RCA album in this category, nor the Columbia Records production featuring Walter Cronkite.

They were first rate, as was Peter Klein's authentic and comprehensive long-player for the Longines people. But most of them were shoddy, incomplete, and of poor physical quality.

I look at sales figures of my two albums now. The Special Markets *Eagle Has Landed* package substantially outsold the original Capitol LP. Both were profitable.

From a different viewpoint, were the Apollo lunar expeditions profitable? American Taxpayers shelled out $26 billion for putting 12 men on the moon and for a collection of 850 pounds of lunar rocks.

Someone smarter than I must answer that question, and it may be many years before a conclusion can objectively be announced. No one questions the brilliance of the NASA achievement. But was it worth $26 billion?

There's a payoff to my exhausting Apollo Eleven coverage in Houston.

A year after my two albums were released I learned that the crafty Kapp, with whom I worked, and who had toiled in Houston on an expensive, lavish multi-disc package for *Time-Life*, was receiving a producer's royalty on *my* two albums. That smarted. Kapp, it was explained to me, had been granted a royalty on each LP sold because he had "suggested" the idea of recording the history-making Apollo mission.

Kapp doesn't work at Capitol now.

23

Music must take
rank as the highest
of the fine arts;
as the one which
more than any other
ministers to
human welfare.

—HERBERT SPENCER (1852)

THE BEATLES WERE still intact in 1967, business was booming, and Chairman Wallichs departed London following an EMI board meeting eager to return to his desk in sunny California.

On the flight into New York he complained to Dorothy Wallichs that he felt ill. In time, physicians at Hollywood Presbyterian Hospital advised the Wallichses that Glenn was afflicted with an uncommon disease known as multiple myeloma which cripples the body's bone structure. There is no cure.

Two men directed Capitol during the chairman's protracted hospitalization. Alan Livingston for six years had served ably as the corporation's president. Stanley M. Gortikov over the same period had risen from the ranks to national sales boss. Together, they embarked on a daring expansion policy in which the term "diversification of corporate interests" dominated their day-to-day conversation in the Tower.

With our merger with a tape manufacturing firm, Audio Devices, Inc., Capitol became Capitol Industries, Inc. Audio Devices operated modern factories in Connecticut, North Carolina, and France. Livingston moved up to the presidency of Capitol Industries and, with Wallichs' and the board of directors' approval, installed Gortikov as president of Capitol Records.

The ambitious Livingston sought still additional acquisitions for the new, muscle-flexing conglomerate. Abrogating a long and mutually beneficial contract with Pan-Americano Discos of Mexico, Capitol set up its own record firm in Mexico City. A productive 1,100-acre orange grove in the fertile San Joaquin Valley near Bakersfield was purchased. Merco Enterprises, a New York rack-jobbing organization servicing more than 700 disc and tape outlets in 46 states with records, tapes, accessories, sheet music, musical instruments, and audio equipment, was acquired. The TL Management Company and Sherman Enterprises of Canada were also brought under the expanding Capitol Industries umbrella.

Capitol increased its real estate holdings as well.

But it was Livingston's obsession to establish the Capitol Record Club on equal footing with Columbia's profitable sales-by-mail operation that dominated his interest. Livingston's fetish envisioned Capitol's Club becoming a multimillion-dollar success, and he set it up carefully with Ed Nash in command. A beautiful ranch-style building to house the club and its employees was hurriedly constructed in the Los Angeles suburb of Thousand Oaks, just off the convenient Ventura Freeway some 30 miles to the northwest of the Capitol Tower. Full-color advertisements were run in a half-dozen national magazines to kick off the club.

"Our object," Livingston told more than a thousand employees at the 1968 Capitol convention in Las Vegas and at Century City, "is to provide the one-third of the nation's population living in rural areas with easy access to Capitol's recorded entertainment and auxiliary products. It is an enormous market and Columbia in no way controls it. Not every record buyer can go to a store and pick up the music he wants; our club will provide those persons with the finest music available."

He advised us that licensing agreements had been established with ABC, MGM, and Warner Brothers-Reprise Records in order to best provide Record Club consumers with the "widest possible variety of recorded entertainment."

Capitol previously had established and successfully operated ASCAP and BMI music publishing firms. Thus, in 1968, its vital arteries extended far into Mexico, Canada, France, and later, across the Pacific into Japan. There Toshiba Musical Industries was founded with Capitol owning 25 percent, EMI 25 percent, and the remaining 50 percent controlled by the Tokyo Shibaura Electric Company.

Japan represents the second largest market for records in the world. It is larger than either Great Britain or West Germany.

The 1967-68 period was one of unprecedented growth for Capitol. Never had the future looked so bright. Even Chairman Wallichs left his bed and gamely returned to his office on a limited schedule.

*　　　*　　　*

On a lower level, I noticed revolutionary changes from day to day.

Clothing, for one. The more conservative men on the a&r floor were all wearing turtle-neck shirts from which hung various pendants, charms, and unidentifiable junk jewelry. The younger producers affected frilly, faggy shirts and vari-colored slacks, mostly striped and flared. Almost to a man, hair was worn long—longer than the Prince Valiant style popularized by the Beatles.

Secretaries had adopted the miniskirt and then the micromini in the wild sartorial revolution that followed in the bumpy wake of the Beatles' fantastic popularity. Now, in 1968, the girls abandoned their graceful, pencil-heeled pumps and began wearing clumpy, klutzy, ugly footware not dissimilar to that worn by soccer players. Facial makeup and well-kempt coiffures disappeared from the Tower. As the decade neared an end a majority of the Capitol femmes discarded their shortie skirts and turned to scruffy slacks and—the sloppiest, most repelling garb of all—unflattering floor-length granny dresses.

Walking from one office to another on the circular floors (so that you always end up at the elevators no matter which direction you take) one also was aware of the pungent mixture of incense and marijuana smoke. Some of the younger producers lit tokes while going over songs or using the telephone or rapping with artists and agents; their secretaries slyly lit up incense sticks to counteract the odor. Some days when the air conditioning equipment was overworked and inefficient the ambience of the twelfth floor community was the same as an Oahu outhouse.

It was in this ribald atmosphere that my old pal and boss Gilmore walked into my office one spring afternoon.

"Well, Dex, they axed me today," he said. "But then I knew it was coming when Gortikov was made CRI prez a few weeks ago."

I hardly knew how to console him. Gortikov and Gilmore had pushed conflicting corporate philosophies for years. Creative, artistic persons will never be compatible with sales and promotion folk. It's like the editorial and advertising staffs on a newspaper, or the butcher versus the fresh vegetables man at the supermarket.

Gilmore's a&r department, the creative men who provided the product that makes or breaks a record company, a television network, or a motion picture studio, quickly became subordinate to the sales and promotion wings as President Gortikov steadily wielded a stronger voice in the corporation's policies.

"Stan is not a Record Man," Gilmore told me, despondently. "He's smart and he's a hard worker but he's making a&r the hind tit on the sow.

"I have fought a long time to maintain our department's strong voice in the company. Wallichs always believed the producers held the key to profits or losses. Gortikov is an ex-overcoat salesman who's convinced that the salesman is the pivotal man. The hell of it is, Dex, our pal Alan Livingston is being conned into believing it."

Gilmore moved off the executive floor the next day and down among the commoners. His successor was a man 20 years younger, P. Karl Engemann, a devout Mormon who had worked for several years as a likable assistant—a sort of male secretary—to Gilmore.

It was soon evident, under the inexperienced Engemann, that, for the first time in Capitol's 26 years, Gortikov's handpicked and personally trained sales and promotion personnel now controlled the company's destiny. The men who produced the records had been downgraded.

Diversification held Livingston's attention. Gortikov concentrated on records. What was the nature of this aggressive, dedicated graduate of the University of Southern California?

I've seen them come and go over my extended hitch with Capitol. None had the drive, ambition and ruthlessness of Gortikov. A onetime member of the garment industry in Los Angeles, I suspect he possessed the highest IQ of any Capitol executive. He worked long hours at his desk directing the sales and promotion activities of the corporation and its subsidiaries. He willingly took innumerable trips to New York, London, and a dozen other cities where industry conventions and conclaves were in session; he proved a tireless, devoted exec who commanded respect wherever he toiled.

But he knew nothing about music.

To Gortikov a record was like a cake of soap, a pair of shoes, or a loaf of bread. He gave the impression, in his dealings with performers, that they functioned like bookkeepers or plumbers.

It was a familiar corporate pattern. Twenty years previously, Decca disposed of Dave Kapp after the death of Jack Kapp. Businessmen took over. Decca's ensuing drop from an industry position of leadership followed. In the 1950s Mercury and MGM overtook the once-prevailing Decca operation to a point where Decca was no longer considered a major label.

Staggering losses incurred by Capitol's Record Club brought Wallichs back into the picture by mid-summer of 1968. Livingston adamantly defended his faith in the sales-by-mail operation, sincerely believing that, in time, the club would turn generous profits into the Capitol Industries money pot.

The books indicated otherwise.

"I don't understand Livingston," the still-ailing Wallichs told me at lunch. "He will not believe the figures we show him—he insists the operation is sound. He never used to be the bullheaded man he is today."

Nor were Audio Devices and Merco Enterprises contributing to Capitol's earnings. Wallichs frequently conferred with Gortikov and British EMI brass whose visits to the Tower became more frequent.

And so Livingston was ordered to resign in July as president of Capitol Industries. Wallichs took over his responsibilities. Despite the Record Club losses, Livingston's last year as the CII topper saw the company tilling a $4,607,000 net income from sales of $106,881,000, the first year Capitol attained its long-sought hundred million gross goal. Buddy DeSylva's original $10,000 investment in 1942 had grown to a net worth of $33 million exactly a quarter-century later.

o   o   o

Livingston's exit meant the end of a prosperous, happy period of Capitol expansion dating back to 1951, a 17-year span in which undreamed-of new heights had been achieved with the a&r staff sparking the rise.

No longer were little blue, crumpled, empty Fizrin packs to be found scattered about the Silo's twelfth floor. Lee Gillette had quit in 1965, only months after Nat Cole died. Cole's passing affected Gillette deeply, and his inability to adjust to the raging rock 'n' roll tastes of the public furthered his desire to leave the scene and occasionally work as a free-lance producer. He was in excellent financial condition; his retirement fund payoff approximated $100,000 cash and he also owned valuable music publishing interests.

I regard Gillette as the best producer Capitol ever employed. He guided Cole, Kay Starr, Tennessee Ernie Ford, Stan Kenton, Peggy Lee, Guy Lombardo, Ray Anthony, and a half-dozen other successful acts through 20 years of not only profitable but artistically laudable performances on discs. He suffered his flops, too, as all producers must. Yet his batting average was probably better than .350 and his home runs were frequent enough to insure him a high niche in the Capitol Hall of Fame, if ever one is established.

Gilmore fared less well after moving off the executive (E) floor and resuming as a producer. It was a difficult position for him to assume. For more than a year he endured the torment of a has-been executive. None of the bosses consulted him. Publishers and musicians no longer telephoned or pleaded for an office appointment. The few acts he continued to record failed to make the charts. Finally, plainly depressed, he vacated the Tower and purchased a boat marina in northern California. Under his old employment contract his sizable salary continued to be paid him through June, 1973.

"I'm happy puttering with outboard motors and breathing the good clean air of the outdoors," Gilmore told me on a recent visit to Hollywood. "But I don't kid myself. I would return to the whole horrible Hollywood hassle if I got the right offer. Records are my life."

Gilmore is a Record Man. Gillette is a Record Man. There are all too few of their caliber around today.

°   °   °

Stan Gortikov assumed the presidency of Capitol Industries when it became apparent, in 1969, that Wallichs' physical condition would not allow him to continue in the corporation's most trying post. He would serve only as chairman of the board.

His move left the presidency of Capitol Records open.

I was on the telephone talking with Joe Abend, Pickwick's a&r chief in their Long Island offices.

"Hey," he yelled, "I hear you've got a new president out there."

"You know more than I do," I replied. "Who is it this week?"

"Salvatore Iannucci," Abend replied.

"Salvatore Who?" I asked Abend. He laughed.

"His last name is Iannucci," Joe explained. "He's a New York University grad who got his law degree at Harvard. I hear he's a brilliant young cat."

"What does he know about records?" I inquired of Abend.

Abend paused. Then, again, more laughing on Long Island.

"That's for you guys in Hollywood to find out."

We soon knew. Iannucci had worked for National General and CBS-TV as an attorney. What he knew about records and the record business you could stuff in the centerhole of an LP.

In his first week at the Tower, the new president called each member of the a&r division into his top floor office. I was booked for 9 a.m. He admitted me at 9:45.

I saw a truly handsome man, not yet 40, and modishly dressed. I took a seat opposite the presidential desk.

"What do you do here?" he demanded, staring sullenly at my graying hair.

"My job is to activate as many of our 80,000 deleted masters as possible and realize income from them," I answered.

"You mean Capitol's old records, the ones we can't sell any longer?" he asked.

"Right, Pickwick issues them under a contract we have which gives them first option on anything Capitol deletes from its active catalog. It's money for them and money for us. And royalties for our artists and the music publishers involved."

"Is that all you do?"

"Not quite. I still produce a live session occasionally. I try to answer questions that come up every day about company activities from years back. I answer a lot of mail from record buyers, songwriters, and aspiring young artists."

"Anything else?"

I continued to explain my day-to-day chores in the Tower as Iannucci stared me down from across his desk. His eyes were like laser beams. He kept looking at his wristwatch.

"Okay," he said after about seven minutes of interrogation. "Tell the girl to send in the next guy."

Some of the a&r men got together late that day. All had left Iannucci flustered and uptight, if not humiliated, by his sullen, cold-steel attitude.

"I can remember," said one neophyte producer sadly, "when it was fun to work here."

24

Today we hear so much musical sound all the time, in trains, in airplanes, in restaurants, that we are becoming deadened to it. Our sensitivity to music is in danger of being lost, just as we are becoming insensitive to the stupid brutality we see so much on television or in the motion pictures. Now I love the cinema and I go to it often. And I think that television is a medium of enormous potential. But we see how modern developments and techniques can be very harmful. Still, we are able to turn off television, or walk out of a bad motion picture or poor concert. You can't walk out of an airplane.

—LEOPOLD STOKOWSKI

RECORD COMPANIES ARE like pro ball clubs. They deal and shuffle for artists in an unceasing battle of wits. RCA seeks a girl singer of the Helen Reddy mold while the Dodgers search for a third baseman. MCA assiduously tries to replace Neil Diamond, who got away; Seattle's Supersonics hunger for a gunning, ball-handling guard like Gail Goodrich. Capitol auditions dozens of rock groups to replace the Beatles; the Rams scout the boondocks for a long-term quarterback. So it goes.

A well-rounded stable of artists is the goal of every discery. Columbia has led the pack in recent years with a balanced roster of every conceivable type of talent, rock through classical. Its worldwide sales gross of $340 million last year led its hundreds of competitors by more than $100 million. Yet a year from now the fast-rising conglomerate that comprises Warner Brothers, Reprise, Elektra, and Atlantic may well push the CBS affiliate headed by Irwin Segelstein down into the second or third or fifth spot, just as the Boston Celtics were at long last toppled in the late sixties.

Capitol has had its years as top dog. So have RCA and Decca, the once-potent label which saved the dying industry in 1934 and which, in 1973, was phased out of existence by MCA's president, Mike Maitland. No one company dominates the charts permanently. The truth is, a record or album the public likes will sell on its own strength, assuming it gets radio exposure. A bad record will not sell regardless of airplay or advertising. Whatever it is, the magic must be within the grooves. No amount of hype—exploitation—will make a winner out of a stiff.

Record men all agree that they welcome hits on competitive labels. "A new singer, a new combo, or a new act brings buyers into the stores and shops and away from their television sets," MCA's Maitland says. "Most of them will buy another album or single. A hit on Capitol or Columbia or whatever label means renewed interest in records, including MCA's. Is there any other business in which competitors delight in seeing the other guy sell a runaway hit item?"

There are many ingredients that make up the $2 billion a year domestic record business.

Some 5,000 albums are issued annually. No more than 10 percent of those are profit-makers. Classical music, for example, has fallen from a 20 percent share of the market to 5 percent in the last two decades, yet more classical records are being sold today than ever before. Why the paradox? The answer is in a booming population growth. There are many more millions of consumers in 1975 than in 1955.

Jazz sales account for no more than 2 percent of the market today. Comedy accounts for another 5 percent. Highly specialized music including polkas, foreign language imports, and documentary productions comprises less than 3 percent of American sales.

Those figures reflect why a single rock 'n' roll hit is the lifeblood of a label. Without the boffy two million sellers there would be no classical output. And no record company.

Kids buy most of the recorded output in the seventies.

Once it was the college student who determined the trends in pop music. Now it is the teenager, the little girl 10 to 16 years old, whose support is sought by most record acts. Radio stations slant their programming to this immature, impressionable audience of millions with their repetitious, deadly monotonous Top 40 formats—the comic strips and toilet bowls of the airlanes.

And that's why, of course, you don't hear good music often. Recording it is a losing proposition. Radio jocks won't play it. So no one buys it.

Radio's execrable Top 40 system dictates the nation's music tastes. Unless it's three guitars and a tasteless drummer, the record isn't broadcast.

Payola runs rampant as it has for a quarter of a century, though it has become infinitely more subtle with the years. One doesn't take a deejay or a program director to lunch and leave him with a $100 bill in a firm handshake; that was the 1950 ploy. New and effective ways to get one's record spun are devised every day.

It's an outright travesty for the Federal Communications Commission to issue frequent publicity handouts deploring payola and to piously assert that investigations are being instituted to eliminate it.

Can FCC investigators prove that Mister X arranged a motel assignation with two willing participants—an influential radio jock and a $100 hooker? Or that Mister X got his record played once an hour for an uninterrupted week by dropping off a color television set to the program director's apartment? I've known promotion men to drive to the suburbs and chauffeur a deejay's wife on her shopping rounds, picking up the tabs and carrying the groceries and new clothing into the house, in exchange for a dozen spins of a new single.

There are hundreds of ways to get the edge on a competitor's record. The FCC, for all its lofty intentions, simply is ill-equipped and too understaffed to eliminate the payola menace. But then there's no way to eliminate similar kickbacks and payoffs to thousands of purchasing agents with companies and corporations throughout the land, either. It is an abominable facet and fact of life.

        ◦   ◦   ◦

America's Mom and Pop shops are long gone. There were more than 5,000 of them in the boom days following World War II and most Americans bought their records there, along with staples like greeting cards, envelopes, stationery, and the then-novel ballpoint pens.

The Big Guys forced Mom and Pop out, one by one and then by the hundreds. Mom and Pop ordered their stock from the manufacturer's sales branch in twos and threes; many of the consistently hot artists like Bing Crosby, Perry Como, Frank Sinatra, Doris Day, Peggy Lee, and Dinah Shore enjoyed standing orders for every record they made.

Not so now.

The national rack jobbers are the purchasing power within the industry now, so overwhelmingly powerful that many record companies act on their suggestions as to what should be recorded.

There are few fixed prices on product. More than 500 record labels vacillate with their own wholesale figures on records and tapes in a woeful lack of unanimity. Yet the rackers and their unignorable bulk purchases of hits have opened up countless new sales outlets—grocery stores, garages, discount shops—and expanded the disc-tape market many times over. So eager are the record companies to write rack business that they cheerfully accept returned merchandise on a 100 percent guarantee basis.

The returns come back by the hundreds of thousands. Warehouses are jammed with them. It is a costly and wasteful practice for which there's no solution. The sales boss who eliminates the return privilege loses the racker as a buyer. So the system staggers along from month to month, inefficient and, at times, intolerable. But no one has conceived a better plan so long as the rackers maintain their purchasing power.

        ◦   ◦   ◦

Changes in sales procedures, changes in promotional practices—no phase of the industry remains as it was a decade ago. The most revolutionary changes of all, however, have evolved within the creative area, the a&r division of the business. No more do a half-dozen staff producers and their assistants work as an integrated platoon, finding songs, discovering new talent, and battling the union clock in the booth with complete autonomy in the day-to-day, night-to-night struggle for hit singles and albums.

This is the era of the independent producer. He finds his own talent, records it, and takes the completed roll of tape to a major discery to make his own deal on a royalty basis. More often than not he retains music publishing rights to his property. He may also demand—and get—a producer's royalty in addition to the conventional artist royalty of 10 to 20 percent of the wholesale price of the record. He may dictate to the record company the precise graphic art he wants on an album's front cover and the contents of the package's liner notes on the back.

The indie producer demands an advance cash payment for his product.

Roger Karshner was employed for 18 years by Capitol, working up from an Ohio salesman to sales branch manager to district boss to vice-president, promotion, in the Hollywood Tower. His experiences are colorfully detailed in *The Music Machine* (Nash Publishing, Los Angeles) which he completed in 1971, shortly after he departed Capitol to set up his own promotion firm. Karshner knows every angle of the game. Here are some of his candid comments on the insane industry situation of the seventies:

"The independent label producers," Karshner expostulates, "ask for astronomical advance payments and impossible concessions and they get them. They get them because the non-creative corporate lawyers and financial wizards and executive heads with the big companies are ???—they really aren't in tune with the elusive nuances of talent and timing as the staff a&r guys were a few years ago. They really don't have feelings and understanding for the street vibrations that gestate record consumerism. All they have are wide ties and hip lips, sideburns and funny suits with overwide lapels, Gucci shoes and hideous fears of lost youth.

"Often," Karshner continues, "record manufacturers involve themselves in label deals that are completely unrealistic and therefore damaging. Anxious to be associated with winners, the manufacturers swallow up great chunks of undigestible fat that constipates their organizations. But all of the industry's biggies want to be hip. They want to be on board the image train and choo choo into the hearts of today's youth market. So they buy big, bad deals from shrewd, independent label bargainers.

"Independent producers appeal to the big industry bosses because they look good, talk about astrology, produce groovy rock artists and eat health foods, and of course they have good track records. The manufacturers shell out big peanuts with reckless abandon to these chattering, musical monkeys. Here are some examples of major label's stupidity:

"Small Independent Label A sold his distribution rights to a major manufacturer. He received (a) a $1,500,000 nonrecoupable advance; (b) a guarantee of 24 percent of wholesale price on every piece of his goods the manufacturer sold (24 percent of a 50-cent wholesale single record equals 12 cents a unit; 24 percent of a $2.30 wholesale album equals 55 cents per unit); (c) a $500,000 marketing commitment; (d) a provision for office space in the manufacturer's home office; and (e) complete autonomy regarding advertising, cover art, liner copy, and merchandising aids.

"Super Small Independent Label B sold his distribution rights to a major manufacturer. He received (a) a $200,000 nonrecoupable advance; (b) a guarantee of 24 percent of the wholesale price on every piece of goods sold by the manufacturer; (c) total autonomy regarding advertising, cover art, liner copy, and merchandising aids; and (d) a complete release of his masters on the various tape products.

"These are typical deals," the cynical Karshner avers. "But there have been hundreds similar to them in the last few years. Only one out of 25 proves profitable to the big company but they are fearful that if they don't make the deal another big company will—and come up with a new Beatles, a David Bowie, or a Carole King.

"Self-ascribed production czars are born daily as illegitimate *enfants terribles* to an industry that sires them. Every successful recording artist becomes a production genius and the industry opens its budgets to them for costly experimentations. Like corporate idiots, the companies gamble millions on rag-tailed talent. One hit record, a best-selling song, opens the sesames of recordom. Even tenuous connections can lead to production agreements, and managers often establish themselves as production aces due to their successful artist associations. Everybody's in the act. Top management gullibility, naivete, and impetuousness has pulled the plug from the industry's profit barrel. Ludicrously negotiated label deals, imprudent producer agreements, general production dishonesty, and double-dealing are taking their toll.

"If," concludes Karshner, "the musical meat packers continue to rule and management continues to play house on Ego Street, the industry had better prepare itself. Yes, brace itself for many turns at the fiscal whipping post."[4]

º   º   º

Capitol Records' president Salvatore Iannucci completed his first fiscal year in June, 1970, with an impressive record reflecting substantial sales growth and increased profits.

Gross sales reached $178,119,000, a 26 percent increase in earnings per stock share, over 1969's record-smashing $153,104,000 mark.

But Chairman Wallichs and Capitol Industries' president Stan Gortikov sensed peril ahead. In their report to stockholders that year they agreed that the future portended difficulties:

"As we enter fiscal 1971, the company shares the concern of the nation's business community as to the basic economic climate. In recent months our industry and the company have felt the impact of changing economic forces which touch all business today. These are reflected in higher costs, customer financing difficulties, consumer buying timidity, and higher than usual product exchanges. It appears that these conditions will prevail at least through the first quarter of fiscal 1971."

Iannucci had no control over the disastrous economic recession that plagued the nation in 1970–71, nor could he put the disbanded Beatles back together again. Those two developments ripped into Capitol's high-flying operation like a cannonball into a balloon. In the year that followed, Capitol's 3,500 employees were reduced by 30 percent; some 1,000 men and women on every level throughout the nation were abruptly terminated in a reign of terror which lowered the morale of surviving employees to an all-time low.

When the Beatles' final album, *Let It Be*, ran its course, Capitol had all too few replacement acts to pull in the sales dollar.

The best was Glen Campbell. His behavior as an artist was, at best, inconsistent. He had come out of Arkansas in the early sixties, managing to scrounge a living as a guitarist in the recording and television studios of Hollywood. Voyle Gilmore was attracted to Campbell's musicianship and earthy, Huck Finn personality. Gilmore signed him to a Capitol binder more as a guitarist than as a singer.

Glen's records moved sluggishly and I recall that several times when his singles and LPs were played in sales meetings in the Tower cries of "stiff" and "dog" were heard. Gilmore refused to drop Campbell. Finally, five years later, Campbell came up with *Gentle On My Mind, By the Time I Get to Phoenix, Galveston, Wichita Lineman, Try a Little Kindness*, and *Dreams of the Everyday Housewife* with a novice, Al DeLory, serving as his producer.

Three young men known as The Lettermen also blossomed late in attaining renown on discs. They sang close harmony, and although they were far from rockers the young record buyers supported them loyally over a period of years.

Few other Capitol performers received such support, however. Capitol's sales plummeted; staggering losses incurred by Merco, Audio Devices, the Capitol Record Club, Capitol's Mexican company, and TL Management compounded the seriousness of the firm's financial position.

Still ill, but working in his office every day under medication that required his taking 40 different pills and capsules every 24 hours, the indefatigable Wallichs, in congress with Gortikov, moved swiftly to avert a catastrophe. They feverishly acted to exchange certain assets of the Record Club for stock in the Longines Symphonette Corporation, stock which later was exchanged for Longines-Wittnauer common stock. They sold Capitol's interests in TL Management. Then they disposed of Capitol's Mexican company, selling it to Mother EMI of England.

Wallichs and Gortikov fired the bosses of Audio Devices and Merco and trimmed the companies' payrolls in an all-out effort to effect a turnaround in profitability of the two potentially valuable Capitol subsidiaries.

Those were dark, despairing days in the Tower. Whatever security and enthusiasm for one's job acquired through the years and decades was cruelly dissipated in the flood of employee terminations, most of them fathers and mothers with children to support. In this trying period of inquisition when pink slips floated throughout the organization, Capitol Industries' management even sought to pare expenses by abandoning the employees' profit-sharing fund.

For virtually every employee the fund was their only claim to security. Gortikov and Iannucci, with Wallichs' concurrence, froze the fund and established a chintzy substitute plan in which 1,554 employees and eight Capitol officers were immediately enrolled in July, 1970. That left 426 longtime employees and five officers severed from the original—and far more bountiful—benefits established by Alan Livingston in the early 1950s.

An old quotation from Sir Walter Scott's *Peveril of the Peak* made the rounds of the gloomy Capitol structure with its numerous vacated offices and empty desks:

"The Tower! How many passages to death did that dark structure present!"

Wallichs' salary as chairman was then $75,000 annually. Gortikov received $80,000 as president. The corporation's 17 directors and officers accepted remuneration amounting to $495,564 in 1970, exclusive of bonuses and stock option privileges.

And when the report to stockholders for the fiscal year ending June 30, 1971, was issued, the staggering, unthinkable net loss for 12 months came to $8,092,000. *Eight million dollars.*° It was the first year ever that Capitol had not turned a profit.

"How," I demanded of Wallichs, "can we sell $143,055,000 worth of records and come out with an $8 million loss??"

He gave me a wry, cynical smile and shook his head slowly.

"It isn't easy. But with the good Lord willing to give me the time, I'm going to take Capitol apart and make it sound again.

"You think there've been changes made this last year? We haven't even started. But now it's management that needs cleaning out. I hope I've got time."

      ❁   ❁   ❁

Unrealistic guarantees to independent producers were made by a&r chief Karl Engemann at the insistence of presidents Gortikov and Iannucci, who persisted in believing that hits could be bought like cans of coffee. Caught in the tornado supplied by his businessmen bosses, Engemann's position rapidly became untenable. Sales and promotion bigwigs in the Tower usurped Engemann's responsibilities; Gortikov and Iannucci constantly pressured him to make outside production agreements and purchase independent masters in a pathetically desperate effort to establish new artists on the charts.

"I'm being used as a messenger boy," the affable but harassed Engemann told me, trying to smile. "It's the ages-old story of the sales guys claiming we're giving them bad songs and bad performers. Yet the bosses insist on my buying up all kinds of unattractive singers and combos from the independent producers whose judgment is no better than those of us here in the Tower.

"It seems that anything we record by Capitol contractees here in the home studios is of no interest to our promotion and sales forces. They think it must come from the outsiders if it's to be sold. I may just walk out of this place and move up to a ranch in Utah with my wife and kids if things don't improve."

They didn't. Engemann and Capitol parted in early 1971. For three years he had given his best in a hopeless position. He was succeeded by Artie Mogull, a onetime music publisher, in a move that astounded most of Capitol's employees. Engemann did not move to Utah. He turned to independent record production. I saw him recently on Vine Street and he still had hopes for life as a rancher.

Chairman Wallichs repeatedly remonstrated with the parent EMI's top brass. With insight and logic, he documented Capitol's weaknesses and offered suggestions for pulling the company from the depths up into prominence—and profitability—again.

"I come in every day and sit at my desk and wonder what the hell is going on," the chairman told me at dinner one evening. "Gortikov never contacts me. Iannucci avoids me. I think the time has come for a showdown."

Wallichs went to Gortikov and demanded that Iannucci be terminated. According to the chairman, Gortikov protested Iannucci's removal "almost violently." But early the next morning, Wallichs told me, Gortikov walked into Wallichs' office and agreed that Iannucci's employment contract should be paid off "in the best interests of the corporation."

Gortikov then assumed the twin presidencies of Capitol Industries and Capitol Records. Iannucci's leaving was greeted with enthusiasm by many Capitol employees. He later became affiliated with Hugh Hefner's Playboy Records, an operation which was still losing money in 1975.

Running two corporations is too much for a man regardless of his capability; Wallichs and EMI's management in England secretly agreed to the appointment of a 37-year-old graduate of the University of Delhi and Oxford University from Calcutta, Bhaskar Menon, to assume the presidency of Capitol Records.

Like the bare-armed Mike Marshall striding to the mound of Dodger Stadium to keep the O'Malley men alive, the diminutive Menon came to the Capitol Tower in a tense and unenviable situation. Capitol was down, an also-ran, a once-mighty industry leader with no place to go but up. And as fellow employees approached me day by day with the same question ("who the hell is Menon?") I was reminded of the stopover I had made in Calcutta 12 years earlier while on Capitol business, and how only one of the EMI staff had dared leave his home during dangerous street rioting to come to my hotel and help me transact business vital to Capitol's international operation.

That man, of course, was the same Bhaskar Menon. He now was my boss and the leader of the nearly 2,000 surviving members of the nervous Capitol family.

He was quickly moved up to Gortikov's position as Capitol Industries' president, a failing, desperate Wallichs demanding Gortikov's resignation less than a month after Menon arrived in the Tower in April, 1971.

The new chief made significant changes in personnel and procedures. In time a newly appointed EMI boss in London, Gerry Oord, made Menon's task easier. Oord, a canny and admired record man for more than four decades in Holland, established an effective liaison with Menon which soon produced a financial turnaround.

Capitol's sales dropped to $129,688,000 for the 1972 fiscal year but its net income leaped to $1,621,000 from the devastating $8 million loss of the previous year. The company showed an even more lucrative effort in 1973 with a net income of $5,624,000 on sales of $142,901,000. More recently the 1974 fiscal year reflected sales of $141,663,000 for a fat profit of $7,322,000.

And so Menon and EMI had pulled Capitol off the floor at the count of nine. "The sensitive and talented men and women who function in all our subsidiaries," he said, not without modesty, "are dedicated to utilizing Capitol's considerable resources and facilities to optimum effect."

At one point in the recovery Menon was charged with employing "too many chiefs and not enough Indians." He had a nimble reply: "I am redressing the balance in favor of the Indians," said he.

Gortikov found a new job, in time. He now is the energetic, pirate-hating president of the Recording Industry Association of America, a position reportedly paying him $100,000 annually.

Chairman Wallichs lived to achieve his goal. Capitol again was in a position of prominence, if not pre-eminence, in the industry. How he managed to remain active, and how he overcame vigorous internecine resistance to his efforts, remains one of the great mysteries bordering on the miraculous. He would say, I'm sure, that God helped him.

Somehow he had crawled out of a hospital bed and toiled through four vexing, exhausting years of turmoil. He was three inches shorter. He walked with difficulty. But his house was in order when he died two days before Christmas in 1971.

Lee Zhito of *Billboard* asked me to write Glenn's obituary. "How many words?" I asked. "As many as you need to tell about the man," said Zhito. I drove home from the funeral and typed out eight pages. Zhito sent a messenger for my copy. I knew my tribute ran hundreds of words too long but when the sheet came out the following Monday not a single line had been cut. It was, Zhito told me, the longest obituary ever published in the 77-year-old weekly.

I got more mail from my Wallichs tribute than from anything I had ever written.

But then Glenn Everett Wallichs was more than a boss to me. For almost 30 years I worked under his direction, with his counsel, even though I may have reported to other execs. He was a man who spoke his mind but always with consideration for another's viewpoint. He welcomed dissenting opinions, and in Capitol's early days there were screaming, heated arguments in which he accepted shocking eyeball to eyeball disputes with employees without prejudice. He was, outside the office, the original Mr. Straight Arrow, a non-smoking, extremely religious Nebraska Methodist who appreciatively eyed the beautiful femmes of Hollywood but never touched. He drank less than moderately. He was thrifty to a point of near-parsimony, yet he never questioned my expense account.

He loved to play records, at home and in his office, and his delight in attending previews of motion pictures with his Dorothy was exceeded only by his fondness for fine motor cars. When Chevrolet brought out its first Corvette in the early 1950s, Wallichs acquired one of the first to be delivered to California. He replaced the engine with a Cadillac power plant and spent an entire afternoon driving a dozen employees around Hollywood to show it off.

He contributed enough money to Redlands University to build a theater on campus. His trips to Hawaii and Europe with Dorothy and their daughters Linda and Susan when they were young were, he once said, the most enjoyable events he could remember.

He made mistakes. Some of the men he appointed to top exec jobs proved incapable. One stole company money. Wallichs erred in setting up certain distribution outlets when the company was young and he overestimated the appeal of certain big-name glamour guys and gals on records from time to time, but he lived the record business around the clock most of his life and the industry is a hell of a lot poorer for his loss. God knows how many of us are in his debt for having been around him.

◦   ◦   ◦

Losing a friend like Wallichs is hard. For me it was all the more difficult because his death came only months after the passing of my big Honduran pal, Carlos Gastel.

Carlos drank more booze day by day than any man I've ever known, yet I never saw him reeling drunk. He was a man of delicate, artistic sensibilities despite his physical immensity and grizzly-bear roughness. He was perpetually good-natured, quick to forgive and tolerant of other's errors. His rank as a personal manager equalled Wallichs' rank in the record business.

The years roll on and the ranks of music men thin. I've recently donned the yarmulke at a dozen Jewish funerals and I've attended almost as many Roman Catholic masses for deceased friends and associates in recent years.

It comes suddenly, like a kick in the ribs, the realization that you are one of the few survivors of the music business of the 1930s. What are all the hundreds of men and women I worked with doing these days? Where are they?

I don't really want to know. Every time I attend a funeral I get a little closer to the answer.

224

25

The good old days of pop music are now, and there will be more tomorrow.

—WOODY HERMAN (1973)

AT LAST COUNT there were 3.6 billion human beings aboard the planet Earth, all of us zipping along at a terrifying speed of 18.5 miles per second in an unending orbit around the sun 933 million miles away.

No wonder so many of us are neurotics. Even the most tranquil men and women have problems these days; just staying alive—hanging on—is challenge enough, particularly if one is involved in the frenzied, unstable, unpredictable music game.

It's a business that dominates the world of entertainment in the 1970s. Its product is enjoyed by an uncountable legion of children, women, and men throughout the world, many of whom have never seen, and will never see, a movie.

British EMI still exports approximately 25,000 hand-wound, non-electric phonographs—like the ones American were proud to use 50 years ago—to the African continent every year. Many companies in Europe and Asia and Africa continue to press and sell 78 rpm shellac discs.

Music is moving away from art more and more and into business. Aesthetic considerations steadily deteriorate as lawyers and business majors assume control of music's creative forces. Upton Sinclair described American businessmen as dishonest and self-seeking. Theodore Dreiser said they were ruthless and savage. Sinclair Lewis saw them in yet another light, as petty and uncreative.

But there are applaudable aspects of my industry which merit consideration, too. Records provide a variety of entertainment and education at a low price, a price that 500 or more competing companies have managed to maintain despite sharply rising costs. For the few dollars an LP buyer today spends he receives two to three times as much music, all of it infinitely better recorded, as he did for the same expenditure 20 years ago.

One of the wings of the industry which reaps little publicity is the budget operation, known also as the economy line. Columbia has its Harmony label, RCA produces the Camden series, and Pickwick, an independent, publicly owned corporation, works with Capitol as its major source of music. There are many others. These labels sell their product for $3 and $4 less than the standard price and they are enjoying uncommon success in the nation's record marts.

Since 1966, I have worked closely with Pickwick's chairman, Cy Leslie, as well as with the corporation's president, Ira Moss, and their a&r producers Joe Abend, Bugs Bower, and Howard Kramer. Most budget discs are manufactured of pure vinyl in full accordance with RIAA standards. Jackets and liner notes are, Moss declares, often more attractive than those available in the original full-price line. "They have to be," he says, "because of the impulse nature of our economy product."

Leslie and Moss compare their operation to that of a paperback book publisher.

"It's the same book at a lower price," Moss says. "But with records, we go one step farther because we can also cull the best of three different LPs and deliver an even better single album than the original. We can also spread music into tens of thousands of stores which would not ordinarily expose many artists on high-priced labels. We believe the budget catalog serves as an introduction of a particular artist whom buyers have heard of but can not afford to buy at full price."

Pickwick must be doing something right. They've enjoyed several years when profits exceeded $5 million. And each year gets better.

The former president of Bell Records, Larry Uttal, is not a devotee of the budget line. A one-time songwriter and music publisher, he is convinced that the standard $6.98 retail price of an LP is too low, and that the manufacturer may be morally justified in charging whatever the traffic will bear for his product. "Nobody in the industry," Uttal says, "is making an excessive profit. Within the retail field, every operator is entitled to price records according to his own merchandising philosophies. It's about time that we realized that the public will pay for exceptional entertainment. I find it hard to believe that the price of a 45 rpm single is about the same as it was when I entered the business 'way back in 1955."

Jac Holzman founded Elektra Records in 1948 while he was a teenaged student at St. John's College in Maryland. Its success brought about the 1963 launching of an Elektra economy series, Nonesuch. Holzman likes to tell his sales staff that every other American home has a photograph, but that millions of their owners rarely buy a record.

"If we are selling 475,000 to 500,000 copies of a hit album," Holzman argues, "we are reaching less than one percent of the nation's population. A smash package should sell 10 million copies; we in the record business must find new sales outlets to reach those potential buyers."

Mike Stewart earned an aeronautical engineering degree at Johns Hopkins University, moved into and out of music publishing, record production, and management firms and since 1971 has served as president of United Artists Records. "In a sense," he opines, "our business is like women's fashions. We try to create a hit pattern on a piece of plastic. We are even more volatile because, once the pattern is created, its life span is extremely short. All the advertising, promotion, merchandising, and selling thrust must be achieved within a brief time period-from a few weeks to perhaps three months—and we must constantly create new hit patterns.

"The consumer," Stewart says, "will buy as many hit records as our industry can produce. Price is not the determining factor in a record purchase."

Somehow the trade talk invariably revolves around money. Especially with corporation bosses. Each covets his share of tasty Brobdingnagian pie.

RCA's Kenneth D. Glancy; MCA's Mike Maitland; Joe Smith and Mo Ostin of the combined Warner-Reprise labels; Jerold Rubinstein, ABC-Dunhill; Ahmet Ertegun, Nesuhi Ertegun, and Jerry Wexler of Atlantic; Jerry Moss, who guides the A&M operation; Irwin H. Steinberg, Phonogram; Goddard Lieberson and Irwin Segelstein, Columbia; Arthur Talmadge and his son, Richard E. Talmadge, of Musicor, and Capitol's Bhaskar Menon—men with astonishingly impressive track records—agree that the $3.2 billion worldwide record gross of last year may attain the $4 billion level by the end of 1976. Quadraphonic discs and tapes are coming on strong despite the international energy shortage. There's gold in them grooves, as they say.

The president of the United States receives $200,000 annually. At the time he was fired in mid-1973, Columbia's Clive J. Davis was being paid more than $350,000 as president of the CBS-owned disc firm.[6] Top execs are worth every cent they accept but only for so long as they maintain industry leadership. They're only as valuable as their last hit.

∘   ∘   ∘

In Hollywood, where I've walked Vine Street every day for so many years, there still exists a sophomoric, decadent caste system among motion picture people. They have admitted television's big names to their dwindling little circle but they snobbishly exclude even the most affluent record folk from their plushy social events in what must be a ludicrous throwback to the golden era of Fairbanks-Pickford frivolities.

Being ostracized, I think, is a blessing. We lowly record people were not present last year at a plushy Friars' Club dinner party honoring comedian Buddy Hackett when NBC's blindly inebriated talkshow host Johnny Carson, on the dais in full view of 1,400 actors and funnymen, urinated into a champagne bucket.

Shades of W. C. Fields. Or Fatty Arbuckle.

∘   ∘   ∘

The blonde in the apple red panties? I'm afraid I never heard from her again after she tempestuously traipsed out of my office, but I'm fairly sure it was she I saw one night on the tube as I caught the close of a program featuring the dancing, singing Golddiggers. Miss Tasteless couldn't dance, either.

∘   ∘   ∘

In 1975, Dave Dexter was awarded a Citation For Meritorious Service by Paul W. Mills of the Veterans Administration for volunteering his time to announce and act as music adviser to the transcribed Here's To Veterans program aired by more than 3,000 American radio stations every week. Mills, at right, said he appreciated Dexter's "knowledge, professional skill, and unfailing civility." (Veterans Administration)

Every week I take a phone call from someone wanting to know about an old orchestra theme song. I receive mail on the subject, too. The Big Band Era may be long gone but it is not forgotten.

Because there is no permanent, accurate listing of world-renowned themes from another generation available to my knowledge, I list here the most complete tabulation ever assembled. Most of the compilation was accomplished over a quarter of century by Bruce D. Davidson of Nashville, a former Capitol promotion executive. It is with his permission that these themes are published.

Band buffs will recall that numerous orchestras employed more than one opening theme. The vicious, protracted ASCAP-BMI imbroglio·to determine control of American music over the nation's airways in 1940 brought about many theme switches. I therefore list more than one for a number of fondly recalled maestri:

AARONSON, IRVING: *Commanderism*
AGNEW, CHARLIE: *Slow But Sure*
ALEXANDER, VAN: *Alexander's Swinging; Alexander's Ragtime Band*
ALLEN, BARCLAY: *Cumana*
ALLEN, HENRY (RED): *Drink Hearty; The Crawl*
ALPERT, MICKEY: *I'm Always Chasing Rainbows*
AMBROSE, BERT: *Tarantula; Hors d'Ouevres*
ANTHONY, RAY: *Young Man With a Horn*
ARCARAZ, LUIS: *Sombra Verde*
ARMSTRONG, LOUIS: *When It's Sleepy Time Down South*
ARNAZ, DESI: *Cuban Pete*
ARNHEIM, GUS: *Say It with Music; Sweet and Lovely*
ARTHUR, ZINN: *Darling*
AULD, GEORGIE: *I've Got a Right to Know*
AYRES, MITCHELL: *You Go to My Head*
BALLEW, SMITH: *Tonight There is Music in the Air*
BAMPTION, CLAUDE: *April Morning*
BARNET, CHARLIE: *I Lost Another Sweetheart; Cherokee; Skyliner*
BARRIE, DICK: *Blue Shadows*
BARRON, BLUE: *Sometimes I'm Happy*
BASIE, COUNT: *One O'Clock Jump; Moten Swing*
BAXTER, PHIL: *I'm a Ding Dong Daddy from Dumas*
BECKNER, DENNY: *You Can Take My Heart and Break It in Two*
BELASCO, LEON: *When Romance Calls*
BELLOC, DAN: *Danny Boy*
BENEKE, TEX: *Moonlight Serenade*
BERIGAN, BUNNY: *I Can't Get Started*
BERNIE, BEN: *It's a Lonesome Old Town*
BESTER, DON: *Teach Me to Smile; Time Signal*
BLAINE, JERRY: *Streamlined Rhythm*

BLOCH, RAY: *Music in My Fingers*
BLOCK, BERT: *Moonglow*
BOSTIC, EARL: *Bostic's Jump; Away*
BOTHWELL, JOHNNY: *Sleepy Alto*
BRADLEY, WILL: *Think of Me; Fatal Fascination*
BRADSHAW, TINY: *Bradshaw's Bounce*
BRANDWYNNE, NAT: *If Stars Could Talk*
BREEZE, LOU: *Breezing Along with the Breeze*
BRIGODE, ACE: *Carry Me Back to Old Virginny*
BRING, LOU: *Love Rides on the Moon*
BROOKS, RANDY: *Harlem Nocturne; Holiday Forever*
BROWN, LES: *Evening Star; Blue Devil Jazz; Dance of the Blue Devils; Yesterdays; Leap Frog.*
BRYANT, WILLIE: *It's Over Because We're Through*
BURKE, SONNY: *Blue Sonata*
BUSSE, HENRY: *Hot Lips*
BUTTERFIELD, BILLY: *What's New?*
BYRNE, BOBBY: *Danny Boy; My Colleen*
CALLOWAY, CAB: *Minnie the Moocher*
CARLE, FRANKIE: *Sunrise Serenade*
CARLYLE, RUSS: *You Call It Madness*
CARPENTER, IKE: *Moon Mist*
CARTER, BENNY: *Melancholy Lullaby; Malibu*
CAVALLARO, CARMEN: *My Sentimental Heart*
CHESTER, BOB: *Sunburst; Slumber*
CHIESTA, DON: *Love Me Tonight*
CHILDS, REGGIE: *Close to Me*
CLARIDGE, GAY: *This is Love*
CLINTON, LARRY: *Dipsy Doodle*
COAKLEY, TOM: *Sweet Georgia Brown*
COBURN, JOLLY: *There's Music in the Stars*
COLEMAN, EMIL: *By the Shalimar*
CONDON, EDDIE: *We Called It Music; Improvisations for the March of Time*
COOLEY, SPADE: *Shame, Shame on You; Steel Guitar Rag*
COON-SANDERS: *Nighthawk Blues*
COOPER, AL (SAVOY SULTANS): *Jumpin' at the Savoy*
COURTNEY, DEL: *Good Evening; Three Shades of Blue*
CRAIG, FRANCIS: *Near You; Red Rose*
CROSBY, BOB: *Summertime*
CROSS, CRISS: *Soft Lights and Sweet Music*
CUGAT, XAVIER: *My Shawl*
CUMMINGS, BERNIE: *Dark Eyes*
CUTLER, BEN: *Yours Sincerely*
DAILEY, FRANK: *Gypsy Violins*

230

DAILY, PETE: *I Want to Linger*
D'ARTEGA: *Cavalcade*
DAVIS, JOHNNY (SCAT): *Hooray for Hollywood*
DAVIS, MEYER: *Just One of Those Things*
DeFRANCO, BUDDY: *Rumpus Room*
DeLANGE, EDDIE: *Don't Forget*
DENNY, JACK: *Under the Stars*
DERWIN, HAL: *My Serenade*
DEUTSCH, EMORY: *When a Gypsy Makes His Violin Cry*
DONAHUE, AL: *Lowdown Rhythm in a Top Hat*
DONAHUE, SAM: *I Never Knew; Lonesome*
DORNBERGER, CHARLES: *If I Had You*
DORSEY BROTHERS: *Sandman*
DORSEY, JIMMY: *Sandman; Contrasts*
DORSEY, TOMMY: *I'm Getting Sentimental Over You*
DOWELL, SAXIE: *Three Itty Fishies*
DUCHIN, EDDY: *My Twilight Dream*
DUNHAM, SONNY: *Memories of You*
ELLIS, SEGER: *Me and My Shadow*
ELLINGTON, DUKE: *East St. Louis Toodle-oo; Take the A Train*
ELLIOTT, BARON: *Stardust*
ELGART, LES AND LARRY: *Sophisticated Swing; The Dancing Sound*
ENNIS, SKINNAY: *Got a Date with an Angel*
FELTON, HAPPY: *I Want to Be Happy*
FIELDS, HERBIE: *Blue Fields*
FIELDS, SHEP: *Rippling Rhythm; Fire Dance*
FIELDING, JERRY: *Carefree*
FINA, JACK: *Dream Sonata*
FIO RITO, TED: *Rio Rita*
FISHER, FREDDIE SCHNICKELFRITZ: *Colonel Corn*
FLANAGAN, RALPH: *Singing Winds*
FOSTER, CHUCK: *Oh, You Beautiful Doll*
FOTINE, LARRY: *Romantic Music*
FOX, ROY: *Whispering; Dreamy Serenade*
FUNK, LARRY: *Rose of Washington Square*
GARBER, JAN: *My Dear*
GARR, GLENN: *I Love You Truly*
GILL, EMERSON: *Weary*
GLEASON, JACKIE: *Melancholy Serenade*
GLUSKIN, LUD: *On the Air*
GOLDKETTE, JEAN: *I Know That You Know; Sweetheart Time*
GOODMAN, BENNY: *Let's Dance*
GORDON, GRAY: *One Minute to One*
GRAY, GLEN: *Smoke Rings*

GRAY, JERRY: *Desert Serenade*
GREEN, JOHNNY: *Body and Soul*
GREEN, LARRY: *My Promise to You*
GRIER, JIMMY: *Music in the Moonlight*
HACKETT, BOBBY: *Embraceable You*
HALL, GEORGE: *Love Letters in the Sand*
HALLETT, MAL: *Boston Tea Party*
HALSTEAD, HENRY: *Cuddle Up a Little Closer*
HAMILTON, GEORGE: *That's Because I Love You*
HAMP, JOHNNY: *My Old Kentucky Home*
HAMPTON, LIONEL: *Flyin' Home*
HARRIS, PHIL: *Rose Room*
HAWKINS, ERSKINE: *Swing Out*
HAYES, EDGAR: *Edgar Steps Out; Stardust*
HAYMES, JOE: *Midnight*
HAYTON, LENNIE: *Blue Moonlight*
HEATH, TED: *Listen to My Music*
HEIDT, HORACE: *I'll Love You in My Dreams*
HEFTI, NEAL: *Coral Reef*
HENDERSON, FLETCHER: *Christopher Columbus* .
HENDERSON, HORACE: *Happy Feet*
HENDERSON, SKITCH: *Anita; Dancing with a Deb*
HERBECK, RAY: *Romance*
HERMAN, WOODY: *Blue Prelude; Blue Flame*
HEYWOOD, EDDIE: *Begin the Beguine*
HICKMAN, ART: *Rose Room*
HILL, TINY: *Angry*
HIMBER, RICHARD: *It Isn't Fair; Am I to Blame?*
HINES, EARL: *Deep Forest*
HITE, LES: *The World is Waiting For the Sunrise;*
        It Must Have Been a Dream
HOFF, CARL: *I Could Use a Dream*
HOLMES, HERBIE: *Love Me a Little Little*
HOPKINS, CLAUDE: *I Would Do Anything For You*
HORLICK, HARRY: *Black Eyes*
HOWARD, EDDY: *To Each His Own; Careless*
HUDSON, DEAN: *Moon Over Miami*
HUDSON, WILL: *Hobo On Park Avenue*
HUDSON-DE LANGE: *Eight Bars in Search of a Melody*
HUNT, PEE WEE: *Twelfth Street Rag*
HUTTON, INA RAY: *Gotta Have Your Love; My Silent Love*
HYLTON, JACK: *She Shall Have Music*
JAMES, HARRY: *Ciribiribin*
JARRETT, ART: *Everything's Been Done Before*

JENKINS, GORDON: *You Have Taken My Heart*
JENNEY, JACK: *City Night*
JEROME, HENRY: *Night is Gone*
JOHNSON, JOHNNY: *If I Could Be with You One Hour Tonight*
JONES, ISHAM: *You're Just a Dream Come True*
JONES, SPIKE: *Hotcha Cornia (Black Eyes)*
JORDAN, LOUIS: *Pinetop's Boogie-Woogie*
JOY, JIMMY: *Shine On Harvest Moon*
JURGENS, DICK: *Daydrams Come True at Night*
KAHN, ROGER WOLF: *Where the Wild, Wild Flowers Grow*
KARDOS, GENE: *Business in F*
KASSEL, ART: *Doodle-Dee-Doo*
KAVELIN, AL: *When Love is Gone*
KAY, HERBIE: *Violets*
KAYE, SAMMY: *Kaye's Melody*
KEMP, HAL: *How I'll Miss You When the Summer is Gone*
KENTON, STAN: *Artistry in Rhythm*
KING, HENRY: *A Blues Serenade*
KING, WAYNE: *The Waltz You Saved For Me*
KINNEY, RAY: *Across the Sea*
KIRBY, JOHN: *Pastel Blue*
KIRK, ANDY: *Cloudy; Until the Real Thing Comes Along*
KNAPP, ORVILLE : *Accent on Youth*
KRUEGER, BENNIE: *It's Getting Dark on Old Broadway*
KRUPA, GENE: *Apurksody; That Drummer's Band*
KUHN, DICK: *Wildflower*
KYSER, KAY: *Thinking of You*
LATTIMORE, HARLAN: *Son of the South*
LAWRENCE, ELLIOT: *Heart to Heart*
LEONARD, HARLAN: *Rockin' with the Rockets; A Mellow Bit of Rhythm*
LEVANT, PHIL: *My Book of Dreams*
LEWIS, TED: *When My Baby Smiles At Me*
LEWIS, VIC: *Blue Champagne*
LeWINTER, DAVID: *Daydreams*
LIGHT, ENOCH: *You're the Only Star*
LITTLE, LITTLE JACK: *Little By Little*
LIVINGSTON, JERRY: *It's the Talk of the Town*
LIVINGSTON, JIMMY: *Just a Little Bit South of North Carolina*
LOMBARDO, GUY: *Coming Through the Rye*
LONG, JOHNNY: *The White Star of Sigma Nu*
LOPEZ, VINCENT: *Nola; On the Radio*
LOSS, JOE: *In the Mood*
LOWN, BERT: *Bye Bye Blues*
LUCAS, CLYDE: *Tonight Belongs to You*

LUNCEFORD, JIMMIE: *Uptown Blues; Jazznocracy*
LYMAN, ABE: *California Here I Come; La Golondrina*
MADRIGUERA, ENRIC: *Adios*
MALNECK, MATTY: *Park Avenue Fantasy; Stairway to the Stars*
MANONE, WINGY: *Isle of Capri*
MARSHARD, JACK: *Aline*
MALTBY, RICHARD: *Midnight Mood*
MANTOVANI: *Charmaine*
MARTIN, FREDDY: *Tonight We Love; Bye-Lo-Bye Lullaby*
MARTIN, PAUL: *On Miami Shore*
MARSALA, JOE: *Don't Let It End*
MARTERIE, RALPH: *Truly*
MASTERS, FRANKIE: *Scatterbrain; A Sweet Dream of You*
MAY, BILLY: *Lean Baby*
McCOY, CLYDE: *Sugar Blues; Lonely Gondolier*
McCUNE, BILL: *Strange Interlude*
McFARLAND, TWINS: *Darkness*
McGEE, JOHNNY: *Just for Awhile*
McINTIRE, LANI: *You're the One Rose*
McINTYRE, HAL: *Sentimental Journey; Moon Mist; Ecstasy*
McKENZIE, RED: *Barb-Wire Blues*
McKINLEY, RAY: *Howdy Friends*
McKINNEY'S COTTON PICKERS: *If I Could Be with You One Hour Tonight*
McSHANN, JAY: *Jiggin' With Jay*
MEISSNER, ZEP: *New Orleans Masquerade*
MEROFF, BENNY: *Diane*
MESSNER, JOHNNY: *Toy Piano Minuet; Can't We Be Friends*
MILLER, EDDIE: *Lazy Mood*
MILLER, GLENN: *Moonlight Serenade; Slumber Song*
MILLINDER, LUCKY: *The Lucky Swing; Ride, Red, Ride*
MOLINA, CARLOS: *La Cumparsita*
MONROE, VAUGHN: *Racing with the Moon*
MOONEY, ART: *Sunset to Sunrise*
MORENO, BUDDY: *Make Me a Cowboy Again*
MORGAN, RUSS: *Does Your Heart Beat For Me*
MORROW, BUDDY: *You're Dancing Tonight; Night Train*
MOTEN, BENNIE: *It's Hard to Laugh or Smile; South*
MOUND CITY BLUE BLOWERS: *Danger*
MOZIAN, ROGER KING: *Midnight in Spanish Harlem*
MURPHY, LYLE (SPUD): *Ecstasy*
NAGEL, FREDDY: *Sophisticated Swing; I'm Writing this Song for You*
NEIGHBORS, PAUL: *Neighbor*
NELSON, OZZIE; *Loyal Sons of Rutgers*
NEWMAN, RUBY: *Rainbow in the Night*

NICHOLS, RED: *The Wail of the Winds*
NOBEL, LEIGHTON: *I'll See You in My Dreams*
NOBLE, RAY: *The Very Thought of You*
NORVO, RED: *Mr. and Mrs. Swing*
NOONE, JIMMY: *Apex Blues*
OLSEN, GEORGE: *Music of Tomorrow; Beyond the Blue Horizon*
OLIVER, EDDIE: *You and the Night and the Music*
OLIVER, KING: *Dippermouth Blues*
OLIVER, SY: *For Dancers Only*
OSBORNE, WILL: *The Gentleman Awaits*
OWENS, HARRY: *Sweet Leilani*
PAGE, JOE: *Alone at a Table for Two*
PANICO, LOUIS: *Wabash Blues*
PALMER, JIMMY: *Dancing Shoes*
PASTOR, TONY: *Blossoms*
PAXTON, GEORGE: *American Nocturne*
PEARL, RAY: *Sunset*
PENDARVIS, PAUL: *My Sweetheart*
PHILLIPS, TEDDY: *Great Big Beautiful Eyes*
POLLACK, BEN: *Song of the Islands*
POWELL, TEDDY: *San Culottes; Blue Sentimental Mood*
PRADO, PEREZ; *More Mambo Jambo*
PRIMA, LOUIS: *Way Down Yonder in New Orleans*
PRYOR, ROGER: *The Whistler and his Dog*
RAEBURN, BOYD: *Raeburn's Theme; Moonlight on Melody Hill*
RAPP, BARNEY: *The Skater's Waltz*
RAVAZZA, CARL: *Vieni Su*
RAY, FLOYD: *Blues at Noon*
REDMAN, DON: *Chant of the Weed*
REICHMAN, JOE: *Variations in G; Little Thoughts*
REISMAN, LEO; *What is this Thing Called Love?*
RENARD, JACQUES: *Coronet; Are You Listening?*
RESER, HARRY: *Eskimo March*
REY, ALVINO: *Blue Rey*
REYNOLDS, TOMMY: *Pipe Dreams*
RICH, FREDDIE: *So Beats My Heart for You*
RILEY-FARLEY: *The Music Goes 'Round*
RINES, JOE: *By the Waters of Minnetonka*
ROGERS, CHARLES (BUDDY): *My Buddy*
ROS, EDMUNDO: *Cuban Love Song*
ROSE, DAVID: *California Melodies; Holiday for Strings*
ROY, HARRY: *Bugle Call Rag; Tiger Rag*
RUSSELL, LUIS: *New Call of the Freaks*
SABIN, PAUL: *Moon Over Miami*

SANDERS, JOE: *I Found a Rose in the Snow*
SAVITT, JAN: *Quaker City Jazz; Out of Space; It's a Wonderful World*
SAUTER-FINEGAN: *Doodletown Fifers*
SCOTT, RAYMOND: *Pretty Little Petticoat; The Toy Trumpet*
SCOTTI, WILLIAM: *My Moonlight Madonna*
SENTER, BOYD: *Bad Habits*
SHAW, ARTIE: *Nightmare*
SHERWOOD, BOBBY: *The Elks' Parade*
SHILKRET, NAT: *Dusky Stevedore*
SISSLE, NOBLE: *I Just Called Up to Say Hello;*
　　　　　　I'm Just Wild about Harry
SLACK, FREDDIE: *Strange Cargo*
SMITH, STUFF: *My Thoughts*
SOSNICK, HARRY: *Lazy Rhapsody*
SPECHT, PAUL: *The Woodpecker Song; Melody of the Evening Star*
SPITALNY, PHIL: *My Isle of Golden Dreams*
SPANIER, MUGGSY: *Relaxin' at the Touro*
SPIVAK, CHARLIE: *Stardreams*
STABILE, DICK: *Blue Nocturne*
STAPLETON, CYRIL: *Sleepy Serenade*
STEELE, BLUE: *Coronado Memories*
STEELE, TED: *Love Passed Me By*
STERN, HAROLD: *Now That It's All Over*
STONE, LEW: *Oh, Susanna*
STRAETER, TED: *The Most Beautiful Girl in the World*
STRONG, BENNY: *I've Had My Moments*
SUDY, JOSEPH: *Reminiscing*
SULLIVAN, JOE: *Little Rock Getaway*
SUTTON, MYRON: *Moanin' At the Montmartre*
TEAGARDEN, JACK: *I've Got a Right to Sing the Blues*
THOMPSON, LANG: *You Darlin'*
THORNHILL, CLAUDE: *Snowfall*
TOWNE, GEORGE: *It's the Talk of the Town*
TRACE, AL: *You Call Everybody Darlin'; Sweet Words and Music*
TREMAINE, PAUL: *Lonely Acres*
TRUMBAUER, FRANKIE: *Singin' the Blues*
TUCKER, ORRIN: *Drifting and Dreaming*
TUCKER, TOMMY: *I Love You, Oh How I Love You*
VALLEE, RUDY: *My Time is Your Time*
VAN, GARWOOD: *Drifting and Dreaming*
VAN STEEDEN, PETER: *Home*
VENTURA, CHARLIE: *High on an Open Mike*
VENUTI, JOE: *Last Night*
WALD, JERRY: *Laura*

WALLER, FATS: *Ain't Misbehavin*
WANER, ART: *Mighty Lak a Rose*
WARING, FRED: *Sleep*
WEBB, CHICK: *Let's Get Together; I May Be Wrong*
WEEKS, ANSON: *I'm Writing You this Little Melody*
WEEKS, RANDY: *Liebestraum*
WEEMS, TED: *Out of the Night*
WELK, LAWRENCE: *Bubbles in the Wine*
WHITEMAN, PAUL: *Rhapsody in Blue*
WILDE, RAN: *Wild Honey; Runnin' Wild*
WILLIAMS, CLARENCE: *Baltimore*
WILLIAMS, COOTIE: *Echoes of Harlem*
WILLIAMS, GRIFF: *Dream Music*
WILSON, TEDDY: *Jumpin' on the Blacks and Whites*
ZURKE, BOB: *Southern Exposure; Hobson Street Blues*

* * *

Will the big bands ever come back?

Perhaps they'll return, but they won't sound like the bands we knew a generation ago. They will feature electric bass, at least two guitars (amplified), and probably an electronic piano-organ. That's the today sound.

Bands would be back within 30 days if someone could devise a way to allot them broadcast time. It was radio—not records—that made bands big in the 1930s. The wretched Top 40 domination of the airwaves today precludes anything artistically laudable being heard by American youth in the 1970s.

* * *

The gleaming, black, pristine disc which we so casually call a record has become so familiar that we take it for granted. How many of us remove the slender platter from its sleeve and consider that its minute grooves, less than one-thousandth-of-an-inch deep, miraculously contain all the complicated information necessary to recreate in our listening rooms the magnificent sound of a 100-piece symphony orchestra?

We accept the near-perfect quality of a record today matter-of-factly, questioning its superb sound reproduction only if we detect a pop or a scratch in the 790 yards—that's almost half a mile—of groove from an LP's outside lip to the label.

A record's soundtrack adopts the form of an Archimedan spiral which, in long-play form, consists of a groove of 90 degrees included angle, 0.0002 inch top width and 0.00015 inch bottom radius On a monophonic disc the modulation is lateral: the stereo groove carries two signals recorded at 90 degrees to each other and at 45 degrees to the plane of the record surface. The groove varies in depth and width because of the differences in phasing and content.

The outer wall of the groove normally carries the channel which we hear through the righthand speaker.

Quadraphonic records are, obviously, even more sophisticated technically. They reproduce four distinct sound channels with remarkable, lifelike fidelity. Yet, for all its magic, the four-channel art falls short of the ultimate. Far more highly advanced attainments within the industry are to be marketed in the immediate future. We will then not only hear the artist but watch him perform as well. In color.

The system nearest to perfection is that developed by MCA of California, which recently allied with the Philips Group of Holland in preparing a miraculous disc which looks like an LP but which is infinitely more complex.

The MCA-Philips Disco-Vision platter contains 12,500 grooves to a radial inch and is scanned by a low power helium-neon laser beam that is electrically transmitted to a family's television set. More than $2 million has been expended in developing the instrument, according to John W. Findlater of MCA. The player unit will sell for about $400.

"One record," Findlater advises, "is capable of storing the social security numbers of everyone in the United States. The laser beam is geared to follow the recorded information spiral without ever touching the disc's surface. Thus a record which we anticipate to sell for $2 to $10 depending on the type and caliber of entertainment it contains will be subjected to no physical wear whatever. It will last forever."

Conventional 33 and 45 rpm records will, of course, continue to be marketed by the 500 American recording companies.

And thus does the long, hard haul from Tom Edison's 1877 efforts progress. From tinfoil cylinders to laser beams in slightly less than a century. The next 100 years can hardly be as exciting if you're a record man.

           ☼   ☼   ☼

Capitol's sentimental observance of the start of my thirty-second year with the company—no one had worked there that long—came two months after my anniversary date in 1974. I was summoned into the office of an Ivy League vice-president and, *sans* ceremony, bluntly told that I was no longer a Capitol employee.

Numbly, I heard the man say something about "early retirement status."

There was no gold watch—I had received a tacky timepiece from the company six years earlier, marking a quarter-century of what Chairman Wallichs described as "distinguished" service, and it had exploded internally three or four months after presentation. There was no publicity release to the trade press, a common amenity. No one among management offered me a farewell luncheon like the scores of others I had attended through the decades for other departees.

Fred Rice, a loyal and valuable Capitol man for 27 years, was called into the same office by the same veep on the same day and likewise retired prematurely.

So at last some of the inmates were, at long last, running the Tower asylum. I felt relieved and tranquil by the time I cleaned out my scarred desk a week later. Corporate profits notwithstanding, "my" beloved company without Wallichs and many others from the old and more felicitous days had sadly deteriorated into something disappointingly different.

◦   ◦   ◦

Editing hundreds of pages of music industry copy, writing a dozen or so news stories, and devising headlines for a majority of news and feature articles for the best weekly music trade journal in the world, *Billboard*, now comprises my daily regimen.

The title assigned me by publisher Lee Zhito and managing editor Eliot Tiegel is copy editor. It's trying, difficult work, and a constant battle against deadlines—under pressures—but the ratio of chiefs and Indians is ideal and most everyone is cheerfully compatible.

I doubt that power-hungry inmates will ever take over the *Billboard* asylum.

Still, there are times when I depart my desk and the frenetic world of Bachman-Turner Overdrive and Grand Funk Railroad to repair to my stereo rig. There I can stack up long-hoarded masterpieces by the truly immortal artists of the 20th century—Boult, Boulez, Previn, Solti, and Ozawa in one field, Ellington, Holiday, Beiderbecke, Basie, Lunceford, Bailey, and so many more in another, all too many of them long deceased.

Some of those precious records, so help me, are chipped, scratched, slightly off-center 78 rpm shellacs. They sound pretty good to my untiring ears and they always will. Who needs Disco-Vision?

—END—

Notes

1. From a biographical article by Louie Robinson in the November 1972 issue of *Ebony* magazine, Chicago.

2. Originally published in an article by James Conaway in *The New York Times Magazine,* 15 October 1972.

3. Tribute to the Beatles by William Anderson was published in the February 1973 issue of *Stereo Review.*

4. From *The Music Machine,* by Roger Karshner. Copyright 1971. Published by Nash Publishing Corporation, Los Angeles.

5. From the Annual Financial Statement of Capitol Industries-EMI, Inc.

6. The CBS Records Group's termination of Clive Davis as president of Columbia Records was reported in a May 1973 issue of *Billboard,* and in scores of other publications. Mr. Davis has since become president of Arista Records.

Index

Edited by Margit Malmstrom
Designed by Bob Fillie
Set in 10 point Laurel by Publishers Graphics, Inc.
Printed and bound by Bookcrafters, Inc.